DIRECTORS IN REHEARSAL
A hidden world

SUSAN LETZLER COLE

routledge, a theatre arts book
new york   london

Published in 1992 by

Routledge
An imprint of Routledge, Chapman and Hall, Inc.
29 West 35 Street
New York, NY 10001

Published in Great Britain by

Routledge
11 New Fetter Lane
London EC4P 4EE

Library of Congress Cataloging-in-Publication Data

Cole, Susan Letzler, 1940–
    Directors in rehearsal : a hidden world / by Susan Letzler Cole,
    p.   cm.
    Includes bibliographical references and index.
    ISBN 0-87830-018-X   ISBN 0-87830-019-8 (pbk.)
    1. Theater rehearsals. 2. Theater—Production and direction.
    I. Title.
    PN2071.R45C64   1992
    792'.028—dc20   92-59
                                                        CIP

British Library Cataloguing in Publication Data also available

ALICE P. LETZLER

summa mater

tibi

Contents

Acknowledgments

In addition to the directors and actors mentioned in the following pages, many persons and institutions have generously contributed time and services on behalf of this project. For assistance of many different kinds I would like to thank:

Those who helped me during the period of research and observation: Julie Archer, Warren Blackstone, Markus Bönzli, Jorge Cacheiro, Lynn Cohen, John Connole, John David Cullum, Suzanne Dieckman, Janie Geiser, Daniel Gerould, Kazuko Hayashi, Jane Hoffman, James Johnson, Nicholas Kepros, Michael Kirby, Bernice Kliman, Kevin Kline, Laura Kuhn, Arthur Lewis, Ruth Maleczech, Martin Marchitto, Chris Markle, Mary McDonnell, Joanna Merlin, Leslie Mohn, Isabell Monk, Frederick Neumann, Bruce Odland, Eren Ozker, Thomas Paulucci, Madeleine Potter, Carol A. Prugh, Marc Robinson, Gaby Rodgers, William Roerick, Jennifer Rohn, Bevya Rosten, Joan Schwartz, Larry Shyer, Elizabeth Smith, Peyton Smith, Priscilla Smith, John Spencer, Ken Tabachnick, Yoshida Tamamatsu, Bob Telson, Richard Thomas, Yoko Totani, Ron Vawter, Wilburt Vera, David Warrilow, Charles Whiteside, Laurel Ann Wilson; assistant directors Robert Aberdeen, Dale Davis, Molly Fowler, Hans-Werner Kroesinger, Ann-Christin Rommen, Marcus Stern; stage managers John Beven, Carol Cleveland, Liz Dreyer, Charlie Otte, Alan Traynor, Susan West, Zoya Wyeth; dramaturgs Norman Frisch and Marianne Weems; filmmaker Ken Kobland.

Those who gave valuable advice during the period of writing: Gloria Beckerman, Irene Dash, Elinor Fuchs, Elizabeth Johnson, Lucille Jones, Alice P. Letzler, Sharon Magnarelli, Alice Mattison, Natalie Miller, Susan Schorr, Richard Sewall, Mary Lee Vitale.

Those who helped me master the intricacies of word-processing: Marty Coyle, Chris Gianniotis, Ben Letzler, Kenneth Letzler, Robert Letzler, Carroll O'Toole, Frank Sokolove.

I should also like to acknowledge the help of the following institutions: Marymount College (Marty Coyle); the New York Shakespeare Festival (Richard Kornberg, Serge Mogilat); CSC Repertory (Kelley Voorhees); McCarter Theater (Dan Bauer); the Guthrie Theater (Dennis Behl); INTAR (Lori Schick); The John F. Kennedy Center for the Performing Arts (American National Theater: Diane J. Malecki, Kathleen O'Boyle); Theater for the New City (Franco-Mario Alessandro); The Women's Project (Julia Miles, Victoria Abrash); Spoleto Festival U.S.A. (Elinor R. Kotzen); Brooklyn Academy of Music (Philip Bither, Ellen Dennis); Yale School of Drama/Yale Repertory Theatre (Robert Wildman, Fran Oliver); Mabou Mines (Frier McCollister, Stephen Nunns); The Performing Garage (Paul Berman, Linda Chapman); La Mama (Ellen Stewart).

I wish especially to thank Albertus Magnus College for an extended sabbatical leave in 1988–90 during which I completed the first draft of this book.

I am indebted to the photographers who generously allowed use of their rehearsal and production stills: Paula Court, Michal Daniel, Johan Elbers, T. Charles Erickson, Martha Holmes, George E. Joseph, James M. Kent, Joan Marcus, Michael Shavel, Beatriz Schiller, Martha Swope, Gerard Vezzuso.

Finally, I am particularly grateful to William Germano, Jason Dewees, Seth Denbo, Michael Esposito, and Susana Favila Myer at Routledge for their careful shepherding of this manuscript through the stages of preparation for publication.

Two acknowledgments remain. I want to thank my husband, David, for his unremitting care for this book and its author, his love and his generosity of spirit. And I want to acknowledge another spirit that infuses this work, that of the woman to whom it is dedicated and who listened to and read every word of it, with loving exquisite attention, even as its completion marked her passing.

Illustrations

Note on Illustrations

Whenever possible, I have used photographs of directors at work in the actual rehearsals I observed. In two instances where no such photographs were available (Fig. 5.2 and Fig. 10.1), the illustrations show the directors in question (JoAnne Akalaitis and Peter Sellars) rehearsing other productions.

Fig. 1.1. Polish director Tadeusz Kantor onstage during a performance of Let the Artists Die *by Cricot 2 Theatre at La Mama. Photograph by Gerard Vezzuso.*

1

A Hidden World

It is almost 7:30 p.m., Sunday evening, October 13, 1985, at La Mama Annex in New York City where Polish writer and director Tadeusz Kantor's *Let the Artists Die* is about to be performed. Tadeusz Kantor is onstage, alternately peering out at the audience and looking at his wristwatch. He exits, enters again, exits. When the play begins, he is onstage, wearing a black suit with an open-collared white shirt, seated prominently on a wooden chair, on a diagonal to the main stage action, his back toward the audience. Throughout the performance the director's hands are in almost continual rhythmic motion, seemingly in response to both sound and action. In addition, his fingers often gesture to indicate sound cues and, occasionally, cues for actors' positions or movements. Once he turns to glance over his shoulder and either speaks or mimes speech to the sound booth. Throughout the one and a half-hour performance the director's concentration on the actors is intense, penetrating. Sometimes he touches or is touched by an actor, or makes eye contact. Sometimes he moves or holds stationary a particular stage prop (a chair, a skeleton-like horse). At one point he is handed an actor's socks, shoes, and trousers; the director neatly folds the socks into the shoes and then folds the trousers, keeping them in his lap until they are later plucked out by the actor who, along with other actors, whirls by him in a circular motion around the stage. Twice the director leaves the stage: once when the exit he sits by requires wider access and again when the full cast is moving in intricate patterns in the small space. The energy level of the actors remains the same, neither decreasing nor increasing visibly, while the director is offstage.

Kantor's characteristic onstage gesture is a kind of world-weary flick of the right wrist. It is an ambivalent and a highly ironic gesture, both calling something into being and dismissing it. The gesture seems to say: "Have done with it," i.e., do it and stop doing it. This is exactly what the director is empowered to command in rehearsal and unable to control in performance. Stopping and starting, energizing and eliminating, presiding over a birth and declaring a stillborn—these are directorial functions which can be enacted only in rehearsal, not during performance. The performance is the after-image of processes set in motion—explored, nourished, made fit for growth, realized—during the "work" of rehearsal.

Kantor's visible presence during performance is a striking stage image of the fantasy of total control and, at the same time, of the irony of the director onstage without directorial power. In his "unsuccessful" attempt to recreate the conditions of rehearsal by intruding himself into performance, Kantor is redefining the boundary, for a director, between rehearsal and performance. The almost involuntary flick of his wrist is an acknowledgment of the director's difficulty in letting go of the actors and of his rehearsal role: he flicks them away but he would be forever "restarting" them, reshaping their life on stage. The Ariels of this Prospero are unwillingly given their freedom in this controlling yet dismissive gesture.

My observation of the rehearsal work of ten professional directors, five female and five male, was completed between June 26, 1985 and October 15, 1989. (In my Epilogue, I describe the additional experience of observing, and unexpectedly becoming the dramaturg for, an amateur production of Sophocles' *Antigone* at the college where I teach.) In all cases I attended at least one performance of the work observed in rehearsal but, throughout, my passionate attention was on "not the result of making but the making itself."[1] In documenting rehearsal as a process, whose traces are often lost in performance, I hope to offer glimpses of a hidden world, a realm usually—and with good reason—veiled to observers. George Bernard Shaw is particularly firm in defense of the theatrical taboo against observers: "Remember that no strangers should be present at rehearsal. . . . Rehearsals are absolutely and sacredly confidential. . . . No direction should ever be given to an actor in the presence of a stranger."[2] Molière, inscribed as a character in his own play *L'Impromptu de Versailles*, proclaims this proscription from the stage itself in a performance of rehearsal:

> *Molière:* Monsieur, these ladies are trying to tell you that they
> prefer not to have any outsiders present during re-
> hearsals.
>
> *La Thorillière:* Why? I'm not in any danger, am I?
>
> *Molière:* It's a tradition in the theater.[3]

To observe directors and actors in rehearsal is clearly a delicate undertaking; it can be perceived as an intrusion upon, and
even a repression of, the conditions necessary to rehearsal (e.g.,
risk-taking, spontaneity, intimacy). But there is no other way to
document the collaborative creation of rehearsal except to be
present there.[4] My previous experience as an invited observer at
Lee Strasberg's Actors Studio and at Joseph Chaikin's rehearsals
of *Trespassing* allowed me to learn techniques of "being present"
that seemed unlikely to disrupt or betray the special conditions
of rehearsal work.[5]

From the beginning I decided to make use of a notebook rather
than a tape recorder. Some interviews were initiated without so
much as a notebook, in corridors or doorways. All interviews
and quoted commentary of actors and directors occurred during
the rehearsal period. When members of the company spoke to
me during breaks in rehearsal, they usually spoke fairly unselfconsciously and spontaneously. Later I might ask if we could
go back over what I heard, checking accuracy and sometimes
phrasing. It is possible that after I became a fixture in rehearsal
rooms, visibly writing almost continuously, my continuing to
write as people spoke to and near me became a part of the
landscape. In almost every rehearsal I observed, I was told that
I appeared to be writing down "everything." Since my focus
seemed decentered, no one in particular at any given moment
appeared to be under the spotlight of my attention. In this tech-
nological age, when to be exposed publicly is increasingly to be
recorded on tape, film, or video, my simply taking notes in a
room of other notetakers—the stage manager, production stage
manager, lighting, costume, set, and sound designers, various
production assistants, speech and text consultants, choreogra-
phers, and, at times, the director and actors themselves—was
perhaps less invasive than I had originally feared.

The following chapters present what, to my knowledge, has
never before been documented in book form:[6] the rehearsal practices of a variety of contemporary American directors.[7] The re-

hearsals I observed range from Peter Sellars' two-actor production of *Two Figures in Dense Violet Light* to Lee Breuer's cast of approximately a hundred performers in *The Warrior Ant;* from JoAnne Akalaitis's opera-theatre workshop production of *Voyage of the Beagle* to Emily Mann's documentary drama, *Execution of Justice* (one of the few Broadway productions written and directed by a woman); from the collaborative creation of script and staging in Elizabeth LeCompte's rehearsals of *Frank Dell's The Temptation of Saint Antony* to the agreed-upon non-collaboration of Richard Foreman with writer Kathy Acker, set and costume designer David Salle, and composer Peter Gordon during the rehearsals of *The Birth of the Poet*. I consider traditional directing styles and texts (Shakespeare's *Hamlet*, Chekhov's *The Cherry Orchard* and *Uncle Vanya*) as well as experimental directing styles and texts (Kathy Acker's *The Birth of the Poet*, Heiner Müller's *Hamletmachine*, Robert Wilson's *The Golden Windows)*; auteur-directors such as Liviu Ciulei, Richard Foreman, and Robert Wilson as well as the collective theatre enterprise of the Wooster Group and Mabou Mines director Lee Breuer.

In the writing of this book I at one point hoped that a single metaphor might unequivocally claim a position of central power. I found a suggestive clue in the etymology of the word *rehearse*, which derives from the Middle English *rehercen* and the Old French *rehercer*, "to repeat," originally "to harrow again": *re-*, "again" + *hercer*, "to harrow," from *herce*, a harrow.[8] A harrow is a heavy frame of timber or iron, set with iron teeth or tines; it is dragged over already ploughed land in order to break up clods of earth, pulverize and stir the soil, uproot weeds, eliminate air pockets that would prevent soil-to-seed contact, and cover the seed. In short, the harrow is a secondary tillage instrument: all the elements of growth are usually present before the harrowing that "fits" the soil for planting.[9] The metaphor of rehearsal as a harrowing—a fine breaking down of the playtext in preparation for a first or simply another planting in the soil of performance—captured my imagination for several months.

And yet metaphors in themselves are provisional: they posit connections, and the very act of positing a connection implies that there are other connections. Against the possibility of one controlling metaphor arises a proliferation of metaphors, many of them substantiated by theatre practitioners themselves. Here, for example, is a list of selected metaphors for the director:

Director as Father-Figure[10]
Director as Mother[11]
Director as Ideal Parent[12]
Director as Teacher[13]
Director as Ghost, Invisible Presence[14]
Director as Third Eye[15]
Director as Voyeur[16]
Director as Ego or Superego[17]
Director as Leader of an Expedition to Another World[18]
Director as Autocratic Ship Captain[19]
Director as Puppet-Master[20]
Director as Sculptor/Visual Artist[21]
Director as Midwife[22]
Director as Lover[23]
Director as Marriage Partner[24]
Director as Literary Critic[25]
Director as Trainer of Athletic Team[26]
Director as Trustee of Democratic Spirit[27]
Director as Psychoanalyst[28]
Director as Listener, Surrogate-Audience[29]
Director as Author[30]
Director as Harrower/Gardener[31]
Director as Beholder, Ironic Recuperator of the Maternal
    Gaze[32]

Of all these analogues, that of the maternal gaze seems the most promising, though insufficient to encompass the whole director-actor experience. Any reader with an interest in the Lacanian concept of the gaze will note intermittent references to it throughout. I shall have recourse to the "gaze" when it seems helpful or suggestive but shall not employ it as an organizing principle of the present book. While this may result in some lack of theoretical rigor, it may at the same time protect against some of the dangers of theoretical rigor.

My own spectatorial relation to the director in rehearsal temporarily reverses the usual subject and object positions and at times puts the directorial gaze in question. Gazing can, of course, be many things. The "phallocentric gaze," which defends against, controls, and wards off the threatening aspects of the female, consigning her always to the object position, is one-way and appropriative. But there is another and earlier kind of gazing: the maternal gaze, which may become the mutual gaze of mother and infant. E. Ann Kaplan raises the question whether it is possible "to imagine a male and female gaze . . . that would go beyond male obliteration of the female, or female surrender to the male, indeed beyond gender duality, into an unconscious delight in mutual gazing that might be less exclusionary and less pained." My observation of directors in rehearsal suggests not that women take on the masculine role as "bearer of the gaze and initiator of action,"[33] but that the director's gaze, if not "beyond gender duality," is more feminine than masculine and that the male director's appropriation of the female gaze is often more acceptable to the actors than the female director's reinvesting of the maternal gaze with its former potency. The directors I observe might well say with Proust: "Our work makes mothers of us."[34]

Should our work also make theorists of us? Edward Snow has suggested that "theory seems always to choose its paradigms as instances of what it already knows." He continues: "While it would be naive to suggest that one can be without a theory, I would still like to think that one could proceed in a different spirit, resisting ideological (fore)closure and treating one's initial terms—'male' and 'female,' for instance—as subject to revision. . . . Even at this late date it may require something like negative capability to make contact with the images that matter to us most."[35] In the attempt to describe any rehearsal, the appropriate spirit of inquiry is exactly that: a spirit of inquiry. I take a much sterner warning to heart: "Even at the stage of description it is not possible to avoid applying certain abstract ideas to the material in hand, ideas derived from somewhere or other but certainly not from the new observations alone. . . . everything depends on . . . [one's ideas] not being arbitrarily chosen but determined by their having significant relations to the empirical material, relations that we seem to sense before we can clearly recognize and demonstrate them."[36]

Metaphors and theories aside, why concentrate on the process of creation rather than on what is created? British actress Dame Peggy Ashcroft has said that "Though rehearsals can be painful, . . . they're the most exciting part of acting, much more so than the performance, because they're the making of it, the giving birth."[37] But why is "the making of it" so fascinating?

In the fall of 1988, I observed Lee Breuer directing the Japanese master Bunraku puppeteer, Tamamatsu, during rehearsals of *The Warrior Ant* at Yale University. Tamamatsu is himself a kind of director who animates a nearly lifesize wood-and-cloth doll so that it becomes the star of the show, seemingly more alive than the puppetmaster. One day, after entering the rehearsal room, I asked, through gesture, if I might hold the precious Bunraku doll. Tamamatsu, who knows very little English, immediately put his hand inside the head of the puppet. (Bunraku puppets have no built torso, just a costumed sack.) He gestured to my hand to take his and follow it until suddenly my hand alone is inside the neck of the doll, bearing its weight, which is substantial—it's heavier than it looks. It is a strange feeling to be exploring the interior workings of the puppet-actor, guided by the Bunraku master. It is a moment when the desire to know "how things work" is met by the failure of facts to account fully for the observed event. To know "how it's done" may take us out of the world of innocence, but no less into a world that resists full disclosure. Finally, the desire to comprehend the mystery is the desire to have the mystery affirmed.

Constantin Stanislavski, perhaps the best known director of his time, has said of rehearsal: "Seventy-five percent of what we do at rehearsal does not enter the performance. If we could retain a hundredth of everything which we find during rehearsal, then in a hundred rehearsals we would have a splendid performance. But, to our regret, it does not always work that way. Don't be afraid to tell an actor, 'Rehearse this way today, but I want you to know that you will not play it this way.' "[38] In the following chapters I document, and analyze, rehearsal work that paradoxically makes possible a performance it seemingly "does not enter."

A few generalizations, expected and unexpected, might be helpful in introducing the different trajectories of the directors I observed. The creative process in crisis—as it usually is—seems to be a kind of hermeneutic circle: the problem has to be fully understood in order to be resolved and yet only the right resolution fully illuminates the nature of the problem. Even playwright-directors like Irene Fornes and Emily Mann depend on seeing the effects of their directing in order to *know* the emerging shape, the physicalized presence, of the written text. It is what Brecht must have discovered in his staging, revising, and restaging of *Mother Courage and Her Children* when he directed his wife in the lead role. What is constructed by the playwright, and reinscribed by the director, is mediated by the physicality of persons and objects, a physicality that leaves its own traces in the process of creation. The frequent complaint of actors that certain directors don't know what they want until they see it enacted in fact calls attention to a nearly inevitable aspect of directing.

A related, equally unanticipated generalization is that "the auteur-director"[39] is to some degree inevitably a collaborator with the actors, even as a director best known for collaborative work may eventually assume a position of central power in rehearsal.

Midway through rehearsal of her play, *Abingdon Square*, Irene Fornes speaks of "the advantage of being a playwright-director: when there is trouble with a line, I just *change* it. If the director is not the playwright, then the actors just have to deal with it." But the distinction between the director-playwright and the director working with others' scripts is not so clear-cut. Fornes's half-playful distinction is deceptive: actors do have trouble with parts of the script that the playwright-director does not necessarily change. As for directors who are not the playwright, there are some who won't change the author's language and stage directions, and many who will, but every director can alter the effect of a troublesome line by placing it in an unexpected context. When an actor has difficulty with a line in rehearsal, adjustments of one sort or another will be made, no matter who wrote the script. In performance, what an actor utters, and how and when and where, is most often beyond the control of both playwright and director.

Rehearsal is the site of the Möbius strip-like relation between authorial and directorial functions. Just as a Möbius strip calls in question our sense of what is "inside" and what is "outside," the playwright directing her or his own play calls in question our sense of where authorial functions end and directorial functions begin. Where we might expect closure, rigid classification, strict demarcation, we find overlap, replication, continuity. Surprisingly, Michael Goldman's wonderful definition of playwriting as "an art of composing in the medium of the actor—of composing in action,"[40] can, without distortion, be applied as well to the work of the director in rehearsal.[41]

It is in this context that a seemingly mundane aspect of rehearsal must be reconsidered: the start-stop process. In starting, stopping, and restarting the rehearsal work that reinscribes the playtext "in the medium of the actor," the director engages the actors in a formal reenactment of the playwright's creative process. It is in this sense that the director may be considered as "standing in" for the author, even when the director *is* the author: not by voicing the playwright's "position" on matters of interpretation or by editing or altering the script, but as the agent of the authorial process itself.

Despite their obvious differences, the first readthrough and the final dress runthrough of a play are singularly alike in their representation of the artistic process as a steady flow onward.[42] In this they are both precursors of the performance itself, and its famous motto: "The show must go on." I vividly recall a performance of one-third of Shakespeare's *Much Ado About Nothing* at the Delacorte Theatre in New York's Central Park on July 19, 1988, in which a drenched Kevin Kline as Benedick continued line-perfect amid lightning, thunder, and violent downpour until the dimming lights commanded his surrender of the role while the outdoor stage gradually became a lake. But this ongoing flow is not a paradigm of the creative process, only one of its illusionistic effects. The *work* of rehearsal work—what, in fact, often makes actors irritable and frustrated—is the forced enactment of the flow *and* the stoppages that are inherent in all creative activity. My own analysis of rehearsal temporarily "stops" a process whose stoppages can only be understood as part of a continuum.

"You do assist the storm," the Boatswain says to Antonio, who is trying to establish the hierarchical ordering of activity amidst a sea-storm in Shakespeare's *The Tempest*. The director in rehearsal is somewhat in the position of Shakespeare's Antonio except that the director, more like Prospero than Antonio, knows that the "storm" is a creation of art, not nature. The director in rehearsal has the paradoxical role of "assist[ing] the storm," the creative flow of energy, by seemingly trying to stop it, interrupt it, at times detour, distract, antagonize it. Finally, the cast, like the Boatswain, will say, "Use your authority. If you cannot, give thanks you have lived so long, and make yourself ready in your cabin for the mischance of the hour, if it so hap. . . . *Out of our way.*"[43]

Fig. 2.1. Joanna Merlin and Amanda Plummer. Photograph by Michael Shavel.

2

Elinor Renfield Directs
The Cherry Orchard

> *"You can observe a lot by watching."*
> Yogi Berra

I begin with the first rehearsal I observed: Elinor Renfield's production of Chekhov's *The Cherry Orchard* in late June and early July of 1985. Rehearsals take place at the National Shakespeare Conservatory on lower Broadway in Manhattan, with performances at the John Drew Theater of Guild Hall in East Hampton from July 12 through July 20, 1985. The cast, characterized by Erika Munk as "distinguished and/or celebrated,"[1] includes Joanna Merlin (Ranevskaya), Amanda Plummer (Anya), Paul Hecht (Gayev), Frederick Coffin (Lopakhin), and William Roerick (Firs). Elinor Renfield is a tireless and intelligent director whose credits include productions in New York, both on and off Broadway, as well as in Washington, D.C. (Arena Stage), Boston, Chicago, and Stamford, Connecticut. Recipient of two grants from the National Endowment for the Arts, she has also taught extensively in universities and conservatories.

Renfield is working not with a repertory company but with an assemblage of actors who bring with them different approaches, training, experience, personalities. She describes the major problem in this production as an excruciatingly constricted rehearsal period of about two weeks; she later remarks of Chekhov, "The text is written as if coded and needs time and care to crack the code."[2] The cast includes actors who are also directors or acting teachers.[3] Many of the actors, as is usual in contemporary American theatre, also appear on television—some concurrently with this rehearsal—[4]or in films.

Notwithstanding its particular conditions and make-up, the *Cherry Orchard* rehearsal is perhaps roughly representative, one version, of a normative directing style in contemporary American theatre practice. While there is, of course, literally no "norm" for such an eclectic art, the documenting of Renfield's directorial style may serve to establish terms of art along with characteristic situations and crises that recur in other productions, as well as a base line by which more experimental directors may be tracked. It is my hope that in this opening chapter the rehearsal of *The Cherry Orchard* can function for the reader, in the same way that it did for the observer, as an introduction to the director at work in the theatre.

Shortly before the cast assembles in a small sixth floor studio in Soho, in the early afternoon of June 26, 1985, my first day of observing rehearsals, Elinor Renfield turns to me and says, "This is too fast. We only have two weeks. We have to do an act a day! I'm frantic." One week later she will remark, in the presence of the actors, "I've never had to work this fast in my life." Today she begins work on act two by setting the mood: "It's a hot June evening, about 6:30 or 7 p.m. [None of this is specified in Chekhov's stage directions, which note only that the sun will soon be setting.] It's interesting to think about how you all got here. Interesting, working class people just drifted away from the house. . . ." There is a long pause, long enough to suggest that what is being transmitted to the four actors is not simply information and that what is being absorbed is individual and private. Renfield tells Dunyasha (a chambermaid, played by Eve Bennett-Gordon) and Yasha (a young male servant, played by Robert Sedgwick) that "there is a definite sexual liaison there." She pauses to describe the as yet nonexistent set, designated by variously colored tape on the studio floor, as she tells the actors what will be on the stage of the John Drew Theater at the beginning of the second act. Karen Ludwig (playing the governess, Charlotta Ivanovna) suddenly muses aloud, "I wonder if we all came here together. I wonder who was here first." The director responds quickly, "I think Charlotta got here first." The actress playing Charlotta immediately suggests an improvisation on how these four characters happen to end up together in the same place (a meadow, near a small abandoned chapel, by the side of a well, an old bench, and some large stones, apparently former tombstones). Renfield gives unqualified support to the *idea* of an improvisation but postpones its enactment until the following week (it is omitted because of time pressures). Addressing the actress whose eerie monologue opens act two, Renfield now says,

"Take as long as you need before you speak. The improv will help us with that. Take your time. Whenever you're ready, we'll start."

Burke Pearson, in the role of the clerk, Yepikhodov, following Chekhov's stage direction, begins to play his guitar. Karen Ludwig, improvising on the stage direction that Charlotta merely take the gun from her shoulder and arrange the strap buckle, aims the rifle at Yepikhodov. The director laughs, but does not interrupt until the actress exits from the playing area, that part of the rehearsal room floor marked to represent the exact dimensions of the theatre stage where the performance will occur. In this small studio, the playing area covers about nine-tenths of the available floor space and creates considerable difficulties for the director in viewing the performance as it will be viewed by the audience in the theatre. Renfield now stops the rehearsal, saying, "Let's call this the first scene of the scene." Chekhov does not divide his four-act play into scenes. Throughout Renfield's rehearsals she is concerned to divide acts into smaller playable units, and to divide these units into even smaller subdivisions, as she and the cast are continually forced to attend to what the director calls the "razor-sharp transitions in Chekhov."

Renfield's comments on the first unit—from Charlotta's opening monologue to her exit, just a few minutes of playing time—touch briefly on Yepikhodov's role (she tells the actor he is too aggressive) but focus on the relationship of Yasha and Dunyasha. She now initiates what will be a period of prolonged attention to the complexities of staging a scene of physical intimacy and sexual implication. The "definite sexual liaison" Renfield has noted is clearly indicated in the stage directions and dialogue (on their first encounter in the opening act, Yasha surreptitiously embraces Dunyasha, who drops a saucer; in the second act, he kisses her and, after declaring that she loves him passionately, Dunyasha impulsively embraces him). The problem for the actors and director is not that of a baffled or disputed reading of the text, as will occur later in both Renfield's and Irene Fornes's rehearsals of Chekhov; nor does it derive from a sense of a complex buried situation as the real fulcrum of the scene. Here, as so often in rehearsal, a problem which initially presents itself as one of relationship or impulse must ultimately be resolved at the level of staging.

Initially Renfield simply asks Yasha and Dunyasha to try another physical position as they sit together on the bench. The initial seated position on the bench indicated by Chekhov is followed by Renfield in her staging of the play, as are almost all the playwright's stage directions.[5] Renfield's note[6] to the actors is open-ended: "Try another position together," yet specifically focused: "Insinuate that your bodies are ready for one another." Yasha's first response is to place his legs over Dunyasha's thigh. The actress expresses a distinction and potential tension, common to every rehearsal, between how a scene *feels*, to the actor, and how a scene *looks*, to the director as audience-surrogate: "I feel as if he's crowding me, but if it looks good, it's okay."

Renfield resituates the actor so that he is leaning against the actress' shoulder, his back toward her; director and actress agree that Dunyasha is free to do whatever she likes behind Yasha's back. Throughout these adjustments, Charlotta remains in character, cleaning her gun, talking to herself. She is seated in the playing area and yet slightly "offstage" to what is occurring there: a casual Chekhovian configuration like that of the scene being rehearsed in which characters present in the same space do not inevitably address their remarks to one another.

The director stops and restarts sections of "the first scene of the scene" in ways that, rather than paralyzing the actors' initial tentative explorations, allow for new outbursts of energy and experimentation. As this tiny unit of the play is rehearsed over and over, no two versions are the same. Renfield, occasionally recapitulating verbally what is happening in the scene, helps the actors to consider what they are doing as a group as well as individually. When Ludwig questions why Charlotta criticizes the singing of Yasha and Yepikhodov ("They sing dreadfully, these people. Faugh. Like shrieking dogs."),[7] Renfield suggests that the Germanic governess' attitude toward the Russian singing is envy, like that felt for "people singing a camp song from a camp she didn't go to." Later when the actress again expresses her difficulty in "justifying" the line, the director, acknowledging that she is unable to recall her previous response to this acting problem, directs Yasha to make the last note of the song "ear-wrenching," thereby allowing the actress to give her line a literalistic reading: the singing really is terrible.

It's not that the director's first interpretation is right and the second wrong, or the reverse: no particular psychologically realistic or literal reading of the line can fully account for its oddness, its indeterminate relation to the situation in which it seems embedded, its uncertain status as a remark not directed, but in direct response, to other characters on stage. In this instance—

and never again—I naively review my notes and privately relay the forgotten early interpretation to the director. By this act I quickly learn that while note-taking stage managers may be asked to resolve disputes about forgotten blocking, directorial suggestions are trickier enterprises. Notes in rehearsal may function as incentives to actors, energizing hypotheses, markers which, like footprints in the sand, are meant to be washed away. As the poet A.R. Ammons says, in the last line of "Corsons Inlet,"

Tomorrow a new walk is a new walk.[8]

Now Renfield turns back to Yepikhodov, the luckless rejected suitor of Dunyasha, who stands, as Chekhov instructs, near the other three characters seated on the bench, and plays a guitar which he persists in calling a mandolin. I overhear the director say to the actor, "You're at a distance. You're at a disadvantage. Play against it." She gives an example. "I'm over here because it's cool under this tree. And it takes . . . guts to consider suicide." After five more minutes of inaudible private conversation conducted off to one side of the playing area, Renfield distills from its psychological context the blocking, the expressive positioning and movement of the actors on the stage: "That's all the scene is about: moving from behind the fence to the tree to beside her to ask if you can be alone with her." Renfield's "That's all the scene is about" is, of course, deceptive; it follows a prolonged discussion of specific elements in the scene. But it is a refrain in Renfield's directorial discourse and suggests that for her the blocking is as much a means of entry into "a text . . . written as if coded" as it is a result of the analytic work of decoding. Thus she continues to refine the physical positioning of Yasha and Dunyasha, but also responds to Joanna Merlin's later question about the exact placement of Lyubov Ranevskaya during a dialogue with Lopakhin, "I'm not certain about that. You'll find your way into it."

At another point, Renfield says to Josh Clark, playing Trofimov, "Blocking will work itself out." While this is clearly not the approach of most of the directors I observe, or even Renfield's view throughout most of her rehearsal, it finds support in Robert Benedetti's instructions to directors: "Think of blocking . . . as a continuous activity which grows naturally out of the tendency of human beings to place themselves in expressive relationships whenever they are engaged in significant interactions in a specific space. When the interaction becomes clear and forceful enough, trust that it will block itself."[9] This "it," however, is complicated, as suggested by the actress' earlier distinction between what feels right and what looks right: the positioning and movement of bodies in space represent, ideally, some kind of coming together or adjustment of the actors' blocking impulses and the director's visual perspective.

Props are not in evidence in this early rehearsal but their importance is never forgotten. In act two, Renfield reminds Yasha that he is "just having a smoke," adding, "The cigar is going to make all the difference. [To stage manager Zoya Wyeth, she says] Let's have it for next time." By her hyperbolic phrasing. "all the difference," Renfield is not simply alluding to the effect of the cigar on other characters as indicated in the dialogue (it gives Dunyasha a headache, Ranevskaya finds its odor disgusting) but also to its function as a physical aid in propping up, so to speak, Yasha's disengagement in this scene.

The addition of a simple prop—a cucumber,[10] a cloak, a piece of candy, a pair of old galoshes—is often more than a simple addition to a scene. It can be an enabling and sometimes a determining factor, especially in rehearsing a play which inscribes its props in its language. But the language of a playtext is always already straining toward the tangible as well as the visual. Charles Segal, writing on classical Greek tragedy, stresses "two systems of communication and representation ... the power of visualization inherent in the image-making power of the word itself and the concrete act of visualization on the theatrical stage."[11] That the director in rehearsal articulates the interlocking of these two systems is suggested in even so slight a matter as the detail of a missing cigar.[12]

Renfield's directorial discourse is often kinetic as well as visual. "There you go, Burke, the winds of fate blowing you upstage again," she says to Yepikhodov, after he has been brushed aside by Dunyasha. Her remark includes both a kind of interior monologue on behalf of the character (Yepikhodov would think of this brush-off in terms of the "winds of fate"; he has just imaged fate as a tempest tossing him as if he were a small boat) and a specific blocking direction: "upstage," a movement away from the audience and thus away from a position of central focus and power on the stage. In Renfield's casual comment are yoked the "image-making power of the word[s]" inscribed in the text and "the concrete act of visualization on the theatrical stage."

But the kinetic implications of Renfield's language are not always so literal nor at times can they be realized except through the voice. For example, in a later rehearsal of act two, she tells Yasha to "put a wink in your voice." Suggesting to Ranevskaya that her comment to Gayev "is loving, though obviously it has in it an arched eyebrow," Renfield clearly does not intend that Joanna Merlin elevate one eyebrow during her speech to Paul Hecht. These directorial notes are not invitations to action but verbal representations and visual reminders of a kinetic supplement in the very act of reading the playtext.[13]

Renfield returns to the problem of staging the "sexual liaison" between Dunyasha and Yasha seated on the bench. She begins by reminding Dunyasha that Yasha will do to her what she does to Yepikhodov. As she speaks, the director mimes an exaggerated pushing away of an unwanted presence. This deliberately exaggerated presentation of a physical action that accompanies verbal analysis is characteristic of Renfield's directorial style. It is a kind of physicalized reading of the text, like that of the actor's body reinscribing the script, but self-consciously detached, more presentational than representational. The director is "performing" a reading of the text on behalf of one actor, then another; the actor is reading a role through the medium of the body.

A related but quite different model of director as reader-critic is Renfield's voicing of the subtext[14] while the actor reads the text aloud. Even as Yasha is telling Dunyasha, "If there's one thing I can't stand, it's a girl who doesn't know how to behave like a lady,"[15] the director is standing close beside him in the playing area, saying quietly, "Yes, you can. It's the only girl you can stand," so that the actor changes his tone mid-speech, giving more complexity to the line reading.

Yasha's speech is preceded by a kiss which, like all rehearsal kisses and embraces I observe, begins in awkwardness. After working closely with Yasha and Dunyasha for four or five minutes, Renfield tells them that the kiss will finally be whatever bargain the actors eventually make. Nonetheless, later that evening, she will work this unit of action again in great detail. But now, after waiting for one and a half hours, a group of three principal actors joins the scene. As the landowner Ranevskaya, her brother Gayev, and the merchant Lopakhin prepare to enter the playing area, Renfield says to Yasha and Dunyasha, "They're coming. It's terror." When questioned semi-facetiously by an actor, "Shall we play 'terror'?" Renfield responds, "Experience terror. Play motion."

As Dunyasha rushes off and a new ensemble enters, a pattern emerges. Renfield characteristically works briefly with each new grouping as a unit and then with smaller groups, finally focusing on individual actors, much as she divides Chekhov's acts into scenes, scenes into units, units into beats. The new group of actors at first seems to have low energy, perhaps because they have been waiting so long to work, perhaps because it is by now mid-afternoon and getting hotter. (It has been decided not to use the room's one noisy air conditioner during these early summer rehearsals.) Speaking to the three principal actors, Renfield says, "Who's going to help me, rescue me? That's the subtext." It seems to me at first that this is Renfield's subtext as director,[16] even Chekhov's as dramatist, as well as that of every character in the play, but it is also a question crucial and specific to this scene in act two.

Acknowledging almost immediately that in her blocking directions she is "giving broad strokes to be filled in later," Renfield suggests that after Yasha exits, Lopakhin, played by Frederick Coffin, "take a back [upstage] cross to the side of Ranevskaya," as if replacing the young upstart by assuming familiarity with a woman whose servant he himself once was. I do not remember whether this cross was retained in performance, but it is a clear example of blocking as directly illustrating a changing dynamic or significant interaction between or among human beings: blocking as a form of literary criticism.

Experimental directors like Robert Wilson or Richard Foreman or Elizabeth LeCompte will expressly avoid blocking that "illustrates" the text. Renfield, on the other hand, characteristically privileges blocking that functions as a kind of objective correlative for a character's "inner life" or for the buried situation in a scene. For example, she says to the actor playing Lopakhin, "I want to try something here. I want you to take this now as a kind of attempted choreography. . . . The degree of Lopakhin's attempted explosive exit reflects the degree of his explosive attempt to get . . . [Ranevaskaya and Gayev] to listen to him." She instructs Coffin to take as much time as he needs to hold Gayev's eye and to decide, in what "becomes a new unit of embellishment," *not* to leave. This "new unit of embellishment," while it seems, strictly speaking, to add a fictionalized detail to Chekhov's inscribing of the scene, is in fact a necessary subtext, and playable as such, in a Beckett-like moment of deferring an expected exit.

Shifting her attention to Ranevskaya in this same unit of action, Renfield now redirects Joanna Merlin's exploratory blocking and also her pace, exposing more fully the director's concern with *Zeitraum*, or space-time. The dancer Sally Hess puts it quite simply: "You really can't talk about time without talking about space."[17] And the reverse is true as well, as is evident in every theatre rehearsal. Joanna Merlin's response to the director's spatial-temporal comment ("You would never run after Lopakhin. Stand up, yes, but don't go to him . . . wait it out.") is to create a breathtaking moment in rehearsal when Ranevskaya rises, asks Lopakhin to stay, and simply *waits* until he turns back to look at her before she continues to speak and move. The tone of begging, suggested in the English translation ("No, dear friend. Please stay."),[18] has been overtaken by a tone of command, and by something more, evoked in part not by detailed analysis of psychological motivation but simply by the directorial note to change the tempo. Renfield has simply *slowed down* the scene, giving Ranevskaya and Lopakhin an opportunity to find a meaningful interaction, a pause whose duration they together create, followed by Ranevskaya's unhurried walk toward Lopakhin.

It is immediately after this that the director responds to the actress' question about Ranevskaya's exact physical position during her next interchange by saying, "I'm not concerned about that. You'll find your way into it." What seems a brusque, even dismissive reply occurs just as the actress is preparing to deliver a speech recalling the death of Ranevskaya's young son and her subsequent suicide attempt. As is often characteristic of early rehearsals, this long monologue is read aloud in a very low voice, almost inaudible, and yet the actress seems to be crying, as the stage directions stipulate but nonetheless quite "genuinely," after the mention of the loss of the child. Renfield hugs the actress after the speech is finished. Perhaps the director's refusal to provide the spatial orientation the actress requested contributes to the feelings of emotional disorientation and dissolution which she expresses so movingly in rehearsal. Perhaps not. In the words of Dame Peggy Ashcroft, speaking for innumerable actors, "Acting is mysterious. You can't get away from it."[19]

Renfield tells Lopakhin that she wants "a sense of a 'new scene' after Ranevskaya embraces Gayev." This new scene includes the entrance of the old valet Firs, played by William Roerick, who is not at rehearsal today. The director first substitutes the stage manager, then plays the role of Firs herself. Suddenly the director enters the playing area as an actor among actors. In fact, she reads the lines aloud without expressive tonal quality or movement, seemingly refraining from "acting" the role, while she gives over her directorial function to the stage manager, Zoya Wyeth, who takes detailed notes on the staging of the scene. After Renfield plays the role of Firs, Frederick Coffin suggests that there is a "new informality" in the line readings and in the staging—for example, characters seem to be in closer proximity to each other than before—and Renfield agrees, adding that Firs "is the archaic element in the scene," is "deaf to everything." Certainly one might detect, or encourage, a new note in any scene Firs enters, as Renfield does in her role as director before she enters the playing area as an actor. But it is suggestive that the scene relaxes as the director plays a character who is "deaf to everything," as if the loss of the director as auditor-spectator along with the change in the formal context of rehearsal is reflected in the acting style. It is also suggestive that Renfield's comments almost exclusively focus on the function and implications of the role she assumes. The director's consciousness and that of the actor creating a role are contiguous but not coextensive, perhaps in the relation of a series of concentric circles in which the outermost circle, ideally, represents the directorial vision and the innermost circle the more intimate space of the actor's imagination.

After abandoning the role of Firs, who has obediently gone silent as commanded by Gayev, Renfield addresses the largest grouping of actors so far, as Ranevskaya's daughters, Anya (Amanda Plummer) and Varya (Cherry Jones), and the student Trofimov (Josh Clark) join the scene. The director first sketches blocking she has seemingly prepared in advance, telling the actors who are now entering where and how to move—running, walking—so that a different kind of energy is invested by each actor in the group entrance. After Renfield describes exactly how she'd like Anya and Varya to enter to Ranevskaya, the actor playing Lopakhin makes a suggestion for an alternate blocking, and without hesitation the director agrees. Renfield, focusing again on a small unit of playing time, says, "This is a scene about how much of a man Trofimov is." To the actor playing the "eternal student," she says, as if speaking Trofimov's interior

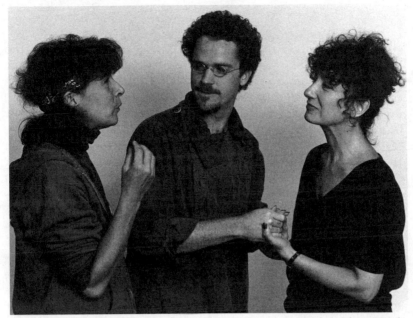

Fig. 2.2. Elinor Renfield with Josh Clark and Joanna Merlin. Photograph by Michael Shavel.

monologue, "This is my passport into the space: I'm using words you [Lopakhin] probably don't understand." It is arguable that the scene is about more, or something other, than Trofimov's manhood, but Renfield's psychological, and at times sexual, reading of a specific situation in the play is often employed as a kind of jumper cable to jolt the actor's awareness of subtextual possibilities.

The increased number of actors on stage (seven, not counting the later brief appearance of a passerby) highlights a recurrent problem in rehearsing Chekhov: the problem of where, and to whom, to direct a given speech. Charlotta, for example, except when she is performing her magic tricks in act three, has no one to talk to, as she herself says, and this is a common puzzling situation of the actors rehearsing the play. Indeed, Chekhov has Gayev address a speech in act one to a bookcase!

Here Renfield suggests that Trofimov direct his remarks, after Lopakhin has baited him, to Gayev and not to anyone else on stage. This choice is not at all clear from the text since both Varya and Ranevskaya address Trofimov directly. Renfield stresses Trofimov's interaction with Gayev as a quarry for other acting choices. She says to Trofimov: "Gayev is your punching bag, your real polar opposite. Dip into Gayev for fuel and then take that energy elsewhere. . . . Also, he's loquacious. You both don't work but each has a different attitude toward it." And she adds, as if it were a logical consequence of her previous notes, "So I'd suggest you go slowly." The instruction to slow down the pace of the vocal delivery, a seeming *non sequitur* in her directorial notes, has the same effect as the earlier blocking direction to Ranevskaya in her response to Lopakhin's abortive exit: it immediately adds clarity and intensity to the scene. Renfield translates the director's usual concern with physical movement in space and time into a kind of "aural blocking,"[20] a shaping of the aural trajectory of speech on stage (in this instance, the trajectory is at first narrowed so that Gayev alone is the auditor) and verbal timing.

What I am calling "aural blocking" is again illustrated by the director's announcement, "We're going to try something here. We're going to break ground here." The ground-breaking, clearly more a harrowing than a ploughing, is the suggestion that Trofimov break up his long monologue on the progress of humanity by addressing different parts of the speech to various foci in the playing area as well as to members of the "offstage" audience. Renfield, reshaping the trajectory of the speech that follows Trofimov's somewhat wandering monologue, asks Lopakhin to deliver the first half of his speech to Trofimov and the second half to Ranevskaya. This is a plausible close reading of the slightly shifting tonal qualities in Lopakhin's speech which could as well be delivered in its entirety to either one of these two characters or to no one in the room. In directing the placing of these speeches, Renfield leads an expedition into an uncharted sound space. In the experimental theatre of Robert Wilson, however, actors will rarely face each other, often not see each other at all, as they speak of situations that may or may not relate to the unnamed characters on the stage.

Near the close of act two and again at the very end of the play, there occurs one of the most haunting and inexplicable sounds ever inscribed in a playtext. A moment of silence on stage is broken by a distant sound, like that of "a snapped string mournfully dying away."[21] Renfield arranges the tableau so that each character is focused on some other character, then says simply, "Now out of that silence comes a sound, a really disturbing sound." She makes a sound, low, raspy, in her throat. Then quickly and without making too much of the moment, she asks the actors "to break the freeze without moving," i.e., to relax their head and body positions as they begin to speak. Renfield has clearly thought out and felt this moment but doesn't make it seem portentous, or rather, doesn't force its portentousness on the actors. One might be tempted to say she simply lets the moment "speak for itself," except that every moment in rehearsal is in some sense chosen—however mysteriously—by its having occurred in the context of rehearsal, a shaping for beholding.[22]

Rehearsal work is a mix of uncanny and prosaic moments. The intrusion into their midst of an inexplicable sound, like the intrusion of the stranger who follows it, does not give the actors as much difficulty as their group exit near the end of act two. Throughout the rehearsals I observe, entrances and exits are apt to be unexpected minefields, like the not-so-simple action of simply walking across the stage during a scene. Renfield has trouble getting five characters off the stage as they continue to converse. Directing the exit so that several lines are delivered "offstage" and others are delivered to no one in particular in the playing area, Renfield knowingly creates a blocking that the actors do not find "natural" or comfortable.

It is 5:30 p.m. and the room is cleared of everyone but the director and two actors. I am allowed to watch a private rehearsal of the final moments of act two. Renfield gives no initial instructions. She watches without interrupting as Amanda Plummer and Josh Clark play the scene in almost inaudibly soft voices. Their inaudibility in so small a room—they are only a few feet from the director and myself—makes the scene seem even more private. The actors, uninterrupted by the director, interrupt themselves at one point and agree to replay one sequence of speeches. This part of rehearsal shows Renfield's understanding of directing as knowing when not to direct, almost as if the scene were too fragile to touch, but might repair, recreate, itself. After the first playing of the scene, Renfield mainly supports the actress' initial choices: "I love the fact, Amanda, that from the minute you came in you're [seated] on the bench." In answer to the actress' quick response, "Why?" Renfield elaborates, "The stillness—to be able to be rooted, not accommodating anybody else. And the end of the act is driven by Trofimov." The simple statement of support, pursued by the actress, becomes a more complex and ambivalent directorial note, more reflective of the density of the text, a suggestion that the actress is rooted and still and also provoked and "driven" by Trofimov. Anya sits on her bench and she says, "What have you done to me, Petya? Why have I stopped loving the cherry orchard as I did before?"[23]

Renfield now gives directorial notes before the second uninterrupted playing of the scene: "You two are getting closer and closer. It's as if the next thing would be a kiss. Sexual tension is rising. . . . 'The moon is rising' [a line near the end of the scene, first spoken by Anya and immediately repeated by Trofimov] is a difficult beat." The "beat," referred to often in rehearsal, is the smallest subdivision of the smallest unit of playing time or action. It is defined differently by different directors as well as by different members of the same company.[24]

When Renfield tells the actors that a certain repeated line in their scene together is a difficult beat, she seems to suggest that the beat here is subtextual. (Later, when Amanda Plummer asks what the beat is in a scene with Gayev, Renfield replies, "The beat consists of 'What are we going to do?' That's also Anya's subtext.") Renfield reads the end of act two as an unacknowledged love scene and Trofimov's repetition of Anya's abrupt *non sequitur*, "The moon is rising," as a clue to a barely concealed affinity (a faint allusion perhaps to the famous moment in Chekhov's *Three Sisters*, completed the year before he began to work on *The Cherry Orchard*, when Masha and her lover Vershinin spontaneously hum parts of Tchaikovsky's opera, *Eugen Onegin*).[25]

Whatever textual or intertextual support there may be for the director's interpretation, Renfield is identifying an acting problem, not its resolution. After the second playing of the scene she sits on the floor with the two actors. She speaks of potential intimacy with Anya as frightening to Trofimov who retreats to his "old pedantic self" and the "distance" this gives him in his relationships. But she speaks at the same time of Trofimov's speeches as "embraces," and she simply mentions the possibility that Trofimov might at one point touch Anya's face and then later join her on the bench (the actors have so far rehearsed this scene without touching each other, Anya seated and Trofimov standing at some distance from her). Later in the evening when the scene is replayed, Trofimov does not join Anya on the bench but touches her face near the end of their dialogue; it is very gentle and moving and receives spontaneous applause from the onlooking cast.

At 7 p.m., after the dinner break, Renfield again rehearses the opening scene of act two. This time the actress playing Charlotta is not present and the stage manager is substituted. (That evening another actor, not the director, will play Firs.) Renfield makes a change in the physical placement of Yasha and Dunyasha on the bench so that Dunyasha is freed from her previous position propping up Yasha's back. Contradicting her earlier note to the actor, Renfield now tells Yepikhodov to act more aggressively to break up, break into, the dialogue between Yasha and Dunyasha. She removes Dunyasha's compact, forcing the actress to find some other way to primp (Chekhov's stage direction indicates that Dunyasha looks into a pocket mirror and powders her face), revealing the reversibility of the implications of her earlier remark that a prop—Yasha's cigar—can "make all the difference."[26] Again altering the work of the afternoon rehearsal, Renfield says, "I'm now trying to follow up the places where Dunyasha is interrupted [by Yepikhodov]." Having focused on Yasha and Dunyasha as a dyad and Yepikhodov as an easily flicked off peripheral figure, Renfield now refocuses: "Burke, I just had an insight." The director moves beside the actor playing Yepikhodov, whispers something in his ear. Yepikhodov again delivers a speech which ends, "Thus, I always carry a revolver. And here it is,"[27] but this time unexpectedly points his revolver at Yasha. Yasha and Dunyasha instinctively sit upright and look attentively at Yepikhodov. As Renfield begins to redirect the couple into a more physically intimate position, Yasha opposes this vigorously, saying, "But he [Yepikhodov] has a gun, he's crazy!" The director, who has introduced the new tension in the scene, does not explicitly ask the actors to play against it. To Yasha she replies simply, "Yes, but don't take him too seriously."

Under Renfield's direction, Dunyasha now experiments with bullying Yepikhodov away from the bench with her body and following him a little way in that same physical attitude. (The next day Renfield will redirect this unit, eliminating Dunyasha's bodily chasing away of Yepikhodov.) Moments in an ever-changing chain of experiments are explored by the actors and then seem to disappear from view.

Now that Dunyasha is liberated from her former position as a prop for Yasha, she is more assertive and appealing. Renfield works again in detail with the kiss, standing close by and often between the actors. Gradually this kiss, initiated by Yasha, becomes ambiguously linked to Dunyasha's subsequent impulsive embrace of Yasha after they hear others approaching. What might have been played as Dunyasha's desperate response to the fact that a rendezvous is about to be interrupted becomes part of a sequence of connected and yet separable moments. During the blocking of the kiss, Renfield says to me with a smile, "This is what directing is." Her remark seems facetious and yet the directing of this belabored kiss is a miniaturized version of the intricacies—the overlapping perspectives, mutual bargains, infinitesimal adjustments—of every shaped moment in the collaborative work of rehearsal.

The relationship of director and actors in rehearsal has many forms, ranging from the director's seemingly tenacious control over acting choices to the actors' revision or reversal of the director's staging of a scene. Sometimes these disparate modes of "collaborative" work follow one another in quick succession. For example, after an uninterrupted playing of the scene between Yasha and Dunyasha, the director demonstrates how the actress might deliver a certain speech with positive pleasure, even self-intoxication.[28] As the actress tries out the suggested reading of the speech, quite successfully, the director stands barely five inches away, between Dunyasha and Yasha, reflecting in her own face and posture the mood she has previously demonstrated which Dunyasha is now enacting. Strictly speaking Renfield is not giving a line reading—anathema to many American actors—but she is in a sense surrounding the actress momentarily with her reading of the line. And yet as I watch, despite what I think I know, the director becomes as much a reflector of what she gazes on as its motivating agent. The mutual reflectivity which I first notice in a woman director and actress recurs in other rehearsals, although—with the striking exception of Emily Mann—usually in more muted forms.

Shortly after this, Renfield's suggested blocking for Gayev and then for Ranevskaya is rejected by the actors. Paul Hecht vigorously opposes the director's suggestion that Gayev move closer to Yasha as he questions him, arguing that (1) Gayev detests Yasha's physical presence, and (2) as a "period character" he would not stand so close to a servant: Yasha breaks the rules, Gayev doesn't. Renfield immediately accepts the actor's view (despite the fact that Ranevskaya has just criticized Gayev for talking to the waiters in the restaurant, another kind of class-crossing familiarity). A few minutes later Joanna Merlin gently suggests that Ranevskaya should not have left the side of her brother as she speaks to Lopakhin. The director immediately supports the actress' sense of the role with its implications for revised blocking. In each case there are at least two, if not three, characters affected by a single actor's placement in space and time: Gayev *and* Yasha; Ranevskaya and Gayev *and* Lopakhin. This might be an occasion for the directorial prerogative to rear its head if for no other reason than simply to adjust the claims or needs of several actors at once. Instead, the director chooses to collaborate with a single actor's impulses. As a result new terrain is open for exploration: Gayev is brought in as a second listener to Lopakhin, allowing Ranevskaya more complexity in her responses as she focuses on both Lopakhin and Gayev. The director suggests that if the scene is to be rehearsed as proposed, Lopakhin should try to move closer to Ranevskaya and Gayev as he speaks. Lopakhin makes this adjustment but is not comfortable with the new blocking of the scene. The director reaffirms her view; the actor again expresses his sense of difficulty with the revised staging. Finally Renfield says, "Fifty-fifty. We'll change part and keep part."

Act two now runs uninterruptedly, with directorial notes given earlier in the day successfully incorporated. The final scene receives applause and the director compliments the actors on having "achieved your first Chekhovian moment." As an exhausted cast prepares to leave the rehearsal studio, Renfield gives the schedule for the rest of the week beginning with renewed work on the first act. Her last words to the company are: "I think we can do a lot with act one tomorrow because a lot is cooking in everybody's unconscious." This is the first of many times I will hear the metaphor of "cooking" in the rhetoric of rehearsal.

Thus ends one day's work in Elinor Renfield's rehearsals of Chekhov's *The Cherry Orchard*. Were I not afraid of imposing on the patience of the reader, a risk already taken in this long opening account, I would have liked to document fully other days in the ever-changing ebb and flow of the rehearsal process. But here instead are selections.

In rehearsal the play's insistencies, spatial as well as verbal, are reflected in the discourse and characteristic configurations of actors in a confined space.[29] At times in the *Cherry Orchard* rehearsals, actors sit in isolated groups taking in and yet not visibly paying attention to the director, who converses audibly with a single actor. Such configurations occur in other rehearsals and yet are distinctive echoes of Chekhov's own dramaturgy, especially his peculiar use of the "chorus scene"[30] in which characters not directly "in" a dialogue seem to be commenting on it. Characters in Chekhov are often simply present in the same space without clear functions. In a rehearsal moment like that in which Charlotta remains seated and talking on stage without directly acknowledging the presence of Yasha and Dunyasha in consultation with the director, Lopakhin rehearses aloud lines from a scene with Dunyasha while standing at a distance from, but still in the playing area with, the actress and the director whose conversation he appears not to hear. Meanwhile, they discuss when Dunyasha is listening and when she is not listening to Lopakhin.

In rehearsing *Execution of Justice* Emily Mann says repeatedly to the actors in their roles as witnesses: "Hear everything. Take it all in." In *The Cherry Orchard* characters rarely seem to be paying adequate attention to other speakers in the room. Renfield compliments Joanna Merlin's playing of a scene in act one between Ranevskaya and Lopakhin: "There's a part of her that's listening and there's a part of her that's not." At another point Renfield says to Lopakhin: "This is why Chekhov is so difficult. . . . You have to tell the truth." One of the truths Chekhov tells is the shifting fragile focus on the quiet human crises in one's midst.[31]

A touching rehearsal of a tiny dialogue between Anya and Dunyasha in act one illustrates the difficulty and delicacy of ensemble work in a Chekhovian scene of conversational bypass. Dunyasha, unable to hold her news in one minute longer, tells the exhausted Anya of Yepikhodov's proposal of marriage. Anya, straightening her hair, brushes Dunyasha's news aside: "You've already told me that. You're always telling me the same stories. I've lost every one of my hair pins."[32] After delivering the first line, Amanda Plummer hugs Eve Bennett-Gordon, saying the unscripted line, "I'm sorry. That was so cruel," as if coming out of her role were a way of getting in touch with it. When she immediately repeats the Chekhov line, there is a slight modulation of her tone which gives a more knowing quality to her seeming indifference. But this is not the solution. The director uncharacteristically stands utterly still, her back at an angle to the two actresses, her arms raised behind her head. The actresses too stand motionless, without speaking. It is a rare moment: a group silence made up of individual silences, another Chekhovian moment in rehearsal.

The director breaks the silence, speaks quietly out of earshot to Anya while Dunyasha twirls a few moments to release tension and then moves closer to watch and listen. The dialogue is rehearsed several times. Anya becomes more abrupt with Dunyasha, as if she tires of this scene as well as the character. Renfield is supportive, reassuring the actress that "the way to deal with temperament is to play the temperament." Whether Chekhov has written a scene about "temperament" or even whether Renfield believes this to be the case may be questioned. But a way has tentatively been found to play a Chekhovian scene of listening and not listening, understanding and not understanding. The most striking aspect of this prolonged rehearsal of a few minutes of playing time is the silence—baffled, meditative, communal. In its own Chekhovian way it tells a truth about rehearsal.

A character's inner life (a term used without quotation marks in these rehearsals although put in question continually by, for example, Robert Wilson) is of continual interest to Renfield. She speaks to Yepikhodov of the "furnace" beneath his obsequiousness; she asks Paul Hecht what makes Gayev need to "fill the space with talk," "sucking up all the air in the room." She elicits the actors' search for inner life through the following means: in her rhetoric of exploration (to Varya in act one, "Something else wants to happen. Let's find it"; to Anya, "See what else is there"); proposals of brief exercises or improvisations (she suggests an improvisation, roughly based on the text but not making use of the scripted lines, in order to investigate Gayev's compulsive need to talk, and a "playground exercise" in which Ranevskaya attacks Trofimov verbally as if she were a child having a tantrum in a sandbox); formal establishing of private moments[33] in rehearsal (she tells Joanna Meriin to repeat and complete the following sentence four times, "I can't live without. . . ." without saying aloud the object of "without": each repetition suggests a deepening emotional revelation, a totally private one); encouragement of full-voiced probing of the interior life of a scene ("Find the full internal voice of the scene. Don't worry about modulation. Later when we try it again we'll take it down to a restraint"); forms of textual analysis that present a single character's submerged point of view (she suggests that for Ranevskaya the situation in the play is one of seemingly infinitely replaceable characters confronting her with their demands and needs so that finally "maybe breaking away is the point").

It is characteristic of Renfield's rehearsals of individual scenes or acts that what might have become fixed or anticipated is continually challenged, refined, overturned, worked against, rejected. Intermittently she articulates every director's awareness that the removal of the rehearsal to the performance stage will inevitably cause alterations in the staging of even the most carefully prepared scenes.[34]

Ghosts are always present in the theatre, and earlier modes of creating life in rehearsal, buried but not dead, reappear in ways that are truly haunting. An example of this begins with Renfield's remark, after some fuss about a missing muff and the use of a coat and hat in a scene between Anya and Varya in act one, that "something else wants to happen. . . . It's something still without being waiting. So what could it be?" In this scene there is a moment when Varya has nowhere to go and nothing to do. Many options are considered and discarded by the director and the two actresses. Renfield enters the acting area and silently replays the scene, thinking in motion. As she stands where Varya had stood while returning Lopakhin's neglected book to the bookcase, she says, "What it's about is not putting the book away; it's about placing, re-placing, Anya." Later she interrupts Varya's speech about Lopakhin's not noticing her to say, "Just fold your life away in that coat," indicating a kind of compulsive fussing with the garment the actress holds in her hands. In performance at the John Drew Theater there is a moment in which elements from that long-ago early exploration are exquisitely realized by the actress—not in the first act, but near the very end of the play, after Lopakhin has failed to propose marriage to Varya. To her mother's question, "Well?"[35] Varya, head down, nods, "no," all the while picking a thread off her coat and gently folding it up as if to "fold . . . [her] life away in that coat" forever.[36]

In her approach to blocking, Renfield takes seriously the tension implied in her summary at the beginning of one day's rehearsal: "Yesterday what we were doing was my telling you what didn't *look* good and your telling me what didn't *feel* good." Her characteristic comment after a blocking instruction is, "But if it doesn't feel comfortable, let me know." The director articulates her working principle when she says to Ranevskaya: "Everything's connected. You make a choice, and he [Lopakhin] makes a choice," adding, "That's why I need choices made now." In rehearsal, choices made by one actor affect the placement, possibilities, and prospects of every other member of any stage transaction.

As roles and relationships are clarified and deepened, as the nature of individual acts, scenes, units, and beats is illuminated and tentatively established, the staging of particular moments changes accordingly. William Roerick tells me that after fifty years in the theatre this is his first experience of a production in which blocking is continually altered during rehearsal. Renfield's approach, visibly collaborative, relies on the interconnected and at times interdependent choices of individual actors in the cumulative building of the final staging. Renfield characteristically encourages actors to resolve some of their own blocking problems (when Yepikhodov can't see Dunyasha, Renfield asks both actors, "How are you going to solve this?"): incorporates actors' suggestions and their improvisations in the expressive placement of human figures in time and space (in response to an inspired spontaneous gesture as Pishchik bids farewell to Ranevskaya, she says, "I love a good acting impulse. It helps my work"); praises the actors' group blocking impulses ("You've found a beautiful picture out there"); unembarrassedly acknowledges the inescapable limitations of any director ("I only have two eyes. . . . I can't see everything. So you have to tell me if you're having trouble with something").

Differences between final dress rehearsal and opening night are legendary in the theatre, but even more striking are the differences between one rehearsal and the next, one moment of playing time and its attempted recreation a moment later. Tortsov, the teacher-director in Stanislavski's *An Actor Prepares*, says: "Each dramatic and artistic image, created on the stage, is unique and cannot be repeated, just as in nature."[37] During rehearsal Renfield says of an improvised gesture, "Wonderful, Mark [Zeller]. Do that again," and the actor replies, "If I can remember it." The director's response, "*I* can remember it," seems reassuring, but even though the director can "remember," the actor cannot recapture and repeat, the improvised gesture.[38] Another version of the same phenomenon occurs when the director says to Ranevskaya, "The opening section of that [act] was brilliant," and the actress replies, "What did I do?" Far from being unique to this production, this kind of occurrence is common in the rehearsals I observe.

A related common phenomenon is what I call "rehearsal going backwards." During one rehearsal of the moment after Yasha kisses Dunyasha, Renfield exclaims in frustration: "Look, you got this yesterday. Don't . . . [ruin] it . . . today." Later one actor says semi-facetiously of the group entrance in act one: "It worked so nicely when we didn't know what we were doing." On the last day of rehearsal in the Manhattan studio, the director warns, "There are some scenes where we've drilled the blocking and we've forgotten what the scenes are about."[39] This kind of running record of debits and credits is part of the interaction between director and actor, actor and play. It's as if the director and actor traverse the common ground of the playtext, coming from somewhat divergent directions; meet at certain points in a nod of understanding; part company; and again position themselves differently to begin the cycle once more.

The directorial eye and ear often catch the actor, as it were, in the midst of acting choices that are still in process. For the actor, rehearsal potentially includes all possible choices, not just those appropriate for performance, as if the right choices must be born in the context of what these choices resist, repel, or exorcise.[40] The rehearsal "workthrough" includes a thorough immersion in what is *not* to be finally chosen for public performance, much like the psychoanalytic "working-through," which "permits the subject to pass from rejection or merely intellectual acceptance to a conviction based on lived experience. . . . working-through is undoubtedly a repetition, albeit one modified by interpretation and—for this reason—liable to facilitate the subject's freeing himself [or herself] from repetition mechanisms." In rehearsal, as in psychoanalytic working-through, a repetition is modified by interpretation. Finally, the psychoanalytic working-through is a "process by means of which analysis implants an interpretation and overcomes the resistance to which it gives rise."[41] In the Renfield rehearsal, about a week before opening night, the actors begin to request uninterrupted runthroughs of parts or all of the play, as if giving notice that the implanting of an interpretation has also overcome the resistance of the director.

There are two directorial prerogatives that Renfield retains with particular firmness. One is the starting and stopping of rehearsal work. Her reply when the actors request non-stop runthroughs of the play is categorical: "When I choose to stop, we'll stop." (Her earlier phrasing is more ambiguously collective: "If we have to stop, we have to stop.") The other principle is fidelity to the Chekhov text insofar as possible. When an actress wishes to omit a line, arguing that it does not make sense, Renfield's response is unconditional: "No, no, Chekhov wrote it and we don't have the license to omit it. He wrote it and *we* have to make it work."[42]

The nature of Renfield's directorial style is suggested in one last example. The performance at the John Drew Theater includes a staging suggested by the director and at first politely resisted by the actor: near the end of the play Lopakhin looks offstage to both right and left, searching for the infirm Firs. It is a literalistic staging of a search for a missing person that gives a slight sense of mystery to Firs's later entrance, after everyone leaves, from the very room which Lopakhin asserts is empty. Throughout rehearsals of *The Cherry Orchard* I sense a tension between the explicit discourse of psychological realism and the director's implicit aversion to a too literal-minded staging. The futile search for the misplaced servant, who will presumably now die locked inside this house, is a staging of a Firs lost and forgotten in a way that defies literalism.

Jan Kott has said, "In theater there is always reality in the illusion and illusion in the reality."[43] This is as true of the rehearsal as of the performance. After the final runthrough in the Manhattan studio, as Firs lies on a rug on the floor delivering his last speech, Renfield leans over and whispers to her stage manager, "That's perfect. That's the perfect picture." Then, uncannily, after Firs's last line, for the first and only time in rehearsal, exactly where there is intended to be created "the sound of a snapped string mournfully dying away," a shutter on the window just behind Firs snaps shut suddenly and loudly. The director gasps.

Fig. 3.1. Michael O'Keefe and Austin Pendleton in Uncle Vanya. *Photograph by Paula Court.*

3

Maria Irene Fornes Directs
Uncle Vanya and *Abingdon Square*

"To be quiet on the stage"

Maria Irene Fornes is a Cuban-born playwright who has directed such stage classics as *Hedda Gabler* and *Uncle Vanya* as
well as her own work; she is the author of over two dozen plays.
Awarded six Obies, among which is the Obie for Sustained
Achievement in Theatre in 1982, Fornes has been the recipient
of Guggenheim, Rockefeller, and National Endowment for the
Arts grants, among others. She conducts playwriting workshops
across the country and directs the INTAR Hispanic Playwrights-
in-Residence Laboratory in New York City.

In the late fall of 1987 I am allowed to observe rehearsals of
Chekhov's *Uncle Vanya* in the fifth-floor La Mama studio at 47
Great Jones Street, in preparation for performance at The Classic
Stage Company (CSC Repertory) theatre in New York from December 13, 1987, through January 2, 1988. As with Renfield's
company, the cast includes actors who have performed on and
off Broadway as well as in regional and repertory theatre, film,
and television; at least one actor, Austin Pendleton, has also
directed. Reminiscent of *The Cherry Orchard* cast, too, is the mix
of varied backgrounds, training, experience, and age (again there
is one member of the company, Margaret Barker, who has been
acting for over half a century). If there is a tendency toward a
predominant acting style among the principal members of the
company, it is that of Method acting. While Renfield relied on
Jean-Claude van Itallie's revised translation of *The Cherry Orchard* and refused to violate Chekhov's stage directions, Fornes
herself revises Marian Fell's early twentieth-century translation
of *Uncle Vanya*,[1] along with Chekhov's stage directions in the
text.[2] A few months before the *Vanya* rehearsals, I also observe
Fornes direct her own play, *Abingdon Square*, performed at the

American Place Theatre in New York, from October 7 through October 25, 1987. Since these rehearsals illuminate each other, I make reference to both in the following pages.

During a break in the *Vanya* rehearsal on November 20, 1987, Fornes tells me that she was originally asked to direct a Shakespeare play at the CSC Repertory but demurred, suggesting instead Chekhov's *The Three Sisters* and eventually agreeing to direct *Uncle Vanya*. When I ask if she admires Chekhov, she responds, "Chekhov is the writer I most admire." Fornes elaborates, characteristically choosing her words with care: "[Chekhov is] so delicate. I don't mean 'polite.' [He] understands things with a refinement. . . . This play is like a fabric that is woven . . . [with] so many delicate threads." She continues, "I never know whether we're doing the first act or the second," adding with emphasis, "The *actors* always know what act they're in. . . . You feel as if any scene could be in any act, but it isn't so." (She clarifies later that "it isn't so" is a supposition.) "I'm not too sure that we couldn't reshuffle scenes. Maybe it . . . [is only necessary] that the play . . . end with Yelena and the Professor's departure."

Fornes's sense of Chekhov's delicately woven fabric clearly does not imply an inevitable narrative sequence, although her musing on reshuffling scenes remains merely musing.[3] Earlier this same day she tells me, as have other directors, "What I'm pursuing is a kind of clarity," but adds, "I think what other directors are pursuing is tension, emotional energy whether it is natural to the scene or not. But I'm finding out from the text what is going on. . . . I think directors and actors are afraid to be quiet on the stage, afraid to be boring, but to be quiet on the stage is as beautiful as it is in life."

This concern for a kind of quiet on the stage, clearly important to Fornes as playwright and director, poses certain difficulties for actors and theatre critics alike.[4] A week later, describing for me what she wishes from the actors in rehearsal, Fornes says: "*For the actor to put himself a little more at rest* than the usual performance requires . . . so [the actor's] thinking process and emotional changes can be seen or sensed by the audience. The moment . . . [the actor's] emotions are pushed, the audience is less aware of what is happening inside" (emphasis added).[5] "I know if a voice comes softer, it will have some music in it. I feel as if the air starts building up the spirit of the time, the place, the author. If a voice is too loud, it can shatter it or destroy it."

On my first day of observing the *Uncle Vanya* rehearsal, Fornes is directing a scene near the beginning of act three. Vanya[6] speaks of the "autumn roses, beautiful, sorrowful roses" and exits. The phrase is repeated by his niece Sonia and then her young step-mother Yelena delivers two lines whose juxtaposition gives trouble: "September already! How shall we live through the long winter here?"[7] Alma Cuervo, playing Yelena, at first wonders if her lines are facetious, for the two thoughts seem to her contradictory. The director, sitting without script in hand, rephrases the speech: "The dreary winter is coming too soon. No matter how much time has passed, it appears that winter has arrived too soon," and suggests that this speech is connected to, and "in the same key" as, the repeated reference to the autumn roses. The actress replies, "So it's all one thought," as if the speech of a single consciousness were a kind of verbal sigh emitted by a group of actors.[8] Following this discussion of the text, the actress delivers her brief speech four times. Each rendering is slightly different, the final version seemingly incorporating something of the earlier explorations so that in these simple haunting lines, even now, as later in performance, the implied contradictions of loveliness and sadness, of time passing too quickly and lingering oppressively, become part of the carefully woven fabric, its delicate colors softly subdued in the actress' voicing.

During Yelena's long soliloquy at the end of this scene, the actress has tears on her cheeks. But Fornes focuses on arms and hands, telling the actress not to let them "take it away." As she stills her hands, the actress' voice becomes stronger. Fornes's emphasis on an exterior stillness, the physical marker of the kind of quietness she often seeks, is quietly challenged. The actress makes the realistic point that at times the human body involuntarily takes over, becomes dominant, and she wishes to show this during Yelena's soliloquy. Fornes's view is different, and is elaborated at various points throughout the rehearsals of *Vanya* and *Abingdon Square*. She says of Yelena, "It's happening inside her, here," touching the actress' face and upper chest just beneath her neck. Afterwards Fornes tells me, "The hands and arms become expressive, but they are taking over, putting a lid on, the emotions."[9] She adds that, in a different scene rehearsed the previous day, she asked the actress "to sit on the edge of the sofa as if she were applying to a convent school . . . very quiet . . . very vulnerable," "just to speak very quietly": "it came out beautifully."

Sitting quietly is as difficult on the stage as elsewhere. Often it is simply a practical necessity, especially in ensemble acting. For example, a week later, rehearsing act one, an actress, having been instructed to sit on a bench until the next pause in the action, repeatedly asks the director, "Irene, what am I *doing* on the bench?" The jokes that surround this incident range from one actor's mock-Stanislavski reply, "You're acting, baby. Never forget that,"[10] to the remark of another that in sitting on the bench the actress is not really *working* and that perhaps she ought to be building the bench. Fornes, who has previously asked the Nurse not to give significant looks to Astroff while Telegin tells his tale of woe, says with a smile: "There's something about movement that attracts the eye. I don't know why."

On the one hand, these directorial notes are different versions of the convention that an actor avoid upstaging another actor. On the other hand, Fornes is trying to encourage an active stillness, particularly appropriate to Chekhov as well as to *Abingdon Square*. How difficult an achievement this is, to create and to evaluate, is illustrated at the end of the third week of rehearsal, ten days before the first preview. Fornes asks one actor to "go very still" after the conclusion of his speech. The actress whose speech follows his asks, "Should I wait longer before I say that line?" Fornes responds, "I don't know, because there's never been enough stillness to tell."

The director asks that the scene be repeated. The actor protests, saying, "I can just be quiet." And indeed his line coincides with this promise. It is: "I am silent. I apologize and am silent."[11] But Fornes needs to see the stillness enacted. They rehearse the scene again, and this time an actress moves in the space of the stillness. Fornes stops the scene, points this out, restarts the scene. Now the actor finishing his speech reaches for his tea. They repeat the scene. The actress who had previously moved delivers her lines and immediately immobilizes herself, arms outstretched. Fornes stops the scene again, saying, "A stillness, not a freeze." Once again the scene is rehearsed. This time I see the hands of yet another actress move but Fornes allows the rehearsal to continue.

In her rehearsals of her own play, in a small studio on the second floor of the Applecorps Theater on West 20th Street in New York, Fornes personalizes that "place" of active stillness. On September 18, 1987, my first day of observing the *Abingdon Square* rehearsals, Fornes says quietly to actress Madeleine Potter, who is sitting on the floor beside the director's chair: "You have to find that hollow, that space, inside you, that place where I am when I write." Fornes is speaking of a long climactic monologue at the end of the second scene of the play in which, according to the playwright's stage direction, "As the . . . speech progresses Marion speaks rapidly as if in an emotional trance."[12] Fornes says to the actress who has now moved into the playing area: "You're transformed now. As if you've suddenly grown into a very tall person," a directorial reinscribing of her own authorial reference to a state of trance. The actress, who has previously been in physical contact with the other actor in the scene, now moves away from him and, in fact, slows down her delivery of the lines. Fornes comments, "Don't move unless you have to." The actress responds, "I have to," but nonetheless moves less as she continues her speech. Earlier, Fornes suggests to John David Cullum that he be less physically active while the actress delivers her monologue. The actor, with some irony, asks: "You just want a body here?" and the director replies, "A body with ears." The actor initially plays this scene as inert and insentient but gradually he becomes "a body with ears."[13] It is doubtful that an audience watching his later performance of lying still on the stage would believe the amount of work required to realize what seems so effortless.

Stillness, seeming non-movement, is an essential condition of all of Robert Wilson's theatre work. While Fornes, unlike Wilson, occasionally makes use of the rhetoric of psychological realism in her discussion with actors in rehearsal, her concern with sloweddown stage time, states of seeming immobility, characters in the presence of characters whose presence they do not seem to acknowledge is, in some ways, as Wilsonian as it is Chekhovian.

Only once has Irene Fornes ever acted. She performed a silent role in one of her own plays: she "didn't move, just wore a dress, loved it, being there on the stage, in the dark." This experience has some connection with the works she writes as well as the author she most admires and her directorial privileging of stillness on the stage. In discussing a workshop production of *Abingdon Square* at the Seattle Repertory Theatre in 1984, Fornes tells the actors that she wanted "a pleasant scene at home, a serenity that comes from people just being together in a room." She eventually wrote scene six, a scene of reading and writing: Marion, the young wife of Juster, sits at a desk writing in her diary; her stepbrother, Michael, the same age as Marion, sits cross-legged on the floor, reading a book; Juster, the patriarch of the family, sits reading aloud an excerpt which Fornes has taken verbatim from *My Garden in Autumn and Winter,* a book by E. A. Bowles.[14] The Artistic Director at that time had suggested that the playwright include a scene, possibly sexual in nature, with Marion and Juster alone together. Fornes chose instead to write a scene in which people who are "not supportive of each other and not necessarily understanding of each other . . . [are] in the same room together trying to deal with the same problem," a scene in which simply being in the same place conveys a sense of being connected. This is a characteristic situation in Chekhov as it is in Fornes's own plays. It is also a telling description of the rehearsal situation itself,[15] and, in a metaphoric sense, it is the situation of the playwright in the process of creating the play. It is what Wallace Stevens describes at the close of his revealingly titled poem, "Final Soliloquy of the Interior Paramour," in which the speaker of the soliloquy is consistently plural: "We make a dwelling . . . / In which being there together is enough."[16]

This sense of characters just being there together in a room recalls the difficulties for both cast and director, already noted in Renfield's *Cherry Orchard* rehearsals, of knowing which verbal, visual, spatial, and emotional fields are operating at any given moment in a scene of ensemble acting. In practical terms, this can simply take the form of an actor's not knowing "where to look."

In rehearsing scene 18 of *Abingdon Square,* actor John Seitz, playing Juster, says to Fornes: "This text is . . . not naturalistic. There is a spare, formal austere approach. I'm asking as an actor: Do I look at her? [his wife, Marion, who sits silent, staring at the floor] at him? [his son, Michael, whom he seems to be addressing and who responds in a single line at the end of the scene]. I hate to talk in these terms because in a way it's talking about results but it helps me." Fornes seems to respond first as playwright: "I feel the sense of spareness is inevitable," and then, perhaps, as director: "but I think it *is* what would have happened." The actor continues, "I really think of . . . [the scene] as daguerreotypes, formal poses for a picture," and the director replies, "But it has to do with how you *feel* about speaking with Michael, not just how it looks." This is a complicated moment in which several issues are overlaid: naturalistic versus non-naturalistic depiction of "reality," results versus process, "how you feel" versus "how it looks." And there is a further potential source of tension.

The actor's candid admission, "What I'm trying to do is to reduce the possibilities," is met by the director's frank reply: "If I had directed the play fifteen times, probably we could trust that there is something rich in certain physical positions. . . . But when I direct a play once, I usually change it, in both the writing and in the directing, because the possibilities do not contain the essence: there are enormous possibilities." The question of "where to look"[17] uncovers the *enormous* possibilities in the minimalist situation of characters simply present in the same space. In this case the actor continues to rehearse the speech, in the presence of the author-director, exploring and shedding various physical movements and overt contact with other actors.

At times Fornes, like Renfield, intervenes in an actor's decision to address, explicitly or implicitly, a particular speech to another character in the scene. An idiosyncratic example is the rehearsal of the opening scene of act three of *Uncle Vanya*, in which Sonia tells her young stepmother, "You feel miserable and restless, and can't seem to fit into this life, and your restlessness is catching."[18] While Sonia's lines in the text seem clearly directed to Yelena and are initially delivered that way, Fornes suggests to Patricia Mattick, playing Sonia, that she not direct this speech to Yelena as if to blame Yelena for the boredom that is "everyone's internal state" in the play. This may seem a disputable interpretation of a speech that ends by characterizing Yelena as a woman who bewitches those around her ("You must be a witch"), but it is an important sign of Fornes's directorial disruptions of literalistic readings of the playtext. Later in rehearsal, Sonia defends Astroff's avid interest in preserving forests against Yelena's criticism of it as an uninteresting preoccupation. Fornes alienates the initially naturalistic delivery of Sonia's speech to Yelena by placing a screen between the chair on which Sonia sits and the bench where her stepmother is seated. When the actress rises from her chair as she continues speaking, Fornes interrupts, saying to her, "Softer, Patty. To yourself."

An earlier, more clearly text-centered illustration of the problem of where to address a speech occurs in the first act when Vanya repeats the word "yes" as he enters a scene of which he has not been a part. Austin Pendleton first addresses his "yes"[19] to the room from which he comes. After Fornes asks the actor to enter more quickly and comments briefly on the state of consciousness of someone just awakening from sleep, Vanya's repeated explosive "yes" is heard ambiguously as a remark to himself, a reply to unseen others in the room where he has been napping, a "choric comment" on the conversation of the old nurse and doctor to whom he enters.

One last example occurs in rehearsal of a two-person scene in *Abingdon Square*. Fornes says to John Seitz playing Juster: "I imagine this is very hard to do because you are speaking but not *to* somebody."

Actors in rehearsal of *Abingdon Square* characterize Fornes as having very firm ideas yet always remaining open to exploration. In the *Vanya* rehearsals, I hear her say to the actress playing Yelena, "Try anything that seems possible." At another point she asks Michael O'Keefe, playing Astroff, to "make a movement," and in response to his question, "Make a movement?" says, "Yes, we'll see where it goes." Working later with the same actor, Fornes says, "As long as something is kept mysterious, and a little bit beyond our reach, the character is whole."[20]

At one point in act two Astroff is described in the stage directions as slightly inebriated. During a two-hour rehearsal of this brief scene, Michael O'Keefe, as directed by Fornes, creates a far spookier state of altered consciousness than that of literal drunkenness, a state physicalized at times by the kind of semi-immobility that often accompanies inner activity. The actor's voice begins to lose its previous naturalistic inflections after Fornes says of the repeated word, "Play!"[21] (Astroff's instruction to Telegin to strum his guitar): "Think of it less as a *command* than as a necessity, as if you were a pilot. It's what you need for the evening or the scene to work, to get the script open at the right page!" As the scene is rehearsed, Fornes interrupts Astroff: "Be less affectionate toward Vanya. It's more as if you're hearing an inner voice that is inviting you into an inner voyage with clues like this playing of the guitar and song, like a ritual." The actor agrees. The scene becomes both weirder and truer. After Astroff's speech, "I feel capable of anything. I attempt the most difficult operations and do them magnificently. . . . Play, Waffles!"[22] Fornes comments: "It's almost there, but let it be true. You're telling about something that really does happen. . . . 'Play' still needs to be said as if you *need* that sound of the guitar. That playfulness keeps coming back in. I think it has to do with habitual vocal tones and voice patterns. You *are* in that place [of inner voyage] that we discussed but you need to break the vocal patterns. In order to break the vocal patterns, you have to really think of the *necessity* of every element." Fornes's interpretation of the instruction to *play* as arranging necessities rather than issuing commands is suggestive of her view of the directorial role in rehearsal.

To Ralph Williams playing Telegin (Waffles), Fornes says, "Ralph, the scene is very different now. It's not just drunk any more. Astroff has gotten darker. You have to be more subdued now in what you're doing . . . because it's gotten more serious. In a way you have to be more concerned about him than about the others, more concerned about what is happening to him than about a person who is drunk and making too much noise." Similarly, after the actress playing Sonia enters the playing area, Fornes tells her that "the scene is now changed, . . . is much darker." Fornes's comments to Telegin and Sonia[23] on the need for new acting adjustments after each has begun to rehearse with the transformed Astroff[24] are a version of Renfield's observation in rehearsals of *The Cherry Orchard:* "Everything's connected. You make a choice and he makes a choice."

A parallel moment, and one of the most striking acting adjustments I ever witness in any single rehearsal session, is the collaborative re-creation of Juster's long monologue in scene 20 of *Abingdon Square.* The knowingly cuckolded husband enters his house and, in the presence of his wife and son, begins to describe a difficult day of work at his office. His speech is simultaneously banal and strange, especially as he focuses on the state of his own clothing: "(*He sits down and . . . takes one of his shoes off*) I take care of my feet. My socks are in a good state of repair. When they wear out I pass them on to someone who needs them. (*Taking off his other shoe*) Others mend their socks. I don't. I don't mind wearing mended clothes. My underwear is mended. So are my shirts, but not my socks. (*With both feet on the floor*) I have always wanted to give my feet maximum comfort. It is they who support the whole body yet they are fragile. Feet are small and fragile for the load they carry. . . . If I treat my feet with respect, my brain functions with respect."[25] Another director might find analogies between Juster's references to his socks and his attitude toward his adulterous wife (in the next scene, he will pass her on to someone else: "Others mend their socks. I don't") or use the discourse of psychological realism to discuss particular stages and manifestations of a nervous breakdown. For several days Fornes has in fact referred to Juster's "demented" state at certain points in the play. Now she says simply, "You take care of your feet. That's how you begin to take care of your life."

After the scene is rehearsed twice, Fornes enters the playing area where the actor is seated on a chair. She stands behind him, with her hands on his shoulders, occasionally moving her hands along his upper arms as she speaks: "Now hold your body carefully. If you let your body go, it will be poisoned. Here, in your brain [touching his head], it's like a generator . . . making electricity at a tremendous speed. It's good, in a sense, because it's keeping you alive. You walk fine, you can climb the stairs, you can wash your hands. Somehow the energy is so intense that, although you can see, you're not able to focus so much on what's going on. You see Michael when you come in but he's a little fuzzy. You can speak to him, to others; it may sound a little mechanical but to you it sounds normal.

"You are even able to notice it is a little somber in the room when you enter. You are talking to them but once you enter this room [Juster first speaks to his wife and son from offstage as he washes his hands before dinner], it's too much of a shock if you actually talk to another person one-to-one. If you do, you may fall apart. You can even tend to your own mechanism so you can take your shoes off. It feels good. But don't relax too much because you might fall apart." All during these comments, Fornes has kept her hands on the actor's shoulders and arms, as she remains standing behind his chair.

The scene is repeated once more. The actor looks very different and talks differently: there is an alien quality about him that was not present before. His pace is faster, his speech rhythms are slightly peculiar. Fornes interrupts the scene: "Don't face them [Marion and Michael] directly. They can shock you, shatter you. They have an energy that could really shatter you." The actor playing Michael, watching and listening to the transformed actor, compliments him. The actors begin the scene again. When John Seitz enters now, everything about him seems slightly askew. He does not look directly at the other two actors. His vocal rhythms are consistently a little odd; the voice itself is a little higher, thinned out. He is, in fact, spooky. His uncanniness seems to come from his own sense of what is necessary "for . . . the scene to work." He has redefined the situation of a man coming home to dinner after a difficult day of work.

The actor cannot, of course, maintain this acting style throughout his monologue on his first attempt, as he himself indicates: "It's in and out, but I'm getting it, I'm getting it." Nonetheless, John Seitz's transformation of the speech is galvanizing and retains this effect later in his finely modulated performance. Fornes congratulates him in rehearsal, adding, "The more rigid it is, the more devastating and moving it is."[26] The actor responds, referring to her earlier directorial comments, "Those are good images. That helps." Fornes's rehearsals seem to illustrate Jerzy Grotowski's remark, "The director's purpose is to create a condition which leads another [the actor] to a new experience; a thousand times it won't work, but once it will, and that once is essential."[27]

Unlike playwright-director Emily Mann, whose revisions of her own play are distributed but not written during the actual rehearsals of *Execution of Justice,* Fornes is literally revising, and often eliminating, words in the playtext as she directs *Abingdon Square.*[28] She frequently discusses with the actors the history and nature, if not the genesis, of the revisions she has made and is making. The actors, rehearsing the outtakes, as it were, as well as the final form of the playscript, are intimately involved in acts of authorial revision which they replicate in their rehearsal explorations of different versions of the text.

In contrast to her characteristic steadily focused concentration on the actors in rehearsals of *Uncle Vanya,*[29] Fornes's eye is occasionally as much on the text as on the performers during rehearsal of her own play. At one point she looks down at the script in a large pink binder in her lap; she looks up over it at the actors, then back at the script. I see her making changes in the text which in a few minutes she reads aloud to the actors, adding: "The more words we take out, the more immediate it becomes." (Cf. her earlier remark to actor John Seitz, "I feel the spareness is inevitable, but I think it *is* what would have happened.") Once, when an actor suggests a revision in phrasing to Fornes, her reaction is immediate and unqualified: "No. That makes it more like grammar." But at other moments she consults with individual actors in making alterations in the phrasing of their lines, sometimes confirming her ear-sense of the line with the actor who will deliver it.[30]

It is striking that while she makes carefully considered changes in the prose rhythm and syntax of individual lines throughout rehearsal, Fornes never attempts to give line readings to the actors. The closest she comes to demonstrating vocal intonation is in a discussion of Juster's question to Marion in scene 28: "What are you doing?" Explaining that she never knows what to stress but can hear a wrong stress, she suggests to the actor that

Fig. 3.2. Maria Irene Fornes's gaze. Photograph by James M. Kent.

each of the four words in the line needs to be made distinct. As she reads the line aloud, she gives the initial word, "What," a slight emphasis. Later, perhaps involuntarily, the actor uses this emphasis when he first repeats the line in rehearsal.

Fornes insists that her primary concern in directing is "for the clarity of what is happening [in the playtext] . . . as manifest in the words." She trusts most not a set of principles but what she calls "a painter's eye" (she was a painter before she became a playwright)[31] and experience: "If I have a feeling that this actor needs to get up and walk over there, then I don't know if it's right until the actor gets up and does it. . . . [What] guides me on how to block scenes and [in the] composition of scenes . . . has to do with energies that happen between shapes and persons. Something happens inside the person when the distance between objects and persons changes." Later she adds: "An unpleasant composition [on the stage] is as much of an irritant as somebody making an unnecessary movement."

Donald Eastman's simultaneous scene setting for *Uncle Vanya*—in which Vanya's study, the sitting room, the dining room, and the garden are present and visible throughout the play—is used by Fornes to allow characters possibilities of spatial definition beyond those indicated by the stage directions in the text. For instance, in the first act, which Chekhov sets entirely in a garden outside the house, Fornes has Vanya's mother seated at one point reading in the dining room and stages the final scene between Vanya and Yelena in the sitting room rather than—as the stage directions indicate—during a walk to the terrace. Early in the rehearsal of this suddenly revealing scene, in which Vanya impetuously declares his love for the professor's young wife, the director interrupts the dialogue between Vanya and Yelena to discuss the intricacies of the actress' blocking: where she rises, crosses, stands, moves, sits. Alma Cuervo verbalizes all her moves, recapitulating her previous blocking, then says: "That doesn't matter. We have a new pattern. . . . What do you want now?"

Fornes is at first silent. There is a slight misunderstanding to be cleared up about just where changes have occurred in the blocking. Now Yelena sits, then stands and moves toward Vanya who crosses to a chair far downstage so that he is not in direct physical alignment with Yelena. The blocking—as it is being explored—clarifies, without realistically illustrating, the relationship of the two characters in the scene: it is a visual-kinetic composition of jerky, discontinuous points of contact. Yelena says to Vanya, "Do you know, Ivan, the reason you and I are such friends? I think it is because we are both lonely and unfortunate," and he replies, "You are my joy, my life, and my youth. . . . Only let me look at you, listen to your voice—" (I. p. 27). As he delivers this speech, Vanya is seated in a chair, downstage right, his back to what would be the center section of the audience, his upper body inclining diagonally left upstage while Yelena stands directly behind him upstage, facing the center section of the audience. (The performance space at The Classic Stage Company is designed so that three-quarters of the stage is surrounded by the audience.)[32] Vanya's face is turned not toward Yelena but toward the couch where she had been sitting earlier in the scene.

Fornes interrupts Vanya's declaration of love to discuss the speech with the actor. The actor now experiments with delivering Vanya's lines while gazing directly at Yelena's face. Fornes stops the scene and enters the playing area. She takes the actor's hands and tentatively explores first how Vanya might seize Yelena's hands and then how Yelena might pull back, enacting what she describes as the actress watches. The actress and director exchange positions; Fornes now stands in the playing area watching closely. As Vanya reaches upward for Yelena's hands, the director interrupts the scene again to suggest that Vanya take Yelena's hands precisely at a particular moment in the speech. Finally, Fornes moves Yelena closer to Vanya and places his right arm around her waist. (This rehearsal recalls, but in a very different key, Renfield's detailed, closely-observed adjustments of the physical positioning of Dunyasha and Yasha on their bench in act two of *The Cherry Orchard*.)

During a break, Fornes points out that the obvious form of resistance if someone seizes your hands is simply to step or pull back. The placement of the actor's arm around the actress' waist helps to secure her in a position that is both physically difficult to maintain and devoid of behavioral verisimilitude.[33] The director wants the actress to remain close by, yet arching back from, the seated actor, who reaches upward to grasp her hands "as if he is a penitent rising from the flames below." She demonstrates for me, grimacing, her head thrust upward, as she raises clenched hands. Fornes's painterly staging[34] of this scene is a close reading in visual form of the delicately woven fabric of the playtext. "When you're trying to pull yourself up, if you are holding on to somebody, you are also pulling . . . [that person] down."

Fornes's staging of the penitent in torment clearly emerges when the scene is rehearsed again in the runthrough after the break. Vanya's arms are upraised throughout the dialogue. Yelena, close to him, her two hands held tightly by one of his, her eyes looking upward in torment, delivers the closing line in the act: "This is torture."[35] But in performance on December 19, 1987, the scene is subtly changed. During intermission Fornes tells me that the actors found the earlier version too artificial. When I ask if she redirected the scene, she replies, "No, *it* changed." The scene as performed is an abbreviated and somewhat more naturalistic staging. What emerges in performance is an allusion to an earlier rendering in rehearsal. Only near the very end of the dialogue do Vanya's arms reach up and, oddly, from my vantage point in the theatre, Yelena seems to clasp his hands near her breast as she delivers her last line, looking upward. Fornes, having watched this performance from the auditorium, confirms that the scene as it now appears does not have the effect she intended and that she prefers the earlier staging. Such is the intricate fragility of moments shaped for beholding in rehearsal.

Like Renfield, Fornes experiences, and articulates, a sense of rehearsal "going backwards." In the third week of rehearsal of *Vanya*, I overhear the director say to production stage manager Nancy Harrington: "Two days ago I thought this was going to be extraordinary, and yesterday I thought it wasn't working. And when we come to tech[nical] rehearsals, I always think we're going backwards, that some beautiful things are disappearing." In addition, there are moments that are discussed, explored, probed, enacted, and then dropped without a trace. One is the attempt to find an opportunity for Marina, an old nurse, to exit and re-enter during act one so that she can bring the professor his tea. Fornes spends perhaps a quarter of an hour trying to find an appropriate staging of what might be thought a simple exit and entrance (there is no such thing), suggested by Margaret Barker, the actress playing the nurse. What is most revealing about this ultimately abortive attempt is Fornes's response when the actress first suggests the need for an unscripted exit for tea-serving: "The reason I didn't think about that is because Chekhov hasn't thought about it . . . but let's try it."[36]

In the rehearsal of her own play Fornes confronts a more serious version of the problem of what the playwright has or has not thought about. At two different points in the rehearsal of

Abingdon Square actors raise the question of the importance and physical presence of Thomas, Marion's child. (Juster believes himself to be the biological parent of Marion's child; Thomas's real biological father is a stranger, a glazier who came once to the house to repair a window.)

John Seitz first raises the issue while rehearsing a monologue in which there is a brief reference to Thomas: "Four years later Marion had a child. I was overwhelmed with joy, but Marion was not. She became more taciturn than ever" (*Abingdon Square*, p. 8). The actor begins by musing that Thomas does not figure much in the scene and in the play: "It's almost as if he's a non-presence." When Fornes comments, "That may be the writer's problem," the actor asks, with a smile, "Can you get the writer to do something about that?" Fornes's response is disarming as she speaks in the role of playwright, "That may be my fault, I've never had a child and I think I do forget the presence of the child in the play."[37] Anna Levine, the actress playing Mary, cautions that *Abingdon Square* should not turn into a play about a child when the child really is not in the play.

The question of to what extent and exactly how the child "is in the play" is later raised more urgently by Madeleine Potter during rehearsal of scene 28, a highly emotional encounter between Marion and Juster. Discussing the nature of Marion's uninvited return to the house from which she has been banished as an adulterous wife, the actress suddenly interjects: "I have to understand this. How much is Thomas, my child, in this scene?" The playwright's response is forthright: "Thomas isn't here [i.e., not in the house; not emotionally present in the scene]. . . . *If Thomas were the issue, this scene wouldn't take place*" (emphasis added).

In the immediately preceding scene with her great-aunt Minnie, Marion has delivered these lines: "I need my child. I need my child, Minnie. I need that child in my arms and I don't see a way I could ever have him again [Juster has kept Thomas hidden, threatening that a court would award him sole custody of the child if there were a divorce, on the grounds of Marion's adultery]. . . . I watch the house. I imagine the child inside playing in his room. . . . I know he's not there, but that's how I can feel him near me. Looking at the house" (*Abingdon Square*, scene 27, p. 10).

Now, in the discussion of scene 28, the actress, following her own sense of through-line, argues passionately for the impor-

Fig. 3.3. Madeleine Potter and John Seitz in Abingdon Square. *Photograph by Martha Holmes.*

tance of Marion's attachment to Thomas. Fornes speaks instead of Marion's attachment to the house itself, of which Marion has said before her marriage to Juster:

> In this house light comes through the windows
> as if it delights in entering. I feel the same.
> I delight in entering here. I delight in walking
> through these rooms and I'm sad when I leave.
> I cannot wait for the day when my eyes open from a
> night's sleep and I find myself inside these walls.
> Being here I feel as if I'm blessed.
> (*Abingdon Square*, scene 2, p. 2)

The distinction between writer and director becomes blurred as Fornes says to the actress: "I feel you want the house from him, and you want Thomas from him, but you want Thomas from *him* more than you want Thomas. You come to rape him [Juster], in a sense." The actress persists, involuntarily quoting a line from the play: "But this child is a baby. 'Where is it?' "

In the final speech of scene 28, Marion says:

> I had forgotten how I loved this house. I love
> this house. . . . I'll tell you a riddle. See if you
> can solve it:
> If a person owns an object, where is it?
> It's under his arm.
> If a person loves an object, where is it?
> It's in his arms.
> If a mother's baby is not in her arms, where is it?
> (*Pause*) Where is it? Where is Thomas? Where have
> you taken him?. . . . How can you do this? How can you
> put me through this? What do you gain?
> (*Abingdon Square*, scene 28, p. 10)

As if feeling the force of the actress' investment in Marion's unanswered question, "Where is it?" but, like her script, unable to answer in literalistic terms, Fornes responds, "You're right. I may forget the child but you don't."

Actors and audiences often need to ask questions whose terms may preclude an answer by the playwright. A familiar example might be: Where are Lady Macbeth's children?[38] In Fornes's rehearsal of her own play, author and director are allied in resisting a certain way of understanding a scene between an estranged couple whose child is being kept by the husband.

Earlier in rehearsal, actor John Seitz describes *Abingdon Square:* "This play constantly defeats our expectancies."[39] This defeating of our expectations—what I call Fornes's "uncanny realism"[40]—is partly related to the director's recognition of the "enormous possibilities" of any acting moment in the play, despite the discomfort this may cause for an actor who understandably needs finally to reduce the possibilities. Implicit in Fornes's stress on "enormous possibilities" is a sense of the enormous range within each possibility. Her works for the stage, in rehearsal and performance, change the actor's and audience's sense of what is possible; in this way, Fornes as playwright and director alters our conventional expectations of what is meant by "realism" in the theatre.

At the beginning of *Abingdon Square,* a fifteen-year-old boy and a fifteen-year-old girl wrestle for a piece of candy. We expect this to develop into a sexual relationship; it doesn't. Instead, the fifteen-year-old girl marries a man old enough to be her father. We expect this to be a Freudian situation; somehow it isn't. A young man and his father play chess. The son thinks he has checked his father's king but loses his bishop instead. We expect the play to dramatize son-father rivalry; it doesn't. Finally, a husband and wife are estranged; the husband keeps the baby. We expect (and so do some of the actors) the custody of the child to be a major issue in the play: it isn't. In each instance Fornes asks us to reconsider a situation and redefine its essence. She wishes, in her directing as well as in her writing, to "eliminate everything superfluous. . . . I don't even like to mimic the gestures and tones of voice of social behavior, which may be 'accurate,' but which are really just a mask concealing a deeper reality."[41]

This "deeper reality" is not always accessible even to the playwright, however. In a disclaimer characteristic of many writers of fiction, Fornes says to an actor during rehearsal of *Abingdon Square:* "The characters know what they're doing but I don't." As director of her own play, Fornes seems at times to discover possibilities in the text unknown to the playwright. Later that day she uncharacteristically interrupts the same actor near the beginning of a scene to explain why Juster offers money to his estranged wife: "Juster is being reasonable. . . ."[42] During rehearsal of a crucial scene between Marion and Juster, Fornes says to the actors: "I never saw this before but. . . ." Speaking as

director refusing interpretative closure, she offers two unscripted options to the actor playing Juster: "It's not in the play
but I think Juster does take on lovers from the street. I'm not sure
whether he is actually doing these things or is having nightmares
about them, but in any event he is confronting his own sexuality."
The "I" here is indeterminate. Fornes speaks also as symbolist
poet/playwright for whom nightmarish dreams are as indicative
of reality as literal experience.

Finally, the context for directorial "knowing" in rehearsal may
at times be indistinguishable from that of the actor. During
rehearsal of a scene that is to be followed by Juster's abortive
attempt to shoot his estranged wife,[43] Fornes silently enters the
playing area and walks to the table representing the desk at
which Juster sits. She stands there, rustling through loose pages
of the script on this "desk," trying to decide whether Juster has
his gun there, among his papers. For a moment I observe the
director and playwright using the same means as the actor to
map unknown terrain. Analytic energy is interchanged with tac-
tile exploratory energies; exploration becomes, for actor and
director alike, a way of knowing in rehearsal. As Irene Fornes
says to actress Madeleine Potter early in rehearsal of *Abingdon
Square:* "Every scene has to be mapped. We all know that. But
the only way to map it is to work it. Then after it's mapped, we
keep working it . . . and map it again."

4

Emily Mann Directs
Execution of Justice

"Take it all in": A Collective Witnessing

When *Execution of Justice* opened at the Virginia Theatre in New York on March 13, 1986, Emily Mann became one of the very few women to have directed her own play on Broadway. A former resident director at the Guthrie Theater, recipient of a Guggenheim fellowship, a National Endowment for the Arts associateship, and, in 1983, the Rosamond Gilder Award for "outstanding creative achievement in the theatre," she has been directing her own plays as well as classical and contemporary plays in theatres across the country since 1977. Her second play, *Still Life*,[1] directed by the author at The American Place Theatre in New York, received Obie Awards for playwriting, direction, and all three performers as well as for best production. *Execution of Justice* was among the six plays considered by the New York Drama Critics Circle for selection as the best new play of the 1985–1986 season. In July, 1990, Mann was appointed Artistic Director of the McCarter Theater in Princeton, New Jersey.

Emily Mann writes in response to my request to observe her rehearsals: "I am very pleased you want to document rehearsal work. Somehow in America, process is a concept little understood or acknowledged."[2] Her rehearsals, like those of Fornes and Renfield, raise—without answering—certain inescapable questions. Is a playtext a map of its own terrain and, at the same time, of the means by which that terrain can be explored and populated? How mimetic, in relation to particular texts, are particular rehearsals, and to what extent is rehearsal's way of exploring a playtext a way of exploring the nature of its own activity? In the rehearsal script, but not in the published version, of *Execution of Justice* the setting is defined as "a series of reflec-

Fig. 4.1. Emily Mann in rehearsal. Photograph by T. Charles Erickson.

tive surfaces." To what extent and with what effect is the director herself one of the "reflective surfaces"?

The New York rehearsals of *Execution of Justice* take place in a sixth floor studio at 890 Broadway. The interracial cast of 23 actors playing 44 different roles has a typically varied mix of age and experience: the actors have appeared in Broadway, off-Broadway, and experimental theatre productions as well as in film and television; one actor, Earle Hyman, has been performing for over 40 years; another, Wesley Snipes, has recently graduated from college.

Unlike Irene Fornes, Mann does not compose or revise her script in the midst of rehearsal. Nor does she inevitably change the playtext even when, as director, she wishes to clarify its meaning for actor or audience. In rehearsal of *The Cherry Orchard*, Elinor Renfield reminds an actress: "Chekhov wrote it. . . . and we have to make it work. . . . We have to stay with the text." Mann's relationship to the text is like that of Renfield, except that the dialogue the director chooses to honor is transcribed, not invented.

Emily Mann characterizes *Execution of Justice* as "theater of testimony."[3] A theatrical reconstruction of an historical event, the trial of Daniel James White for the murders of "the liberal Mayor of San Francisco, George Moscone, and the first avowedly gay elected official, Supervisor Harvey Milk," on November 27, 1978, the "words come from trial transcript, interview, reportage, the street."[4]

Describing *Execution of Justice*, Mann says: "All the trial stuff is transcript—boiled down, of course, distilled, but in keeping with what was said and meant. I decided to stick with this pure a form because I wanted the rigor and discipline of keeping to the facts as much as possible."[5] At one point in rehearsal Mann says to an actor: "I know it's transcript. I wish I could change that word to make it clearer." Instead she suggests that the actor "think" her revised phrasing as he delivers the line as written. Later in rehearsal, although highly sympathetic to another actor's complaint that certain lines make his character (a police officer) appear "generic," Mann does not offer to rewrite but instead suggests that the actor "soften . . . [the speech] here," partly by slowing down the pace. In her role as director the playwright alters the speech without changing the text.[6] As Robert Benedetti remarks, "An action performed quickly is a different action than the same action performed slowly."[7] (I understand his statement to apply to speech as well as to action.)

The playwright's intention to remain faithful to "what was said and meant" by actual persons living through literal events is more difficult than it appears. Five rehearsal revisions, dated February 5, 1986, contain specific clarifications of meaning and corrections of grammatical constructions. Here, for example, is the original version of part of Dan White's confession:

> Yes, my aide picked me up but she didn't have any idea ah
> . . . you know that I had a gun on me or, you know, and I went
> in to see him an, an he [the mayor] told me he wasn't going
> to, intending to tell me about it.

This is changed to:

> Yes, my aide picked me up but she didn't have any idea ah
> . . . you know that I had a gun on me or, you know, and I went
> in to see him an, an he told me he wasn't going to reappoint
> me and he wasn't intending to tell me about it.[8]

The added words, "reappoint me," make clear to the audience what is implicit but elliptical in the text. That four of the five rehearsal revisions, including this one, do not appear in the published version of the play suggests a tension between the playwright's fidelity to "what was said" and the director's fidelity to "what was . . . meant."

The director tells the actors before the first runthrough: "So much of the play is about witnessing and testifying. . . ." A witness is "one who is called upon to be present at a transaction in order to attest to what took place."[9] In rehearsal the company itself bears witness to the recreation of an historical transaction.

In Mann's rehearsals of *Execution of Justice*, to an extent uncharacteristic of any other director I observed, there is an emphasis on thinking rather than on the free play of feeling or impulse. Again and again her discourse reveals this directorial approach and its relation to the nature of the playtext: "This is a complicated play. It's all thoughts. . . . If you're wandering and if you're not analyzing everything you hear through your own diagnosis, the scene loses its validity. It becomes too funny. Always be hard on yourself and bring yourself back to your own thinking. You've got to stay alive mentally. Mind-power . . . Good [complimenting the cast at the end of a day of rehearsal]. . . . It's well thought-through. . . . Think the thoughts because we are watching you think, watching a whole community think. . . . A collective witnessing."

In Mann's theatre of testimony, the actors reflect and reflect on a communal process ("watching a whole community think") which they also embody ("a collective witnessing"). The playwright's imperative to the audience is the director's imperative to the actors: "Hear everything. . . . Take it all in. . . . Take in everything."

How difficult a task this is, for actors and audience alike, is vividly illustrated when video equipment is brought into the rehearsal studio. The cast competes not only with documentary footage of the historical events they are recreating (e.g., the touching candlelight ceremony of mourning for the deaths of Milk and Moscone) but also with instantaneous images of themselves on video monitors as they react to the verdict reached by the jury in the trial of Dan White. For the director herself there is a competition between different kinds of "reflective surfaces," a potential conflict between the demands of the camera and the demands of theatre. At one point in rehearsal, Mann says to actors Mary McDonnell and Jon De Vries, "I like what you're doing on camera; I don't like the stage picture."

For the audience as well there is a distracting array of simultaneous images competing for attention: the live actors performing communal actions; the over-familiar, seductive images of the faces of the actors on closed circuit television as they perform; the footage of actual events in San Francisco. In the final moments of act two, for example, individual members of the large cast respond variously to the announcement of the conviction of Dan White on the reduced charge of voluntary manslaughter, with a maximum sentence of seven years and eight months, for the slayings of Mayor George Moscone and Supervisor Harvey Milk. Live actors compete with footage of the San Francisco riots in May, 1979, following the verdict, and also with images of themselves on monitors. The camera, by focusing on one actor at a time, creates an "intimacy" not provided by the staged event, an "intimacy" of a kind familiar to a nation that watched, for example, televised images of faces witnessing the Challenger explode and crash, images then played over and over until they seemed part of an old newsreel.[10]

The problem the play poses for the actors in rehearsal is the problem it poses for its characters and its audience: how to achieve a collective witnessing in which one is expected to "take in everything" and "stay alive mentally." *Execution of Justice* puts the same kind of pressure on actors and audiences as do the life-events it dramatizes.

The director's emphasis on "mind-power" seems at times in conflict with the deeper resources of successful acting. For example, in the most intense scene in the play, Dan White's approximately twenty-minute confession to police officers, the initial sentence is followed by the stage direction: (*sob*). When I first see this rehearsed, John Spencer, playing Dan White, is crying so profusely that the actor playing the police inspector leaves the scene and returns momentarily with Kleenex to wipe the face of the actor whose hands remain handcuffed behind his back. Continuing to cry during his confession speech, the actor loses his lines several times, saying at one point, "I don't know where I am" (an unscripted line). At the end of the scene the director compliments Spencer: "John, it's wonderful." She rubs his shoulder and back quietly, then walks away, still visibly moved, to compose herself. The director's note, "Think the thoughts because we are watching you think," suggests a self-consciousness that is often a part of acting, even when one is acting out-of-control. Dan White's breakdown during his confession speech is extremely difficult to perform, partly because the actor, like the character, approaches a state in which a certain kind of "mind-power" is no longer possible.

In the next rehearsal of the confession scene the actor is clearly struggling for more control. But crying is the right physicalization for him; when he turns off the crying he turns off an essential subcurrent of which it is a manifestation. The actor's face is wiped dry of tears several times before he can continue. When he is silent during the police interrogation, his face seems to register the struggle of a consciousness coming out of shock, trying to open up an event to itself, "take it all in," replay it with emotions that are surfacing as if for the first time. The dilemma of the character, who becomes accessible to his own impulses by replaying them for an "audience" of policemen, is the dilemma of the actor playing for a theatre audience—and the rehearsal of the confession speech stages that dilemma:

> But I just kinda stumbled in the back and he [Mayor Moscone] was all, he was talking an nothing was getting through to me. *It was just like a roaring in my ears* an, an then em . . . it just

came to me, you know, he . . . What I was going to do now, you
know, and how this would affect my family, you know, an, an
just, just all the time knowing he's going to go out an, an lie
to the press an, an tell 'em, you know, that I, I wasn't a good
Supervisor and that people didn't want me an then that was
it. Then I, I just shot him, that was it, it was over. (emphasis
added)[11]

Invariably, after rehearsal of the confession the actor is shaken.
Mann places the one "recess" (intermission) in the play shortly
after this scene, which concludes the first act.

Excluding testimony recorded in official documents, Mann
says of her playscript: "There's not a line in this that wasn't in
some way said to me."[12] Her authorial role as a kind of ear-
witness is complemented by her rehearsal role as observer. At
the end of the second week of rehearsal Mann says to Mary
McDonnell (playing Mary Ann White) and John Spencer (Dan
White): "May and John, I'm going to leave alone what's going on
[between you] in that red square [marked by tape on the floor].
. . . It's lovely. I'm going to leave it alone. *I'm just going to watch
it*" (emphasis added).

But watching it is not leaving it alone. I am told by Assistant
Director Molly Fowler when I discuss my seating location in the
rehearsal studio that Mann prefers observers of her rehearsals
to be invisible to her, as if she does not want to observe herself
being observed. And this is completely understandable since
"seeing oneself being seen"[13] is the very process the director is
engaged in with the actors in rehearsal. Ellie Ragland-Sullivan,
describing the connection between Lacan's theory of the gaze
and Sartre's *regard*, notes that for Lacan, "The *regard* is not simply a glance cast from the eye, nor a glance from reflective consciousness, because the *regard* has the power to activate within
consciousness an awareness of unconscious motivation and in-
tentionality." Thus, "a person may feel scrutinized by someone
whose eyes and physical being are invisible. A mere suspicion of
the presence of others can trigger an inner resonance: a window,
darkness, a feeling—and suddenly the window itself becomes a
regard."[14] The director-figure is crucial to the process of "seeing"
in rehearsal, even when the director is not literally gazing at
the actor. It is Lacan's theory that "the gaze is one of the first
structuring mechanisms of the human subject. It was introjected
as a part-object in the pre-mirror stage before the eye acquired

its function of seeing and representing the subject, and, conse-
quently, before there was any sense of alterity."[15]
An earlier account of the process of "seeing," which also has
some application to rehearsal, is that of the eighteenth-century
idealist philosopher George Berkeley: *esse est percipi*, "to be is to
be perceived." Northrop Frye, in his study of William Blake,
writes: "The acceptance of the *esse-est-percipi* principle unites
the subject and the object. . . . If to be is something else than to be
perceived, our perceptions do not acquaint us with reality. . . ."[16]
Without debating whether Berkeley, Blake, and Frye are right
about the nature of "reality," it is possible to say that for the
actor in the theatre, to be perceived is to be. The actor acting in
rehearsal does not exist until perceived by the director, who acts
as surrogate for the eventual spectator. The "reality" created by
the actor is first completed in the director's gaze, a gaze I have
gazed at over and over in rehearsals. This gaze, more maternal
than patriarchal in its origins,[17] represents the ultimate collaboration in the rehearsal process, the birthing and nurturing of the
imagined life of the playtext as present "reality." Dramatic texts
in the process of becoming theatrical events are, in the words of
Marianne Moore's definition of poetry, " 'imaginary gardens
with real toads in them.' "[18]
It seems particularly appropriate to "a collective witnessing"
that the director arrange two early semi-public viewings of
runthroughs of the play. During the first of these Saturday morning rehearsal "performances" with invited guests, I am seated in
"the gallery," a section of seats placed upstage in the playing
area where actors sit when not performing during rehearsal and
where, in the theatre itself, some members of the audience will
sit. In her verbal notes to the company before the runthrough
begins, Mann says, "I want you to *feel through* the play, not just
produce an effect because there are people out there watching
the runthrough today." What follows is a detailed documenting
of a unique experience in my observations of rehearsal.
Seated in the gallery I watch the director watching what I can
no longer observe, only remember, for in the gallery I see the
backs of the actors and the face of the director responding to
them. As Dan White enters, Mann's face is pained, aghast. (His
entrance is preceded by the enlarged image on the video monitor
of Acting Mayor Dianne Feinstein whose announcement of the
double murders seems, paradoxically, to be that of an actress
carefully modulating powerful emotions.) When a police officer,

played by Stanley Tucci, and Sister Boom Boom, a political activist played by Wesley Snipes, begin to perform the next scene, I watch Mann become the ideal audience, reacting as if for the first time to Snipes' strutting, mocking, ironic, truth-telling Boom Boom and Tucci's racist, anti-gay cop. Sitting in the silent gallery, the actors performing between us, I see the director as the cast sees her throughout rehearsal, and as they will not see her during public performances in the theatre. When a prospective member of the jury, her back toward me, is questioned by the defense attorney, the face of the director displays the changing emotions of the actress as I recall them from previous rehearsals; then Mann's face reflects, in quick succession, the varied emotional states of three more would-be jurors under interrogation and also the grimace of the defense attorney. For the first time, I see the words being spoken by the actors forming on the director's lips.

Now a new element is added as I watch. Even while the expressive face of the director continues to register, sequentially, the impulses of the actors, she snaps her fingers at the appropriate moment, delivers the single cue, "Lights." Although she seems as intensely present to the rehearsal "performance" as it is possible to be, she is both inside and outside the experience of the play; she is a reflector of the actors' impulses and the audience's responses, and yet always something else, something more, allowing her, in the words of Teresa de Lauretis, "a view from 'elsewhere.' "[19]

The day before this runthrough, Mann rehearsed what she calls the "Cyr chorus," a group of actors whose speeches intercut the emotional testimony of Cyr Copertini, appointment secretary to Mayor Moscone, as she describes the events preceding and following his murder by Dan White. In this rehearsal Mann asked five actors to sit in a circle and then joined them in the playing area. As the prosecuting attorney elicits from Cyr Copertini the prosaic details of Dan White's behavior and conversation just a few moments before he entered the mayor's office, three other characters—White's jailer, a friend of Moscone, and a young mother—tell their own stories. At the end of this seated rehearsal of the "Cyr chorus," in which the director has taken part silently, one actor says, "It's like a wake," and Mann nods in agreement. She has created a physical staging, not to be repeated in performance, in which the author-director becomes a mourner along with the actors. Mann initiates, and joins, a circle of intimacy, a performance of mourning, but she is, at the same time, observing, witnessing, the configuration she establishes.

When the scene is rehearsed "on its feet," it moves much more quickly and its speeches are less pause-ridden. No longer a series of independent phrases or phases of consciousness, the choral wake becomes an interweaving of voices, voices in eerie intimate contact rather than making way for each other, voices building a cumulative resonance as they find a common nucleus, a small paradigm of the rehearsal process itself. Eventually Mann, now watching from outside the playing area, asks Lisabeth Bartlett (the young mother) to move downstage right, while Suzy Hunt (Cyr) remains center stage. The immediate effect of this revised blocking, which Mann offers tentatively as an experiment, is to elicit a more subdued performance from the repositioned actress.

In the runthrough I see the effects of the director's restaging. The redundancy of two emotionally wrought weeping women (Cyr and the young mother) is rendered in a newly interesting way. As the "choric" speeches (in the Chekhovian sense) draw the actors into intimacy with each other, the audience seems to hear and see a single Picasso-like woman whose face (that of the young mother) and back (that of the appointment secretary) are both visible to the spectators, wherever they may be seated. The gallery audience sees the face of the young mother and the back of Cyr Copertini; the auditorium audience sees the face of the appointment secretary and the back of the young mother. In this staging "upstage" and "downstage" lose, exchange, their expected meanings.

As I observe this scene from the gallery I see, for the first time since the beginning of the runthrough, Mann's head turn away briefly from the actors to make a note.

Shortly after this the director looks down as she makes two more notes, first when an actor giving testimony seems to be having trouble with his lines and the scene slows down for a moment, and then when another actor needs a line cue and some blocking seems unclear. Mann, whose assistant director sits next to her, does not dictate notes during the runthrough, preferring instead to "take it all in" herself.[20]

Just as abruptly as the director's note-taking begins, it stops, for there is a crisis slowly emerging in the runthrough, a crisis whose nature I can detect only through the director's responses to it. As Dan White begins his long confession, the emotional climax of act one, Mann's body posture and facial expression tauten to maximum intensity. The actor seems to be having trouble, though I cannot see his face. Mann says quietly, in an undertone, to the actor: "Excellent, excellent; stay in the scene, please." The faces of the audience seated behind the director are preternaturally still. The director's head and upper body move rhythmically forward and backward. The thumb and forefinger of her right hand move with incredible staccato-like rapidity, her large expressive eyes focused on the actor. It is now so quiet that I hear the director's indrawn breath across the room. The actor stops moving; the director stops moving. They are both still for a moment, then the actor continues his confession-speech and the director continues the rhythmical movement of head and upper torso back and forth, the right forefinger resuming its staccato beats on her knee.

This is the first time the company has rehearsed before a "public" audience rather than the "private" audience constituted by the company members.[21] I hear the director emit a loud release of breath, then another. She is seated about ten feet away from the actor, directly in front of him. Her chair has been moved to the left side of the rectangular director's table so that there is nothing at all in the space between actor and director. It is as if she is trying to send her breath into the actor, literally to inspire him.[22] At the same time she seems close to crying, as if deeply moved by the actor's giving himself to this moment, daring to try to do what she has asked of all the actors at the beginning of the runthrough: "I want you to *feel through* the play, not just produce an effect because there are people out there watching the runthrough today." Only at the very end of the confession-speech does Mann make a brief note, taking her eyes off the actor for an instant. There is a twenty-minute recess, and the actor is escorted "offstage" (i.e., out of the playing area), his face, now visible to me for the first time, streaming with tears. Mann walks over to speak to him; I overhear only the beginning of her sentence, "I'm sorry about. . . ." There is no further revelation of what has happened. The actor remains alone for some time after the director leaves his side.

Two actors immediately ask how I liked the first act. When I mention my sense of difficulty in never seeing Dan White's face, one actor, Adam Redfield, mentions that he has only seen this scene from the back, has never seen Dan White's face during the long confession speech. My usual perspective has been exactly reversed. I am now observing the director and the audience from the perspective, over the shoulders, of the actors.[23]

After the intermission, during a scene I have not seen rehearsed before, Mary Ann White (Mary McDonnell) movingly testifies about the nature of her early marital relationship and her husband's "moods" of sexual apathy and depression; the director's face is again taut with pain but her body is relatively still, her arms crossed over her chest. I am struck, as the actors must be, by the variety of ways in which she signals empathy. What again complicates this responsiveness is the director's characteristic reflection of both the actors' expressive choices and the audience's reactions to those choices. For example, from behind the back of City Supervisor Carol Ruth Silver, a witness for the prosecution (played by Marcia Jean Kurtz), I observe the director's face involuntarily mime the actress' bemused silent reaction to the question of the defense attorney, "Is it *Miss* Silver?" and then see her smile, along with the rest of the audience, at Miss Silver's deftly timed, "Yes." A few minutes later Mann's face tenses during the rising tones of a shouting match between Silver and the defense attorney; then she laughs aloud at Silver's quiet attempt to defang the lawyer's innuendos. Near the end of the runthrough I notice Mann's eyes moving around the playing area, as she takes in the physical staging, making one last note. The runthrough is followed by spontaneous applause.

After a break, during which the invited audience leaves the rehearsal studio, Mann addresses the entire company before giving individual notes to the actors: "Everyone, congratulations for a very fine first runthrough. There's a lot going on in the room. I think it's clear to me now after only two weeks of rehearsal where we've come to and where we have to go. . . . Basically, it's thinking faster, tightening . . . so the rhythm of your scene becomes part of the emotional stakes for you, so you're just not pacing. . . . I really saw the emotional arcs for each of you. Basically the staging is right and the choices we've made are right. I'm very pleased by this. I'm really hearing *all* the gradations from all sides and I'm getting all the context, so bravo. Those are the major tasks and we've done them."

Mann is defining the director's role as much as she is identifying the needs and achievements of the actors in rehearsal. The director "saw" each emotional arc, heard "*all*" the gradations "from all sides," registered "all the context." The repeated emphasis on "we" ("where *we've* come to and where *we* have to go," "the choices *we've* made," "Those are the major tasks and *we've* done them") is not gratuitous. It is neither the royal "we" of power nor the slightly inauthentic, overly chummy "we" of a forced camaraderie. The director is embedded in this intimate collective achievement, as her discourse assumes, and her final directorial note is necessarily partly self-reflexive: "The hard task is to keep everything going, to take in everything, to preserve all that variety and yet to keep a clear line going for the audience. . . ."

In a detailed analysis of the first runthrough, the director discusses a missed exit with an actress who explains that she was so affected by the summation speech of the prosecuting attorney that she momentarily forgot she was in a play. She explains metaphorically: "[I] left the room." Literally, of course, she *failed* to leave the "room": there was an awkwardly long pause during which Mann repeatedly asked her to "leave" until the actress finally took her exit. The paradox of the semi-public runthrough is that it combines performance values with rehearsal vulnerability. The actress later says to the director, "I lost some lines." Mann replies, "Yes. Why?" The actress explains, "Because some new stuff came up, but I don't want to name it," and the director responds, "Now we just have to craft it, find a safety valve."

The discussion that follows the second semi-public runthrough illustrates rehearsal's tendency to make use of all means at its disposal for its own purposes. One actress acknowledges that the cast was nervous and Mann quickly responds, "Yes, but that's what it's like to be in court." The nervousness created by simulating performance conditions is used in rehearsal to induce a more intense enactment of courtroom jitters. Another example of making use of "natural instinct" to heighten the illusion of natural instinct is Mann's note to actress Isabell Monk (playing Gwenn Craig): "I hate to be so precise but I will be." Asking Monk to move exactly when a certain word is spoken by another actor, Mann adds: "You did it this way the first time you ever did it. It was your natural instinct."

But the most illuminating aspect of this second post-performance discussion has to do with the role of the director as observed observer. As already suggested, Mann functions partly as audience-surrogate in rehearsal. When the actors begin tentatively to observe other less receptive, less invested observers, they are not always reinforced, energized, nourished. At first, the members of the audience—the collective witnesses of a collective witnessing—are discussed somewhat impersonally and speculatively. One actress is pleased that the invited guests provide "the reverberations of the city." Director and cast, assessing a woman in the audience who was weeping and two men who looked angry, muse on whether the play offends the spectator's political alignments or preconceptions about acting. Gradually, actors reveal more specific forms of observing those who observe, or fail to observe, them. One actor mentions a man in the audience who fell asleep during his long climactic speech. Another actor says that he attempted to "take part of [a] . . . speech" to a particular bearded gentleman in the front row. Several other actors immediately protest: no, no, he's not the one to look to, ever. These comments may seem commonplace to the experienced theatre practitioner, but they suggest the power of the gaze as "one of the first structuring mechanisms of the human subject." In the semi-public runthroughs the actors are beginning to transfer the power of the gaze from the director to the audience. Eventually the gaze of the director-figure will become the *regard* of a mostly invisible audience seated in a usually darkened theatre. The transitional state of this transference of power from director to audience is revealed when an actress startles Mann by asking if she voiced an expletive during a certain scene in the runthrough. After another actor quickly clarifies that this term of disgust was uttered by someone in the audience, the actress replies, "Well, that made me go." On the one hand, Mann's role as witness is clearly being co-opted by the audience. On the other hand, even as she is beginning to be divested of one of her directorial functions, her perceived presence "can trigger an inner resonance."

Like other directors not rehearsing in the actual performance space, Mann is explicit about the physical restrictions on her viewing of rehearsal. For example, she characteristically adjusts actors' positions in the playing area in relation to the "red square" center stage. Yet, after asking the prosecuting attorney not to "nick the corners of the red square" in his opening speech, she quickly adds that she will have to see exactly what this red square looks like in the theatre. Later she responds to a question posed by the defense attorney: "I almost can't tell you until I get on stage and can see the whole stage picture. . . . I actually can't answer your question." In the rehearsal studio Mann is forced to sit "ridiculously close" to the actors; she needs to "get into the theatre" to see the actors "at a distance." Even the sounds of the actors' voices cannot be accurately evaluated outside the performance space. Discussing when Nicholas Kepros, playing the judge, should be artificially amplified, Mann says, "I don't know about vocal adjustments until we're on a stage. . . . I don't know about certain physical adjustments until we're on stage. . . . I don't know how to do any more in here. . . . I think we're done in this room!" (This is the last day of rehearsal scheduled in the Broadway studio.)

On the first day of technical rehearsal in the Virginia Theatre, a large Broadway house of 1100–1200 seats, Mann tells the company, "Today is a day we've been waiting for for a long time and we're ready. . . . This stage was built for you. . . . Find your reality out here [on the stage]. . . . These lights are very very hot and very exciting. . . . We're really going to be lighting moment by moment so please bear with us. It may be tedious at times. If you see a potential problem with crossovers, exits, entrances, quick changes, please tell me immediately." I am again sitting in the gallery, now a raised platform of four rows of comfortable plush theatre seats, upstage center, where the actors are assembled. Mann stands downstage center, her back to the empty auditorium, as she talks to the company. Suddenly the lights come on: they *are* very hot.

While the cast physically explores the theatre space, Mann studies the set, designed by Ming Cho Lee. For the next fifteen minutes while the actors move around backstage, their voices sometimes audible, the director moves around in the auditorium, viewing the stage from different perspectives. As she observes the set, I observe on the director's table an article from that day's *Asbury Park Press* in which the playwright is quoted: "When I put down one side, I always tried to hear the other. If I said, 'Here is black,' then I'd have to show white, and gray would come. . . . I've done probably five cycles of 360 degrees. That's what this play does to you. You find out there are no simple, easy answers."[24] The author's exploration of multiple moral and political perspectives is reenacted in the director's present exploration of multiple visual perspectives, while the actors make their own physical explorations backstage.

The stage setting Mann studies is itself a kind of Möbius strip. It is stark and abstract and is accompanied by a large photomural which depicts on the inside of the walls of the Virginia Theatre the exterior of the San Francisco Hall of Justice, with small trees and large bushes visible in front of its façade. We in the auditorium are outside the Hall of Justice, while the stage depicts the inside of the court, where some members of the audience will be seated in the gallery. Thus the audience, like the director before them, is both outside and inside the courtroom, the place where justice is "executed."

Earlier, in the rehearsal studio, Mann has told the company that she is working with the staff at the Virginia Theatre to preserve the intimate setting of the play in the large Broadway house. This attempt proves to be unsuccessful, and becomes one of the many paradoxes of this production. *Execution of Justice* is a theatre piece which is not quite a documentary, although every word is documented; its set, which makes use of photographs and film footage of actual places and persons, is nonetheless non-naturalistic; finally, it is "a collective witnessing" of a public event which plays best in an intimate setting.

When the actors first enter the stage of the Virginia Theatre, they look small and slightly disoriented. They are competing with a newly installed sound and video montage, the beat of a city in tension. Despite their having been given time to explore, the only real exploration for the actors is to rehearse in the new space. But new explorations are occurring without the actors. As lighting designer Pat Collins works with some of the 250 light cues (there are just under one hundred sound cues), the director watches and comments, often asking for adjustments in duration and intensity of light. Standing beside them in the darkened auditorium, Ming Cho Lee watches the effect of these changes on the set he has designed. Sound designer Tom Morse is now brought into discussion with the director, and adjustments are made in the volume and timing of sound cues. Moment by moment, the director in collaboration with the lighting, set, and sound designers makes a series of seemingly minute choices which change the effect of what is heard and seen by the audience. At one point, director and lighting designer agree on a lighting change which the set designer finds "beautiful." Ming Cho Lee then suggests a corresponding change in his set in order that the lighting change have its full intended effect. Although the cast has been given its required ten-minute break, actress Suzy Hunt happens to walk across the stage just as the set and lighting designers are experimenting with new choices. The director says, "Yes, that's perfect," as the actress' body inadvertently reflects the newly adjusted lighting in the re-imagined set.

What is striking is that the director and her three designers—lighting, set, and sound—are now performing, in a different mode, the same exploratory roles previously enacted by the cast and director in a relatively bare rehearsal studio. Just when one might expect the process to be coming to its completion, the process is intensified. With the first preview just four days away, more and more exploration occurs in the performance space as more and still more components are added, labored over, adjusted, and re-adjusted. The final authority remains that of the director whose use of that authority is expressed in continual collaborative creation.

The actors are once again part of this process. The director speaks privately to John Spencer, asking him to hold a certain position a few seconds longer, then returns to the side of the lighting designer, saying, "I've just made an acting adjustment that will help you." In the ideal interaction between actor and designer, negotiated by the director, designers enhance what actors create and actors make adjustments to enhance designers' effects. The figure of the Möbius strip is the appropriate emblem of a process in which precisely identified causes and effects are as illusory as the theatrical reality created by that process.

Just before I make my final exit from the technical rehearsals of her play, Emily Mann suggests that I be recorded running on a hard surface in spike heels, becoming "immortalized" on audio tape, as the sound designer says, for use in the performance. The play begins and ends with "hyperreal sounds of high heels on marble,"[25] always associated with Mary Ann White running to meet her husband praying in church after he has murdered Moscone and Milk. The director has indirectly issued an invitation to me to come out of the observer role and into the process itself. Because I cannot remain in New York, I am unable to leave this audible imprint on the experience I am attempting to record. But I still feel that somehow I am reflected there. For as I document rehearsal work, I recognize that I am one more reflector of a collective witnessing, an observer recording a process that perhaps has in it traces of my own presence. Emily Mann's allowing me to observe the observer observed is the knowing and self-defining gesture of a director committed to a theatre of testimony.

Fig. 5.1. JoAnne Akalaitis. Photograph by Martha Swope.

5

JoAnne Akalaitis directs
The Voyage of the Beagle

"Quiet, boys. I'll direct this."

Writer-director JoAnne Akalaitis is a founding member of Mabou Mines, "one of America's most respected theater troupes,"[1] and has worked with the company since 1970 as performer, designer, and director. Akalaitis has been directing plays in New York City and across the country since 1974. She has also written and directed a feature film based on her award-winning theatre piece, *Dead End Kids, A History of Nuclear Power*, performed by Mabou Mines at the Public Theater during the 1980–1981 season. The recipient of five Obies for Distinguished Direction and Production, a Guggenheim fellowship for experimental theatre, a Rockefeller Playwright Fellowship as well as Rockefeller and National Endowment for the Arts grants for *The Voyage of the Beagle*, Akalaitis directed Shakespeare's *Cymbeline* at the Public Theater and Genet's *The Screens* at the Guthrie. In August of 1991, she was appointed Artistic Director of the Public Theater's New York Shakespeare Festival.

The rehearsal I observe is preparation for a script-in-hand "workshop"[2] production of *The Voyage of the Beagle*, with text by Akalaitis and music by Jon Gibson, presented by the American Music Theater Festival at The Triplex in lower Manhattan on April 18, 1987. It is described in the program notes by Eric Salzman as "a poem-in-progress about a theory, a non-narrative story about a journey. . . ." The journey is Charles Darwin's five-year circumnavigation of the world as ship naturalist on the M.S. Beagle. The theory of evolution, published almost three decades after he embarked, had its origins in Darwin's detailed journal entries, later published as *The Voyage of the Beagle*.

Rehearsals of Akalaitis' *The Voyage of the Beagle* take place in an upstairs studio on West 16th Street. The cast is a small, vital chorus of eight boys and four adult actor-singers.[3] In the following pages, I shall emphasize features of rehearsal (use of a children's chorus and professional singers) that are not representative of Akalaitis' career as a whole, yet may illustrate certain aspects of her approach to directing, a process she characterizes as "one of the most complex, complicated human activities—and more manipulative than I would like it to be."[4] Even in describing a rehearsal which, Akalaitis cautions me, is unusually "efficient," more "putting together, construction, than deep investigation, exploration," I recognize, as I do at every rehearsal I have observed, the appropriateness of Darwin's words from *The Voyage of the Beagle*: "Whilst viewing such scenes, one feels the impossibility that any description should come near to the mark, much less be overdrawn."[5] Although this eminent director is represented here only by an abbreviated period of rehearsal on a work-in-progress, that very limitation makes it possible to raise the question: What can preparation for a script-in-hand workshop production reveal about the rehearsal process?

Akalaitis tells me that she usually begins her rehearsals by inviting the actors to dance or move rhythmically to some music she associates with the script, but does not attempt this in workshop. In the first audition for *Voyage of the Beagle*, selections are based on singing ability. Second auditions are held to determine how well the singers work together as actors. In a postperformance discussion with the audience, the soprano remarks that in her first audition, for which she prepared an aria, the director asked her to move through the room as she sang. In the second audition, with two other actors, she was asked to read certain texts aloud in various ways and to improvise a dance. Even in a workshop production, the audition—a crucial component in shaping the rehearsal experience—is itself a highly condensed form of exploration.[6]

Akalaitis may not be conducting a "deep investigation," but there are signs of the exploratory nature of rehearsal everywhere, even in so seemingly slight a detail as the sound of a glass breaking. After the cast has left on the evening before the performance, Akalaitis asks sound designer Stephen Cellum to play over and over a tape of about a dozen different sounds of breaking glass. After some time the director finally decides on sounds nine and ten. In response to the designer's question, "Is this what you wanted?" Akalaitis says, "It's different from what I mentally meant but I like it."

Even what Akalaitis "mentally meant" seems to be rediscovered in rehearsal. She says at one point, "I'm marking through. I've never heard this dialogue spoken." First asking the tenor to deliver a long speech unaccented, she subsequently encourages him to speak with an English accent. Later in rehearsal that day she interrupts the tenor: "That could be a little less dry." The singer now delivers the lines with greater expressiveness: the accent is diminished, but the speech is more effective. Toward the end of rehearsals, Akalaitis encourages alto Yolande Bavan to use "the rhythm of an Indian accent" in one of her speeches. After the accent becomes more pronounced, the director cautions: "*Don't* do too much. It plays." The trying out of accents is a mode of experimentation, not a fixed means of characterization.

On two separate occasions Akalaitis seems belatedly to confirm her own authorial decisions as if discovering their structural force or use only in rehearsal. There is one section in the playtext that Akalaitis finds "terrible": a series of corny Tarzan and Jane jokes. One singer resists the director's initial desire to eliminate this section. Akalaitis later speeds up and de-emphasizes the joke sequence so that it functions as a transition from the "Drink" section, a hearty round sung by the quartet, to the "Argentina" section, a long speech by Darwin on the massacre of Indians. This use of the joke sequence, seemingly discovered in rehearsal, is in fact indicated in the script: "The company rushes around (moving into the next scene) telling jokes."[7]

As is characteristic of a workshop production, certain elaborate stage directions in the text are not attempted, e.g., "On stage naked children rise from the mud. An angel (SOPRANO) in slow motion falls singing."[8] But as the soprano sings a text taken from Shelley's "Mont Blanc," the director interrupts: "Ellen, I think you should take a *really* slow cross. It really seems to call for that." The indication of tempo is rescued from the abandoned stage direction and transferred to the soprano's walk across the stage, but Akalaitis' phrasing seems to suggest a directorial perspective rather than a playwright's prerogative: "*It* really seems to call for that," as if the script speaks to her from a site outside the province of authorship. After the full dress technical rehearsal of what she describes to a visitor as "a work-in-progress," Akalaitis says simply, "I saw some things," and then remarks, "I think we should try something new every day."

Characteristic of her directorial rhetoric is her response to composer Jon Gibson's demonstration of a certain weirdly smothered sound he wishes to incorporate, that of a hand beating from inside a drum: "I like it . . . for now." Receptive to suggestions from sound and set and costume designers, as well as from the music directors, Akalaitis retains final authority but in the context of ongoing exploration. After telling the musicians, "My direction to the singers is . . . more aggressiveness, more gentility," Akalaitis says quietly, "I don't know what the result will be." Earlier she remarks, after suggesting adjustments in sound levels that are intended to reduce the tension between the competing sounds of the singers and the musicians, "What I just said to do, do—and then I'll probably change my mind later because it probably won't work."

A last example is Akalaitis' "great idea," later rejected. The stage direction in the text reads: "A cloth is flung across the stage and a fan placed on it. DARWIN regards it carefully, flings himself on it and crawls across stage."[9] On my first day of observing rehearsal, Akalaitis says to the cast: "I have a great idea! Want to hear it? At the end of this [speech], we'll have a long wind fade [and] . . . the cloth will wave." After carefully directing the sound of the "long wind fade," provided by production assistant Mary Ann Marek, Akalaitis says with excitement: "This is going to be great." As the slow fade of the wind, carefully synchronized with the moving cloth, continues to be rehearsed, it seems gradually displaced by the presence of the adult singers. During rehearsal on the day of the performance, the director announces, "We're blowing off the cloth and the fan. . . . Anybody want twelve feet of pink silk?" Akalaitis characteristically does not analyze intensively either causes or effects. Her positive responses take a form reminiscent of other rehearsals I have observed: "It's cooking," "It plays." Rejected choices are announced with a lack of fanfare, as a matter of course: "Anybody want twelve feet of pink silk?"

My emphasis in this chapter on sound problems—and by implication on the director's ear rather than on her gaze—reflects in part the nature and tensions of a musical theatre piece. Miking and other aspects of artificial amplification create problems in the performance space. Rehearsing on the Triplex stage, baritone Cris Groenendaal, playing Darwin, complains, "I feel in competition with the music. I can't hear myself. The music drowns me out." Polite, controlled, the director replies: "I'm doing my best here. *I'm listening*" (emphasis added). The singer acknowledges this response in an immediately subdued voice, "Okay." Here the director's reassurance that she is listening replaces the reassurance that she is remembering (as in *The Cherry Orchard*) or watching (as in *Execution of Justice*) or rewriting (as in *Abingdon Square*) in the midst of crisis. Later, in rehearsing the choir, Akalaitis says, "I want everything. I want to hear the syllables the boys are singing and to hear the names of the prehistoric animals. . . ." Emily Mann's imperative, "Take it all in," is baffled in the *Voyage* rehearsal by the artificial amplification of the sounds of human voices and live or taped musical instruments.

The baritone has trouble hearing himself; the tenor, Jeff Johnson, has trouble hearing the soprano, Ellen McLain, who says she can't hear the other singers on the stage. The director, listening to the quartet from different sections of the auditorium, says to the musical director and sound designer, "I could use more of their voices myself." The problem is temporarily and partially solved by Akalaitis' request that the sound level of the synthesizer be lowered but difficulties in hearing continue to shadow the director's attention to the words of the text. She says to one singer, "You *are* heard. Don't panic," and to the cast as a whole: "Big note. There's a lot of language here, spoken and sung. . . . Nonstop efforts have to be made to make the language clear without slowing down the piece and without making it sound like a BBC documentary."

Darwin says, "If it were not for seasickness, the whole world would be sailors."[10] Darwin's own seasickness, recorded in his journals during the voyage of the Beagle, becomes a metaphor for the rehearsal experience of auditory disequilibrium. The director's notes are like a rudder, indicating new shifts as changing conditions dictate even when the final destination is not visible. The precise coordinates of every moment of stage time must be plotted, assessed, readjusted. Like Darwin, the director is an explorer who seeks truth in minute particulars. And, like Darwin, the director is not immune from disorientation during the voyage but finds her bearings in the midst of storm. Akalaitis, still dissatisfied with the sound of a spoken-and-sung section of the play, although her sound designer is satisfied, says, "I think I'm losing my judgment." She is not, and afterwards succeeds in encouraging a final necessary vocal adjustment: the downward modulation, with some playfulness added, of the very high, strained sound of one singer.

On the last day of rehearsal Cris Groenendaal's microphone loses power and he asks the director what the cast should do if the microphones fail during performance that evening. He quickly adds, "I won't know if my mike does fail. . . . Oh, for the days of unamplified performance!" Amplification is tricky, the sound designer explains to me later, especially for professional singers who are used to practicing in rooms where they can hear every nuance. Once miked, the singers cannot really hear their own voices as they need to. And if the degree of loudness is raised beyond a certain point by artificial amplification, the quality of the sound will be altered, possibly distorted. The problem is not simply that musicians' sounds are overwhelming singers' voices but that the artificial amplification provided by body microphones creates disturbances in the actor-singers' ability to monitor, control, even hear the actual sounds they make.

I am suddenly brought into the process I am attempting to record when the director asks me if I can hear the words sung by the soprano, audible in certain parts of the auditorium but not in the center section where we now sit. The sound designer does not want to increase the sound level of the singer's microphone because she will then "*sound* artificially miked." He suggests moving the body mike from the singer's chest to her shoulder. The director resolves the problem not by readjustments in the placement or use of the microphone but by reblocking the scene so that the actress walks diagonally downstage right, facing the audience at an angle that is consistent with her movement across stage. The crisp enunciation of the words of the text, in question until now, is clearly heard.

Auditory problems affect lighting as well as blocking. At one point the boys' choir is wilting, holding their scripts in odd ways, slouching, looking randomly at their feet and everywhere. Assistant music director Joseph Baker, who works closely with the boys, has told them to hold their scripts in such a way that they can see him. Akalaitis says, "Don't hide your faces behind the books [scripts], boys." A few minutes later she stops the rehearsal and enters the stage. The problem is now vocal delivery: "Pronounce the syllables. Enunciate, enunciate. And don't push. . . . High, simple, clear voices." As I overhear the director's words, I see lighting designer Stephen Strawbridge moving on the stage, giving eloquent silent hand directions to the lighting assistant to change the size and intensity of the spots. The director returns to the auditorium, the choir continues, Akalaitis says to the assistant music director, "I think the boys are singing too loud." The assistant music director asks the choir to sing in alternating groups in order to reduce their volume but Akalaitis does not want smaller groups of loudly singing boys. "I would like them *all* to sing it but softly. If they can." She then repositions the choir further upstage, behind three rows of chairs placed downstage right. The lighting designer groans audibly and resets the lights.

The adjustments I am describing may seem too technical or trivial to be of interest. But no alteration in rehearsal is unimportant or without consequence: no component, even in a workshop production, is an island "entire of itself."[11] The component, however, that does at first seem like an island within the workshop is the boys' choir.

The choir is made up of boys of varying age (the youngest seems about eight and the oldest about fifteen) and height (one so small as to be half the height of the tallest). They have sung in school choirs and most have had some professional experience in television, film, and theatre. When they first enter the rehearsal studio, except for the fact that they all have identical green, yellow, and orange notebooks containing scripts tucked under their arms, they look like any small group of kids during school recess. Akalaitis, in the postperformance discussion with the audience, remarks that the "boys' choir was an early idea" in creating a theatre piece "that deals with generations, and millions and millions and millions of years, and holocausts. . . . [It] seems very human and energizing to have children on stage, to witness their innocence, which we know they're not," adding that children seem "a natural and inevitable presence to have on stage."

One of the boys gives his view: "It was a trying time for the children. It tried our tempers. We had two weeks to become a boys' chorus and I think we did." This view from the underside of adult perception (the boys seemed to try adult tempers) is worth noticing and may have its own Darwinian implications. The children's presence puts in question certain rehearsal conventions usually reflected in theatre practice. Darwin says, "The perfect equality among the individuals composing the Fuegian tribes must for a long time retard their civilization. . . . Whether we look at it as a cause or consequence, the more civilized always have the most artificial government."[12] The children, who often arrive with their own mothers in tow,[13] do not automatically privilege "the maternal gaze" of the director, herself a mother of two children. Nor do they necessarily associate the directorial

presence with patriarchal authority. They seem at times oblivi-
ous to the special conditions of rehearsal work, as if nothing but
the performance itself is "real."

In the script there is an indeterminate stage direction: "Someone walks across stage with a sign: ON-TO-GE-NY-RE-CA-PI-
TU-LATES-PHY-LO-GE-NY."[14] In rehearsal Akalaitis asks all the
boys to participate in enacting this stage direction, each boy
carrying a large blank sign on which eventually will be written
the syllables of the entire sentence. She explains the meaning of
the hypothesis, assigns syllables, and arranges the sequence. As
the adults sing, "Ontogeny recapitulates phylogeny," each boy
struts across the playing area with almost total stage presence.
But when the director asks them to return to their original positions, the boys all become distracted by the slides of prehistoric
animals that are being projected on a large screen behind them.
Forgetting the director's request, completely obliterating rehearsal decorum, the boys talk loudly and animatedly to each
other, clustering in front of the screen, gaping at it, their backs
to the director who, laughing, finally manages to attract their
attention. The scene is rehearsed several times, the adults singing
while the boys walk, one by one, from right to left, and then left
to right, with their blank signs. Watching this staging over and
over, the director decides to try having the choir sing the sentence
as they walk. The smallest boy is unable to pronounce "recapitulate." The soprano is brought in to sing the sentence very clearly
and the boys repeat it after her in their beautiful high voices.
The boys then sit in the folding chairs vacated by the adult
singers and rehearse by themselves the pronunciation of "Ontogeny recapitulates phylogeny." The director, beginning to look
slightly harried, is called out of rehearsal to attend to the first of
many problems with adjustments in the sound mix of music and
sung words.

After the dinner break I discover the boys arm-wrestling; when
they finish that they make finger-shadows of rabbits' ears on
the screen where earlier they had been transfixed by images of
prehistoric animals. Rehearsal begins and the director asks one
boy to read aloud a speech with words that are fairly difficult to
pronounce. Corrected occasionally along the way, his delivery is
complimented by the director: "Good. Do you think you can do
it?" Zachariah Overton replies, "Yes," and the speech is scheduled for rehearsal the following day.

Exploration of the possibilities of her text is an exploration of the possibilities of her actors as well as of the auditory and spatial conditions of the performance space. Akalaitis now experiments with the blocking of the debate between Thomas Huxley and the Archbishop of Oxford on the question of evolution, performed by the baritone and tenor and witnessed by the rest of the cast. The Lecturer tells us that in this memorable debate of 1860 Bishop Wilberforce sent the room into an uproar when he "begged to know if it was through his grandfather or his grandmother that . . . [Huxley] claimed descent from a monkey" and that Huxley then "rose, very stern," and "said something like this. 'I am not ashamed to have a monkey for my ancestor but I would be ashamed to have . . . [connections] with a man who used great gifts to obscure the truth.' "[15] In creating the blocking for the soprano and the children, Akalaitis first asks two boys, Joey Rigol and Reuben Gaumes, to enter and walk toward Ellen McLain. Then three other boys are directed to enter in a group from upstage right. There is a pause while Akalaitis stands in the playing area, thinking on her feet. I have seen every director do this at some point in rehearsal, as if only in the physical site of the staging can the staging problems be finally resolved. She changes the second group entrance to upstage left and the final group of three boys now enters from the opposite side of the stage.

The Lecturer begins to speak, introducing the debate between Dr. Huxley and the Bishop. After all the groups have assembled on the stage, a boy suddenly asks, "What are we doing?" And the director replies, "I'll tell you in a minute." A few years earlier, speaking at a forum for women directors, Akalaitis remarked that she likes "to start with *any* physical choice—accent, glasses, limp," adding that it can of course be thrown away: "I think it's important *not* to interpret the text, until very late."[16] Here those preferences are illustrated, if in a skeletal way. The boys are positioned and the interpretation is postponed, not because the child actors are incapable of understanding but because this is how Akalaitis prefers to work. Only now does she answer the boy's question, "What are we doing?": "You're playing grown-up men. You're watching intently, you're sort of clumpy [she adjusts their physical positions]." Her notes to the boys reveal an emphasis on the presentational rather than on the naturalistic ("you're playing grown-up men," not "you are grown-up men," is an appropriate remark to children and characteristic of her directorial style); on the use of the natural to create the illusion of the natural ("you're watching intently"); and on the physical as a liberating aspect of acting: she has said that "what is mechanical is truly liberating."[17]

The same child actor asks Akalaitis, "Do we have any reactions? Like facial reactions?" She replies, "Just whatever it means to you. . . . This is the greatest debate of the century." When the baritone rephrases, "Like Luke and Darth Vader in *Star Wars*," the boys' eyes light up knowingly. The director herself does not refer to good guys or bad guys. She speaks of physical and vocal choices which may or may not have interpretive resonance. An example is her later comment to the boys: "The organ music is *so* loud that you're going to have to project your voices. Think of your voices as a ball you're going to have to throw out."

Akalaitis' discourse often seems purely utilitarian. She explains to the choir as they watch the debate: "Do you know what 'upstage' means? . . . The focus is on them [the baritone and the tenor], " and later, "What's going to happen, boys, is that Ellen [McLain] is going to talk. I want three of you guys [names them] to exit now. Then the rest of you exit slowly later before the next scene. . . . So, is that clear? You don't want to take the focus off Ellen. *Very* quietly go off the stage." (Instruction in "not upstaging the soprano," although usually less explicitly phrased, is not limited to child actors.) Later, I happen to overhear a private version of this directorial note when Akalaitis tells the boys in a very low voice, "Stop jiving [in your seats]" while the adult actors are speaking or singing.

Sometimes the avoidance of interpretation may appear manipulative. During the debate on evolution, the Bishop argues, "It is obvious to all that a man is qualitatively different from the lower beasts."[18] At the phrase "lower beasts," Akalaitis tells the boys to respond. The result is a wild array of noises, some inappropriately silly. She then says, "Everybody inhale." This produces exactly the effect she wants.[19]

A blocking direction may be grounded in the act of making physical choices and still have a resonance over the heads of the actors, as it were, once it is enacted. In the "Housekeeping" section of the play, rigid rules of domestic life are enunciated by the adult singers while the boys' choir becomes "a procession of child servers carrying giant sickly colored, plastic models of Victorian favorites."[20] Discovering blocking for her own stage direction as she rehearses, Akalaitis arranges for the boys to carry plates across stage, from left to right and then the reverse, on a diagonal cross and upstage parallel to the back wall of the rehearsal studio. Now she says to the boys: "Everyone's walking differently. Everyone, follow me on stage. It goes *walk*, and *walk*, and *walk*, and *step*, and *step*, and *step* [speaking slowly as she walks in the playing area]. Now this is the look I want [demonstrates]. Make your eyes wide—zombie-like. . . . Don't go heel-toe [as the boys rehearse]. Go heel and heel. Place your feet firmly on the floor. . . . Show me your looks. Let me see your look, Joey. Don't smile." They begin the "Housekeeping" section again. The seemingly impulsive choice of the phrase "zombie-like" eliminates certain random movements in the procession of child servers carrying giant plates just as it temporarily introduces a sense of stiffness and artificiality that eerily connects a world of zombies and Victorian conventions for "successful housewives."

I recall watching Joseph Chaikin in the winter of 1982 rehearsing highly gifted actors whose attempts merely to walk on stage in a mourning procession were overly stylized or self-consciously "tragic." After prolonged experimentation, the problem was resolved only when the musicians asked to join the procession, finally replacing the actors on stage. The solution produced a processional walk whose hidden function was to provide what Chaikin called "a joyous movement, a kind of dance," as a component of mourning, a performance of ambivalence. The musicians' natural non-stylized walk—counterbalanced by the extraordinary sounds of their instruments—was a staging of mourning and dying as journey, natural and uncanny.[21]

In a much abbreviated and less exploratory way necessitated by the restrictions on a workshop production, Akalaitis eliminates unwanted theatricality in the procession of the child actors. Her solution is to replace randomly chosen movements with a single stylized walk for all the zombie-like servers at a Victorian feast. Earlier I watch the rehearsal of another procession in which Akalaitis, like Chaikin, uses what is natural to create the illusion of the natural. The boys' choir is "changing the Crystal Palace into a jungle,"[22] by carrying branches across the stage and placing them in a tray on a table. The director, as she physically demonstrates placing a branch in the tray, says to the boys: "Just be natural, [just be] yourself."

A later direction to the children to cross the stage, "just as yourselves" is echoed in a problematic note to the tenor concerning a line delivery: "I think it should have no attitude . . . just you, Jeff." But who *is* "Jeff" in the midst of the circumstances of enacting a playscript, especially when he is not assigned a particular character? It is a question which rehearsals of experimental theatre work can easily raise for an actor.

In their responses and questions, the child actors continually come up against the exploratory nature of rehearsal. During the debate scene, Akalaitis tells the boys not to mark up their scripts, that she is just "trying things out"; she tells them simply to think of her directions as "reaction one, reaction two. . . ." She asks groups of boys "to follow" the debater nearest to them whenever he moves. A child actor asks perceptively, "Should we follow them just with our faces or with our feet?" After a pause, Akalaitis says, "With your faces and with your feet, *just a bit.*" She asks one group of boys to rush, with audible dismay, across the playing area toward the other group. The boys ask how, and on which side (upstage or downstage) of the debaters, to run. Akalaitis responds immediately: "Just play it by ear." They run, she watches, she asks them to run again with a group sound of great dismay and then to continue to move, "taking baby steps" (she demonstrates physically), as the debaters feint and pace up and down. The authorial stage direction Akalaitis is blocking is non-specific: "The children in slow motion perform debate mudras," mudras being defined elsewhere in the script as "formalizations of psychological gestures."[23] These group physicalizations will be revised in later rehearsals and become more subdued, e.g., vertical and horizontal nods of the heads of seated boys in black robes responding to seated black-robed debaters. In this first rehearsal of the scene Akalaitis is clearly experimenting or "constructing" through experimentation. She asks the cast to rehearse the debate once again, with the stage manager calling out tentative blocking cues so that she can "see the structure."

One might think it would be simpler, even normal practice, for a director to work out in advance such details of the staging of the playtext, especially her own. And yet in every rehearsal I have observed, despite the most careful pre-planning of directors like Robert Wilson, Liviu Ciulei, Richard Foreman, or Peter Sellars, even a director restaging a prior production is forced to explore new renderings of the playtext in a particular space with a particular cast.

In her first rehearsal of the debate, Akalaitis, intently watching blocking she has tentatively created, is still searching for a staging of the end of the scene. Musing aloud, she considers having certain actors faint. The boys go wild over this idea and are asked to take their seats by the stage manager. As the director discusses cuts in the text with the adult actors, the sounds of the boys singing to themselves waft over us in the small rehearsal studio, a gentle comment on the convention of patient waiting during the inevitable delays that are part of rehearsal work.

The boys' choir is expected to dance as well as sing and time is spent in teaching them the box step and the tango, at which they become quite proficient. With startled delight I later watch Irene Fornes demonstrate and teach a tricky little two-step to Madeleine Potter and John David Cullum in rehearsals of *Abingdon Square*. Akalaitis herself teaches the boys to dance the tango in the *Voyage* rehearsals. But the blocking and the synchronization of the dance steps suddenly evaporate during the final afternoon of rehearsal before the performance.

The boys enter dancing a tango that is not coordinated either with the music or with each other. Akalaitis calls a halt to the rehearsal and walks down to the stage from her seat in the auditorium. All the boys immediately begin explaining, complaining, telling the director what is wrong and what needs to be done. Above the uproar I hear the director's calm firm voice: "Quiet, boys. *I'll* direct this." She redirects the boys, counts out the dance steps, rescues the tango. The boys enter as before in a line, each (with the exception of the leader) placing his hands on the shoulders of the preceding boy. In perfect synchronization they dance a slow tango on a horizontal upstage cross from left to right. The same dance step is repeated from right to left, but with the faces turned toward the audience. The tango is repeated once more upstage from left to right, now with both bodies and faces turned toward the audience. Then the boys move downstage, one by one, forming couples, and continue to dance as the soprano and tenor sing. All this is the directorial inscribing of the single stage direction in the text: "On stage, children try to dance the tango."[24] The tango step is executed perfectly in the performance that evening.

During technical rehearsal the previous day, a well-dressed man I had never seen before enters the darkened Triplex theatre and sits directly behind me, watching. After awhile as he prepared to leave, he leans over and whispers, "Can I ask you a question? It seems like they're going to an awful lot of work for one performance." I smile and say, in response to his unasked question, "I'm just an observer."

In the midst of rehearsal, JoAnne Akalaitis, like Irene Fornes and Emily Mann, is attempting to explore, by enacting its possibilities, the nature of her own script. Theatre critics tell us that we have today a uniquely "director's theatre" and theatre historians remind us that the director is a fairly recent phenomenon, first documented in the nineteenth century. It is my undocumentable speculation that as soon as there is an author of a script and an actor of that script, the directorial impulse is present, however imperceptibly, even if author and actor are one.[25]

Akalaitis' choice of Darwin's text suggests a final observation. The "evolution" of the director might be analogous to that of certain self-fertilizing hermaphrodite organisms which, as described by Darwin, inevitably "intercross with other individuals."[26] My focus, however, is not on the origin of the species—not on the birth of the director but on what the director helps to birth. The rehearsal process, one would like to think, assures the survival of the fittest in the struggle for the life of the theatre.

Fig. 5.2. JoAnne Akalaitis and Isabell Monk rehearsing The Screens *at the Guthrie Theater. Photograph by Michal Daniel.*

Fig. 6.1. Elizabeth LeCompte watching the Wooster Group in rehearsal. Video print.

6

Elizabeth LeCompte Directs
Frank Dell's The Temptation
of Saint Antony

The Invisible Director: Creating in Company

Elizabeth LeCompte is a New York avant-garde director exclusively engaged in collective theatre work. She is one of the seven core members of the Wooster Group, a splinter of Richard Schechner's Performance Group, formed in 1967. Since 1975, when Schechner relinquished his leadership of the theatre collective, LeCompte has directed the new Group, which rehearses and performs in its own theatre, a converted commercial garage in lower Manhattan (Soho). The Wooster Group originally included two actors, Willem Dafoe and Spalding Gray, who have achieved independent prominence, particularly in film. This is not altogether surprising since the Wooster Group is continually exploring the relations between theatre and film, "working at the point where the lens and the stage interact, contradict, complement, even interchange."[1]

James Leverett describes the Wooster Group as "arguably the most aesthetically radical, socially and politically provocative theater to be found anywhere today." What Leverett calls the "collage exploration"[2] of LeCompte's theatre characteristically involves years of preparation and revision in rehearsal. Indeed, it is only as I begin to write this chapter that the Wooster Group presents to the public the final form of the theatre piece whose first day of rehearsal I observed exactly four years earlier. The Group's process of collaborative creation and development requires the same devotion and patience in the critic as in the company itself.

My first day of observing rehearsal of *Frank Dell's The Temptation of Saint Antony* is unique in may ways. It is the only occasion on which I am invited to attend the first readthrough,[3] a readthrough that occurs *before* the play is cast as well as *before* the script is created. It also occurs in the absence of LeCompte's collaborator, Peter Sellars, as part of the special arrangement between the two directors, and in the presence of other art-making (actor Willem Dafoe is completing one painting and beginning a second throughout the afternoon rehearsal). Unique to the company are factors very familiar to me. For the first time the Wooster Group sits together around a table reading a text aloud[4] and for the first time the director chooses "to use a very tight plot" (based on the storyline of Ingmar Bergman's *The Magician*) "as a mask for the piece" she is creating.

The rehearsal readthrough of Bergman's *The Magician* takes place on a hot afternoon, September 20, 1985, in an upstairs room of The Performing Garage, the theatre on Wooster Street owned and operated by the company. Fourteen people are assembled, including the director and dramaturg. The reading aloud of Bergman's text is interspersed with analysis of what is read. Written on a blackboard, behind the long rectangular table at which the actors—with the exception of Willem Dafoe—sit, are the words: "ACTION, NOT IDEAS," and LeCompte stresses the need to establish the basic "actions" in each scene. The actors eat as they speak, as if equally nourished by the acts of reading and eating.[5] There is laughter, vitality, a sense of fun, despite the heat and growing humidity. LeCompte takes an active role, reading aloud stage directions and synopses of action. The actors deliver the lines of dialogue fairly tonelessly in normal speaking voices.[6] At one point Ron Vawter parodies an "acting voice." Intermittently certain members of the Group deliver lines in more actorly ways. Always there is some laughter to confirm and counteract self-conscious acting styles. At one point LeCompte's turn to speak comes after she has begun to eat potato chips; she at first speaks with a naturally muffled voice, then exaggerates the sound of obstructed utterance. Later she is forced again to read a stage direction with a voice thickened by food. She reads quickly, as if in allusion to the rapid, unintelligible voice of Ron Vawter hurrying through the text in the Wooster Group's earlier performance of (. . . *Just the High Points* . . .).[7] The self-reflexive style of the company in rehearsal is also one of its characteristic styles in performance.

Intensity in this rehearsal is reserved for vigorous debate about the elusive nature of the events in the Bergman screenplay. LeCompte offers her views in the tone of one participant in a discussion, but when the time comes for a final decision, actors and dramaturg defer to her. At one point an actress comments, "You can't say it's irrelevant if he [Bergman] wrote it in." Defending the point just made, LeCompte replies, "Sure you can." After awhile LeCompte asks actress Kate Valk (who later plays a role I designate as the director figure) to read aloud the stage directions so that she can "think."

LeCompte reenters the reading of the text at her own insistence to deliver the speech of a ghostly figure, the actor Johan Spegel. The actors applaud her rendering of the lines, but her reading is, in fact, a striking misreading. The lines in the text are: "I haven't died, but I have already started to haunt. Actually, I think that I'm a better ghost than I am a human being."[8] In her misreading of the final phrase, LeCompte devalues her appropriation of the actor's role even as she reinscribes her ghostly role as director, the "invisible artistic guiding presence"[9] shaping the work of the theatre collective: "Actually, I think that I'm a better ghost than I am an actor."

As the readthrough continues, the actors' voices gradually take on more resonance and their concentration intensifies, as if they are drawn in by the text they are reading, despite their occasional tone of light irony. Boundaries between "reading," "analyzing," and "acting" become tenuous. The text seems increasingly porous under the collective scrutiny of the company. The basic "actions" of the screenplay are implicated in its voicings, sounded in the throats of these actors.

The readthrough, like every other Wooster Group rehearsal I observe, is interspersed with judgments on the text (e.g., its dragginess: "it just goes on and on. . . ."), digressions on contemporary actors and acting styles, allusions to current social issues (the AIDS crisis), phone calls for the director or dramaturg, late deliveries of supplies.

All these elements recur in the performance of *Temptation*. Onna comments on a passage from Flaubert, read aloud verbatim by Sue, "We need something . . . more . . . modern." Onna refers to Glenda Jackson or, in alternate performances, Vanessa Redgrave, and Dieter refers to the Yale School of Drama or, in alternate performances, the Actors Studio. Partly quoting Albert Goldman's book on Lenny Bruce, Onna says, "I didn't realize you could get a serious disease from playing with a dirty needle." Sue tells Frank as he is gazing at videotapes of the nude company improvising, "Frank, you've got a phone call on line two." Later Onna makes a routine out of this, "I'm going to do my telephone number, Phyllis. Brrring . . . brrring . . . Oh! the telephone's ring-ing. I'll get it." Groceries, referred to several times by Onna, are finally delivered by Sue at the end of the play.[10] In themselves these moments are not self-referential but, taken together, they allude to the texture of Wooster Group rehearsals.

As the afternoon of the first readthrough wears on, individual Group members' needs jar slightly, momentarily. After two and a half hours of work, one actress, Peyton Smith, rises from the table and demonstrates the action of staggering backward to illustrate the point she is making about a particular scene in the Bergman screenplay. Her physical demonstration is striking in itself and as a jolting reminder that up to now the establishing of "action" has been conducted entirely through reading and discussion of the text. After four hours of work in a room where the temperature is over 85 degrees, the actors seem visibly un-comfortable; several stand, pace, or recline on mats on the floor. Still, at 6 p.m. when I prepare to leave, there is a palpable surge of excitement as a complicated and ambiguous moment in the Bergman screenplay is decoded.

Elizabeth LeCompte, asked for a copy of the script she is re-hearsing, says, "The first year of performances is the final stage of finishing the script."[11] My discussion of *Frank Dell's The Temp-tation of Saint Antony* is a collaging of observations of Wooster Group rehearsals during the fall of 1985 and the spring and early summer of 1986, with occasional retrospective glances based on "open rehearsals" in April, 1987, work-in-progress performances in the fall of 1987 and 1988, and performance of the final version of the piece in the fall of 1989, at The Performing Garage.

The theatre piece whose trail I am following is the third part of a trilogy called *The Road to Immortality*, consisting of *Route 1 and 9*, (. . . *Just the High Points* . . .), and *Frank Dell's The Tempta-tion of Saint Antony*. The source-texts, or "pretexts,"[12] used in the construction of *Frank Dell's The Temptation of Saint Antony* proliferate throughout rehearsal and include the following mate-rials:

(1) the story line and certain characters as well as excerpts from the dialogue of Ingmar Bergman's film, *The Magician*

(2) Gustave Flaubert's nineteenth-century epic drama, *La Ten-tation de Saint Antoine*, as translated by Kitty Mrosovsky, along with selected passages from Flaubert's letters, edited by Francis Steegmuller

(3) passages from Geraldine Cummins's book, *The Road to*

Immortality: Being a Description of the Life Hereafter, With Evidence of the Survival of Human Personality (1932), in which Cummins establishes contact, through trance, with a deceased nineteenth-century writer and founder of The Society for Psychical Research[13]

(4) recordings and films of performances of Lenny Bruce (Frank Dell is an early pseudonym used by Lenny Bruce); excerpts from journalistic accounts of the last days of Bruce's life in the late summer of 1966

(5) "Channel J" videotapes of the nude company improvising lines in response to an off-camera reading of Flaubert's *Saint Antony* by actress Nancy Reilly (Cable Channel J in New York featured late-night nude talks shows)

(6) Ken Kobland's film, *Flaubert Dreams of Travel But the Illness of His Mother Prevents It*, made in conjunction with the Wooster Group and inserted as a kind of interactive text in the evolving theatre piece

(7) distillations of the Flaubert text into a series of dances choreographed by Peter Sellars and rehearsed with the actors while LeCompte, by prearrangement, was not present

(8) such eclectic visual "texts" as a still photograph of French film-maker Georges Méliès as Satan; reproductions of Kurt Schwitters' collages and a Hieronymous Bosch painting of St. Antony flying on a frog; a book entitled *Ghosts in Photographs*, brought to rehearsal by actor Jeff Webster; eventually a reproduction of a production still showing Willem Dafoe as Jesus in Martin Scorsese's highly controversial *The Last Temptation of Christ*, which, by a remarkable coincidence, was being filmed during the latter stages of the development of the Wooster Group's *Temptation*

(9) Georges Méliès' film, *The Devil and the Statue* (1902)

(10) a videotape of a young actress, Ursula Easton, reading lines from Flaubert's *Saint Antony*, several months before her death

(11) a plot-line continued from the Wooster Group's (. . . *Just the High Points* . . .) in which Frank Dell and his theatre troupe impersonate a dance company, Donna Sierra and the Del Fuegos

(12) the Wooster Group's own videotapes and audio tapes of the company in rehearsal as they construct, rehearse, and analyze the script (Since the actors view or listen to these tapes intermittently throughout rehearsal, the tapes become additional "source-texts" in the collaborative creation of *Temptation*.)

(13) texts written by playwright Jim Strahs in workshop with the Wooster Group as well as excerpts from Strahs' *North Atlantic*, first performed by the company in 1984

(14) dialogue excerpted not from any written text but from rehearsal improvisations

Almost all of these materials find their way into the final version of *Frank Dell's The Temptation of Saint Antony*.[14]

Temptation has been described as an exploration of "the relationship between religious ecstasy, insanity and social repression,"[15] "part mystery play and meditation on morality, part an in-the-theater burlesque filled with tricks, gags, and numbers,"[16] an identification of theatre with magic or an act of clairvoyance in which "emanations of the dead [are] filtered through a living medium, like the ghost of F.W.H. Myers speaking through Geraldine Cummins to explain the plight of 'the newly dead, those tumultuous waves of life that break daily and nightly like the tides upon our shores.' "[17]

Frank Dell's The Temptation of Saint Antony is also explicitly a theatre work about making theatre work, and thus about the collective creative process of rehearsal. Director and conceiver Elizabeth LeCompte has said repeatedly: "The piece is about the making of the piece, always."[18] Actress Peyton Smith, one of the members of the Wooster Group, confirms this: "It's about making art and failing at making art. Then we succeeded so well at failing that it became painful. It's about being up there, being naked, trying to make up a world, and failing. . . . We wanted to make a piece about making a piece, . . . [about] know[ing] that you have to stand up there and do the wrong thing." Each night before performance in the fall of 1989. LeCompte says to Smith: "It's a rehearsal. Perform it just for me as if it were a rehearsal."[9]

"Stand[ing] up there," "do[ing] the wrong thing," "being naked," performing for the directorial gaze are all familiar elements of the rehearsal process. What every director might wish to say, "Perform it *just for me*," takes on a different inflection for the Wooster Group: "Perform it just for me as if it were *a rehearsal*." In the former case, a director might wish to control and reshape the alterations, accidents, improvisations that occur once performances begin. In the latter case, the director privileges the exposure of the making itself and its inevitable corollary: "doing the wrong thing." As Richard Foreman has said, "It is those continually REJECTED choices of the backdrop, never articu-

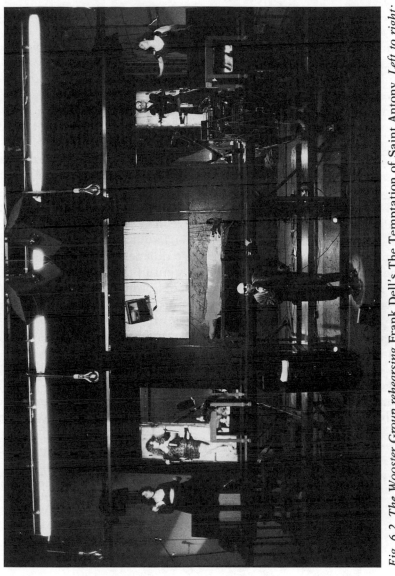

Fig. 6.2. The Wooster Group rehearsing Frank Dell's The Temptation of Saint Antony. Left to right: Kate Valk, Anna Kohler, Michael Stumm, Peyton Smith. Below stage: M.A. Hestand, Jeff Webster. Foreground: Ron Vawter. Photograph by Paula Court.

lated yet always present as the un-thought 'possible,' which give plasticity and depth and aliveness to what is chosen."[20]

In LeCompte's *Temptation*, a theatre troupe on the lam rehearses: "Paula, Paula, bring the lights up, the lights. Phyllis, Phyllis, guess who's coming up here. Dr. Jacques Dieter wants to see us rehearse 'Spell of Flesh' number. Remember that one? You'd better dust it off, babe." There are many additional allusions to rehearsal of a show within the show, as well as comments on performance: "Tonight is my last performance. I'm leaving the show. I'm leaving the theatre."[21] But the play-within-the-play structure is enclosed within another theatricalist mode. "Phyllis" and "Dieter" are characters in the play, but Paula, who is asked to bring the lights up, is Paula Gordon, the person literally operating the lighting board during the Wooster Group's performances. This kind of self-referentiality produces a double, if not a triple, exposure of the process of making theatre.

In *Temptation* the Wooster Group impersonates a theatre troupe impersonating the Del Fuego dance company as it rehearses and then performs a magic show for an invisible backstage audience. The theatre troupe's leader is a figure who incorporates Lenny Bruce's Frank Dell, Flaubert's Saint Antony, Bergman's Magician, the fake Dr. Del Fuego, actor Ron Vawter, and director Elizabeth LeCompte. That Frank Dell is, in part, a director figure is suggested in LeCompte's comments:

> What I'm doing in this piece is paraphrasing texts. The activity is centered around the character of Frank Dell who's trying to recreate *Saint Antony*, but it's his *Saint Antony*. In the story line this man is trying to get away with using other people's texts by paraphrasing them, rather than stealing them outright. And that hooks up with my feelings about texts, about the object-ness of the written word and its inherent lifelessness without the intervention of an interpretive or outside consciousness.[22]

In rehearsal, the director reauthors "other people's texts," providing, along with the actors, "the intervention of an interpretive . . . consciousness."[23]

There are, in fact, two director figures in LeCompte's *Temptation*, one female (Onna, played by Kate Valk) and one male (Frank, played by Ron Vawter). Both are involved in the discovery or recovery of text and subtext. Frank asks: "Look, you got that Cummins book? . . . Would you mind reading some to me?" Onna says to Jacques: "What! Wait a minute! That is not your line. This is not free improv here. Your line is 'I'm hurting myself, baby.' Now try it. . . . I think you need a little subtext. (*Onna smashes bottle across Jacques' face*.)" Frank: "Let's have a little enjoyment then. . . . Let's have a little dance. . . . (*crosses to stage left monitor, looks at dancing genitalia*)."

Both Onna and Frank note and correct problems in staging and acting. Frank addresses the offstage assistant to the director, James Johnson, listed in the program as "Himself" playing "J.J.":

> Wait a second . . . this is not the [right videotape; a Western has replaced the "Channel J" tapes] . . . J.J., put that into fast forward . . . fast forward . . . let's see [this "error" occurs in every performance]. . . . Cut! Cut! (*Lights black out, music out*) That . . . That's going to take a little more work than I thought. . . . Try to do a little better with the enunciation, ok? Diction's poor. Think diction.

Onna comments on Jacques' delivery of his lines: "No, no, we need a lot more from you here." Frank urges, "Sue, stick with the script. . . . OK, Sue, stick with the lines." Onna remarks later in the play: "Wrap it up, Frank." Finally, Onna speaks these repeated lines, suggestive of the directorial gaze: "Does a glance talk? Does a look see something? Who can read other people seeing, what other people say when they see?"[24] The Wooster Group is staging the problematic of reading texts and making theatre.

British film director Jon Amiel has said, "The problem with good directing is that it's often the art that conceals itself. . . . To a certain extent, the aspiration of a good director should be to achieve anonymity."[25] I hope partly to rescue Elizabeth LeCompte from that anonymity even while detailing the collective nature of the creative work of the Wooster Group. In their rehearsals I witness a company literally constructing a script. And yet, as dramaturg Norman Frisch suggests, "Rehearsals are about the play that Liz [LeCompte] is trying to see in front of her."[26] The dramaturg's statement is especially interesting in that its emphasis is not on private vision but on the director's seeing what is "in front of her," suggesting the function of the directorial gaze as controlling context in the work of the theatre collective.

In early November of 1985 LeCompte begins rehearsal by reading aloud an article from *The Washington Post* discussing the Wooster Group's imminent visit to the Kennedy Center for the Performing Arts, under the aegis of the American National Theater, where they will perform Jim Strahs' *North Atlantic* and present "open rehearsals" of *Temptation*. She then comments on the previous day's work, "I like it and I don't like it. . . . When you guys get too much of a presence, I don't like it: it's too much like a play." In the late spring of 1986 she will say of *Temptation* in rehearsal at The Performing Garage: "It's got the preciousness of art in this space. It didn't when I saw it in Washington [at the Kennedy Center's Free Theater]. . . . Basically, we're trying to find the mode for the beginning, whether it's story or rehearsal."

In the early stages of rehearsal LeCompte associates the narrative "mode" with the storyline of Bergman's *The Magician* and the rehearsal "mode" with Flaubert's *Saint Antony*. Eventually the temptations staged by Flaubert's Hilarion, demon and former disciple of Saint Antony, become part of the magic show presented by Bergman's itinerant troupe, the Magnetic Health Theater of Albert Vogler. In addition three other "shows" are incorporated in LeCompte's *Temptation*: the stand-up comic routines of Lenny Bruce, the performance of the fake Del Fuego troupe, and the nude colloquies of the "Channel J" videotapes.

LeCompte's method of construction is aptly described by Flaubert's Antony in his opening monologue: "It's a matter of knowing the natural affinities and repulsions of things, then setting them in action. . . ."[27] Her characteristic approach to blockages in rehearsal is to encourage exploration of new possibilities: "Make up something. It may not work. But I just want to *see*. . . . You have free rein. Do what you want. . . . Maybe I'll throw it away but I've got to *see* it" (emphasis added).[28]

Throughout rehearsals the company reads various kinds of texts which they ransack for stage life. Their own spontaneous improvisations in rehearsal are recorded on videotape and studied later for selective appropriation. A black-and-white videotape of Bergman's *The Magician*—with English subtitles but no sound—is literally "read," not heard, by the company during rehearsal.[29]

In the fall of 1985 I observe the company watching a film of Lenny Bruce in performance, reading aloud from the transcripts of his trial for obscenity.[30] Even as they study documentary footage of a controversial comedian whose intonations, speech rhythms and diction will be replicated in Vawter's monologues, the actors are observing reading as performance. The "story" of LeCompte's *Temptation*, the protracted action of the piece, is the reading of texts.[31]

At the beginning of rehearsal on November 10, 1985, LeCompte tells the company, "We're making a subtext script, a subtext action script and a psychological subtext script." She holds a notebook divided into two columns. Stage directions based on Bergman's *The Magician* appear in the left-hand column and are transformed into "a subtext action script" in the right-hand column. Underneath, spanning both columns, is the "psychological subtext script." Asking if the company "could help me finish writing this," LeCompte is not simply revising or editing a play in the midst of rehearsal but engaging the entire cast in the earliest stages of creating a script. The conceptual difficulty of even finding an adequate form for the complexity of the text she is constructing is suggested by Kate Valk: "It's hard to know how to write it." LeCompte replies, "Yes, we all have to find our systems," as if the operative forms of the working scripts are as numerous as the members in the company.

The day is spent in communal writing of subtext scripts. Le-Compte begins by dictating a Bergman "action script" (e.g., "Tubal eating," "Granny poking ground," "Albert smoking pipe"). Together with the company she transforms or relocates these actions so that they become part of another action script ("Cubby eating," "Fanny poking/tapping the walls,"[32] "Albert smoking . . ."). The company then begins to create a "psychological subtext script" (e.g., the fake Del Fuegos "are informed by Cubby that they are being sued for right of publicity"; "the company's passports are missing"; "the company is performing in the cocktail lounge at 9 p.m."). Additional subtext is considered: Annette talks with Albert about the book she is reading on the survival of the human personality after death; there is a phone call from the living dead.

After scene one is tentatively established LeCompte says, "Both the *Saint Antony* and the Lenny Bruce are going to have to be laid over . . . [these subtext scripts based on Bergman's *The Magician*]." Peyton Smith comments, "This helps but the problem for me is the *talk*, what we say. . . . All this action and . . . only five lines of dialogue."

The Group begins work on the next scene:

Bergman action script	*Wooster Group action script*
"Tubal sighs and belches."	"Cubby relieves himself."
"A uniformed man . . . opens the coach door."	"Tony comes in and Cubby gets rid of him."
"Tubal tries bribing him."[33]	"Cubby tries bribing Tony. Tony shoves Cubby . . ."

Psychological subtext script

"Cubby tries to bribe Tony because Tony is complaining that there are too many people in the [hotel] room. A church bell rings, reminding the troupe that they have to rehearse Flaubert."[34]

As the preceding examples suggest, "psychological subtext" and "action subtext" seem at times to overlap. The various subtexts are now modified and clarified.

Later in the afternoon Vawter reads aloud from a book on the construction of a play: a necessary element is a "hint-wait pattern," consisting of "a hint, a wait, and a fulfillment." The company discusses various hints and waits in Flaubert's *Saint Antony*. LeCompte considers having certain of these prescriptions for playwriting printed in the program or inserted intermittently in the performance by voice-over. It is always hard to fix the tone of the Wooster Group: it is characteristically both playful and serious. Vawter again reads aloud from the same book: "The best way to show mental process in character is to have your characters in a situation where they have to make a quick decision," and continues to read silently during breaks in rehearsal. These components of conventional play construction do occur in the 1989 version of the piece the company is just beginning to construct.[35] But more significant is the reading aloud of a text on text-making in the process of creating scripts that allude to other scripts, subtexts that allude to other subtexts.

At the end of the day I suddenly see all about me reflective images of my own activity: a theatre of actors bent over notebooks, pens and pencils busily at work, one eye on the source-text (*The Magician*), the other on its gradually evolving incorporation in a new text so interlayered[36] that "it's hard to know how to write it." Ten persons (seven actors, the director, the assistant to the director, myself) sit writing quietly in a room; they make one kind of text and I, another. Bergman's screenplay exists as a thing apart, alluded to in the left-hand column of the action text. It is reanimated and transformed by the adjacent text in the right-hand column, as by the implications of the psychological subtext below, and eventually by the "laying over" of text fragments from Flaubert and Lenny Bruce. The Wooster Group's collective creation in rehearsal is also a thing apart from my attempts to express it in a text that transforms a living process into "the object-ness of the written word." And yet the process itself is the primary "source text" of all I write.

One week earlier, on Sunday, November 3, 1985, Peter Sellars, at that time the Artistic Director of the Kennedy Center's American National Theater in Washington, D.C., makes one of his periodic visits to The Performing Garage to spend a day rehearsing the Wooster Group. It is part of his arrangement with Elizabeth LeCompte that in their initial collaboration as directors of *Temptation* they never observe each other's rehearsals of the actors.

It was in 1983 that Sellars, then the director of the Boston Shakespeare Company, first proposed to LeCompte a directorial collaboration on a theatre piece based on Flaubert's *La Tentation de Saint Antoine*. The situation of the fake Del Fuegos rehearsing a play called "The Temptation of Saint Antony," the coalescence of Saint Antony and Lenny Bruce as a lone visionary/hallucinating figure, and the encircling narrative of Bergman's *The Magician*, along with the "Channel J" videotapes, the film by Kobland, and fragments from Strahs' *Have Seen the Tree* are added by LeCompte. The connection between the semi-pornographic "Channel J" tapes and Flaubert's Saint Antony as mediated by Lenny Bruce is made clear by LeCompte: "Lenny Bruce always dreamed of getting into film. We imagined that if he were alive today and made movies, he might have done Channel J-styled tapes. . . . I think of him as a moralist who just couldn't believe that people were as bad as they were. In his final years he was very much like a visionary in the desert with the question left open as to whether he was insane or divine or whether the two have to go together. It's a question that I ask over and over and that runs through all of our work."[37]

In addition to translating and adapting selected passages in Flaubert, Sellars choreographs six dances, of which two are staged: the Queen of Sheba Dance and the Devil Dance, the latter set to the ballet music from Gounod's *Faust*, the former accompanied by music of Art Tatum. Sellars, who gradually withdraws from the directorial collaboration, is listed as assistant director in the fall, 1987 program and "Dance Doctor" in the fall, 1988 program. In the fall, 1989 program he is thanked for "his help and support all along the way."

In his casual opening comment to the assembled company, Sellars anticipates the next four years of LeCompte's rehearsal work on *Temptation*: "It's odd. I've changed my mind several times about this but I'll figure it out." The cast, holding copies of Mrosovsky's translation of *Saint Antony*, sits on risers in the auditorium of the theatre, with the exception of Dafoe who lies on the floor. They take notes on pads of paper as Sellars creates his *Temptation* text. The director selects lines from Flaubert which do not follow each other sequentially but occur in different parts of the Queen of Sheba's opening monologue and assigns each line to a different actor. He asks the actors to read these lines aloud five or six times in a particular sequence and then says, after praising the readings, "That was Episode One. Please mark it." He begins immediately to establish Episode Two in the same manner. Sellars does not arrange to have photocopies of his "text" simply handed out in advance to the company. Instead, director and actors sit together looking at the source-text, each actor first laboriously finding the individually assigned line and then writing it down, "creating" a new text. As Sellars dictates, he also quickly alters and edits the English translation. For example, he assigns the following sentence, "You can't imagine what a long way we've come," then instantly changes "a long way" to "how far." He assigns "I'll depilate you" unaltered, and then a much earlier sentence, "There, the green couriers' asses have died of fatigue," to Willem Dafoe, eventually asking that the actor omit the word "couriers" in future. Peyton Smith's unaltered lines are, "what is it? . . . what are you thinking of?" and Jeff Webster's line is the stage direction, "*She inspects him.*"[38]

Like LeCompte, though in what seems a fairly straightforward manner, Sellars is exploring in the company of the actors. He says at one point, "I thought I had worked this all out in advance, but I'm changing my mind. I'm considering some new things. . . ." A clear pattern emerges in Sellars's construction and revision of three episodes. He first assigns selected lines to individual members of the company, and asks that these be read aloud in sequence several times. He then makes alterations in the assignment and arrangement of lines and suggests adjustments in vocal delivery. After individual episodes are established, he asks for readthroughs of a sequence of episodes, suggests further adjustments, and concludes by saying cheerily, "Shall we stage this?"

The cast, positioned around the director in a kind of sprawling circle, now leaves the auditorium and enters the stage. Sellars, hesitant at first, stands up, looking at the actors. He tells them to make a forward bow, saying as he demonstrates, "I think it's this way. . . . But maybe I'm wrong."

Both LeCompte and Sellars have the kind of power granted to a director working in an openly acknowledged context of experimentation. If either one says, "Do this," it usually means, "Try this, so that we can see whether we want to do this." In a sense, the Wooster Group is the closest approximation I know to a company of directorless, self-generating actors. It sometimes seems that a director need only ask them to begin. It is not surprising that LeCompte and Sellars create or construct scripts in the midst of these actors, "figure things out" in rehearsal. Both directors enter the theatre with ideas, strategies, connections already conceived in private, but the operative creative process in rehearsal is visibly communal. Sellars's directorial style as I outline it here may appear more orderly or controlling than LeCompte's but if she is more wildly exploratory in her work with the Wooster Group, she is also more powerfully, and ultimately, in charge.

Like LeCompte's, Sellars's directorial approach does not privilege psychological realism. He tells Anna Kohler that in the scene he is choreographing she is "an elephant in heat in love with a monkey" (Dafoe). At one point Sellars asks the actress to utter a loud elephant noise. She tries; he tries; she tries again; he tries again and is greeted with cries of appreciation from the cast. "Raw talent," someone says and offers him the role. Working on the staging of Episode Three, Sellars stands close to the actors and pauses, silently thinking for several minutes. The cast is quietly attentive. He begins talking out his thoughts, asks Kate Valk to sit, then changes his mind immediately, asks her to stand up. This self-correcting reversal of directorial blocking is presented casually but carefully. Sellars's pace is one of good-humored efficiency. He sits much closer to the actors on the stage than does LeCompte. He has come from a distance and needs closeness; she is very close to the company and needs distance. Sellars, like LeCompte, participates in and yet occasionally edits the characteristic semi-facetious tone of the Wooster Group. After a runthrough of Episode Three, he says to the cast: "Oh, this is ravishing. This is the height of drama. This is the flowering of late high German romanticism we've been looking for. . . .

Beautiful, very beautiful." In response to an ironic glance from
one of the actresses, he repeats, "No, this is ravishing." Later he
will say, "As this dance goes on, we deal with the famous attitude
problem. It'll soon have to be acted 'dead-serious.' No irony. Zero
humorous stuff." An actor asks, "No irony?" Sellars replies, "No
irony. Zero." In June, 1986, LeCompte, rehearsing the dance
choreographed by Sellars in her absence, says to the cast, "Part
of what makes this Devil Dance work is that you're totally involved in it. If you step outside it and 'comment on it,' it doesn't
work."[39]

Not stepping outside the work is especially difficult for a company that explores "the point where the lens and the stage interact." The actors in the Wooster Group, even more than most
actors, are continually watching themselves, not only in the literal or imagined gaze of the Other[40] (the directorial gaze), but
also in their frequent viewings of videotaped re-presentations of
their rehearsal work. In this November rehearsal, the cast suggests that a runthrough be taped. Sellars, after observing the
actors from the risers, invites them to join him there after the
runthrough so "you can *see* where it needs to be jazzed up, where
characters need to be made more exciting, but it's good, it's good.
. . . *Let's look at it*" (emphasis added). Sellars's last note has been,
"more inner-oriented," paraphrased by Vawter as "look inside
ourselves."

Now I watch the company looking at themselves, laughing
appreciatively at times as they gather around the video monitor,
sitting where the director had been sitting as he observed their
rehearsal performance on stage. Sellars's invitation to the actors,
"Let's look at it," is an invitation to see what the camera sees,
rehearsal work already framed by a highly selective lens.

During LeCompte's rehearsals, the "Channel J" videotapes of
the nude cast are frequently studied by the entire company. In
performance Vawter will pause to stare silently at these images
of himself and others on two monitors placed to stage right and
stage left in full view of the audience. The "Channel J" videotapes,
made by LeCompte herself in late November, 1985, present the
point where the directorial gaze and the lens "interact . . . even
interchange." In such moments of self-viewing in rehearsal and
in performance, the actors become their own spectators, their
gazes functioning as "the final signifier of significance."[41]

If Sellars initially shares with LeCompte the "privilege" of the
directorial gaze,[42] filmmaker Ken Kobland collaborates with her

Fig. 6.3. Anna Kohler, Willem Dafoe, Peyton Smith, and Kate Valk in the film, "Flaubert Dreams of Travel But the Illness of His Mother Prevents It," *from* Frank Dell's The Temptation of Saint Antony. *Film by Ken Kobland.*

in the interposing of the camera's eye. Unlike Sellars, Kobland, who has worked with LeCompte in previous productions, watches her rehearsals for several weeks. He later shoots a surrealistic film, made with the Wooster Group in Washington, D.C., and titled *Flaubert Dreams of Travel But the Illness of His Mother Prevents It*, sections of which appear in the final four episodes of *Temptation*. Remarking that LeCompte is "more expansive," has "more largesse" than he, the filmmaker emphasizes that she "works with oppositionals, with opposing aesthetics." He describes their collaborative process as "very interactive and organic" (wincing at the word "organic"). Kobland responds to LeCompte's "initial conception, initial visual scenario," in the form of a "rough film," "*another text* which she can manipulate . . . and play with." His work takes its impulse from, comes out of, rehearsal and returns to it "as an original text."[43]

It is in the spirited interplay and ever-changing modulations of what may seem the glacially slow evolution of rehearsal work that I feel the power of LeCompte's directorial presence and vision. Her ability to re-focus a scene, a gesture, then a collage of gestures, challenges and revivifies the individual and collective energies of the company. At one point, she half fears that her directing brings the theatre piece too close to the filmic texture of Bergman's *The Magician*. This is partly due to her remarkable ability to sharpen and frame even those moments in her productions that most appear to be accidental or improvised.

But LeCompte's "experiment in intertextuality"[44] has its pitfalls and dangers. In the spring of 1986 I observe a series of at times painfully illuminating crises. On May 29, 1986, as the Group prepares to rehearse a levitation scene based on Bergman's *The Magician*, the loosely woven mesh of *Temptation* begins to unravel. LeCompte suddenly says, "There's a clash here between the scripts [Bergman and Flaubert]. . . . We're in trouble here. . . . Let me think." During the ensuing discussion voices in the company overlay each other in ironic opposition, like the texts themselves: "Maybe it's that we do away with *The Magician*. . . . and yet we still need a story" (LeCompte);[45] "Maybe it starts out with *Saint Antony* and then degenerates into a magic show" (Frisch); "Maybe the bed needs to fly . . ." (Valk, alluding to Hieronymous Bosch's painting of Antony flying on the back of a frog); "We could get rid of *Saint Antony* completely. The problem is that *Saint Antony* won't fit" (Michael Kirby); "It does fit but it won't literally fit: it won't *smash* together" (LeCompte); "Layered on top of *The Magician* could be a superficial reference to *Saint Antony*" (Frisch); "What's Lenny Bruce doing in this?" (Kirby). LeCompte paces back and forth while the company continues an intense colloquy very difficult to transcribe accurately.

Finally LeCompte says, "I'm not going to [resolve] . . . this until I get the visual right [still pacing]. . . . Take the back wall down." The stage at The Performing Garage is a rectangular platform with two downstage troughs crossing its width. The upstage part of the platform is hinged so that it can be raised or lowered, "like a page of a giant book." When the upstage wall is lowered, it becomes a floor, "as if . . . [a] room were magically opening out or the viewer suddenly moving in."[46] Paula Gordon lowers the back wall. Discussion continues, pauses. LeCompte says: "*It's got to be found in what we've got. Maybe it's in the visual image we've already got. . . . Let's give it a try. . . . The image is of a crowd [under the bed] with arms upraised like this [demonstrates]. It's not what you're doing [lifting the bed, as if it is levitating] but how you're doing it. We've got to get away from the literal. Maybe I'll throw it away but I've got to see it*" (emphasis added).

After the wall is lowered, LeCompte briefly considers dropping the levitation scene, views the "Channel J" videotapes, and finally asks Ron Vawter to "fly" by lying on top of Michael Kirby's body as Kirby lies face down in bed, downstage center.[47] The cast dances an exuberant Devil Dance as the "Channel J" tapes continue to play. Watching the rehearsal, LeCompte says, "I'm not sure how but somehow the dance and the flying seem right." She asks Peyton Smith simply to read aloud lines from *The Magician* script, commenting afterward, "We're getting somewhere, getting somewhere. . . . Now he [Vawter] could be playing *The Magician* as well as the Flaubert." Unhappily I must leave at 6 p.m., half an hour before the rehearsal ends, as general manager Linda Chapman, entering with a telephone message, remarks on the high energy that is now palpably present in the theatre. The problem of synchronizing seemingly disparate scripts seems to be temporarily resolved.

The following day, May 30, 1986, before rehearsal begins, LeCompte comments on her working method as a director. She tells me that her characteristic response to "an impasse" is to move as far away as possible from its literal terms, "turn it over," seek out its opposite, or return to rejected material. Often, she says, a dance serves as resolution, or context for resolution, of a dilemma. The Devil Dance, choreographed by Sellars but provisionally rejected by LeCompte, "opened up a space" for the coming together of the Bergman and Flaubert source-texts. LeCompte now begins rehearsal by discussing the dance and what follows it: "I'd like to knock our way through this. . . . The dance has to stand apart."

It is an extremely hot day in the city and the actors seem slightly groggy. LeCompte, fully recharged, says to the company, "I wasn't thinking structurally yesterday. I was thinking thematically. . . . I had always wanted to finish off the Bergman story as this other strong current [Flaubert] is coming through. . . . What I'm looking for now is lust and death and the end." "What we're all looking for," murmurs Peyton Smith. The Group discusses two different climaxes as possible endings: Bergman's screenplay ends with a timely deliverance (the King of Sweden invites Dr. Vogler's Magnetic Health Theater to perform at the palace); Flaubert's *Saint Antony* ends with a vision (the face of Christ radiates inside the disc of the rising sun). LeCompte wants the Bergman and Flaubert endings to occur successively, not simultaneously, but there is no agreement on which source-text to privilege.[48]

In the midst of the new impasse LeCompte again returns to rejected material. She sits quietly for about fifteen minutes re-reading the introduction to *Saint Antony*, looking for what she remembers as its "much darker," "more ambiguous" underside. She finds, and reads aloud to the company, Mrosovsky's description of Flaubert's own rejected image:

> Manuscript fragments show that he had earlier considered introducing at the end of the episode on the gods *a very old and reviled Christ, repeating his passion obscurely in the modern world. One doesn't know at what point this idea was dropped, but it would certainly have impaired the simplicity and impact of the chosen final image.* The increasing importance of the rising sun can be traced throughout the three versions. In the first Flaubert simply indicates a few pages before the end that the sun rises; for the second he dug into his Grecian travel notes for a dazzling and dramatic description of sun and clouds; but only the last version concludes with Christ's face shining out of the sun (italics mine).[49]

LeCompte seeks out a rejected impulse in the painstakingly slow evolution of one of her source-texts, an impulse similar to her own need as director to explore the underside of her materials, to embrace oppositions at work in the creative process itself.

After a short break the company views the last twenty minutes of the videotape of *The Magician*. I notice that at the end of the film Bergman-as-director highlights an image not mentioned by Bergman-as-author. In the published screenplay, Bergman describes the final scene:

> The coach sways through the gate, turns the corner slowly and climbs the hilly streets, which glisten in the afternoon sunshine.
> The other carriages follow.
> In this way the mesmerizer Albert Emanuel Vogler makes his triumphant entrance into the Royal Palace.[50]

In the videotape, as in the screenplay, the rain suddenly stops and bright sunshine floods the end of the film. (The cast comments on the fact that there is no sign of the effects of the rain at the end of the film.)[51] Among the final visual images is that of a hanging lantern swinging back and forth above the street as Vogler's coach makes its way to the royal palace. The focus on the swaying lantern rather than merely on the (scripted) swaying coach suggests, if ever so slightly, the disjunction between director and author even when director and author are the same person, just as the movement of the light-source, its swinging back and forth, suggests the revisionary process in rehearsal.

After their viewing of scenes from *The Magician*, the actors again perform the Devil Dance. LeCompte's response is tempered: "Well, in the light of day . . . [laughs] it's a little rough." The resolution of the previous evening's dilemma is itself unraveling. LeCompte makes adjustments, asking one actor to remove himself from the dance (despite a protest by one of the actresses) and eventually re-introducing him in the scene in another role. LeCompte's stated reason for eliminating the actor from the Devil Dance is that his presence is distracting, tempting her to redirect it. Later, when someone in the Group suggests that she rechoreograph the Queen of Sheba dance, LeCompte replies, "I don't want to redirect it. I want to take what's good and throw away the rest."

In explicitly refusing throughout rehearsals to create her own replacements for the original visual, kinetic, and written "texts," the director reveals her characteristic stance: "source-texts" exist to be scrutinized, searched, struggled with, made to yield stage life through "the intervention of an interpretive . . . consciousness"[52] that is largely, though invisibly, her own. LeCompte stages neither Flaubert's *Saint Antony* nor Sellars's distillations of it as dance. She stages the problematic of staging any text.

On June 1, the earlier crisis in intertextuality recurs and deepens. LeCompte says, "It's very possible we may cut all the *Saint Antony* material at the end and not use any of it but right now I think we really have to work through the *Saint Antony* material." She begins to read aloud from the script. The cast discusses the implications of the role of Hilarion in Flaubert. LeCompte's young son, Jack, enters the theatre. He runs to his father's arms and whispers to Dafoe. He does not interrupt his mother, who is still working intently with the actors and the text.

When I next observe rehearsal a week later, LeCompte evaluates the work-in-progress: "It's good. What I mean is, basically it's a mess but I know where we're going with it, up to the bed scene. . . . but I haven't got the tone of it clear. There's also the confusion about where the *Saint Antony* comes in. I also have the Ursula [Easton] tape and don't know where that fits in. . . . And the Lenny Bruce material—I'm not sure where that comes in."

The "mess" LeCompte alludes to is partly a phenomenon I have already noted[53] in which rehearsal work unaccountably "goes backward," losing vitality or fluidity: "I'm also having trouble with the dances. The first time I saw the Sheba dance I thought it was great but now I'm really seeing it. . . ." The crisis is also, as this last comment suggests, a matter of seeing and the shifting nature of seeing what is "in front" of one.

The director, nine months after the first readthrough, is not assisting at a birth but still mapping the terrain. Describing the interplay between the videotaped and the live performances of the actors, she says, "The two cancel each other out. If you're watching the tapes, you don't see the faces of the actors. . . . It's almost as if I have too much information. . . . I either have to go to Kitty Mrosovsky's text of Flaubert and edit, cut it down, or go to Peter's Flaubert text and edit it. I don't know what the rest of you think." There is some discussion and then general quiet among the company. Together the director and cast raise questions: "What is the dance part of? the Bergman script? the Flaubert script? a separate script?" LeCompte says, "My tendency is for some kind of [consistency in] voice." New translations of Flaubert are suggested but LeCompte replies, "No, that's not the problem. The problem is I'm interested in the original. *Where is Flaubert?* . . . I'm trying to figure out *what* in Flaubert I'm really interested in: certain sounds, certain images. I think the only way I'm going to find out is by *hearing* it. So we're going to have to try different parts of it. . . ." She balances one aesthetic, "It's got to be found in what we've got," with another, "Maybe we shouldn't have any Flaubert in it. . . . or set Flaubert diametrically apart from the rest, not sprinkled through," but "the only way . . . to find out is by hearing it." Exploration continues.

The next day LeCompte begins rehearsal by saying, "I want to take it back to see what's not working." She returns to a version of rehearsal work presented earlier at the Kennedy Center's Free Theater but inappropriate in the smaller performance space of The Performing Garage. Wigs and a long black flounced skirt worn over a blue bathing suit appear; many running shoes are removed. Rehearsal begins but is halted after two minutes by a technical problem. The actors stop. The "Channel J" videotapes continue to play. LeCompte says to the cast, "While we're waiting for the sound glitch to be fixed, I'll read to you."

Using a hand microphone in order to be heard over the sound of the overhead fans and the considerable noise of the tech crew at work, she reads aloud from an article in the *New York Times*, describing a recent AIDS epidemic in Belle Glade, Florida.[54] During the reading the cast and director editorialize intermittently in a way that is reminiscent of the first readthrough of the Bergman screenplay. As LeCompte and Vawter engage in intense discussion, I see over the actor's shoulder the "Channel J" images of his face alternately smiling and crying on the video monitor. Images from the stage suddenly seem to enclose the interchange between director and actor. "Real" discussions, born of reading and acts of interpretation, seem to be monitored by a taped performance of responses to a reading, endlessly playing.

The sound problem is resolved, and the director begins the piece again, then stops it five minutes later. She restudies the script, makes some slight verbal revisions, starts the runthrough from the beginning, stops it immediately: "Hold on, don't say anything for a minute [silent pause]. . . . I know we don't want to dramatize. . . . Let's start and Ron, say just the first phrase, then give us some Lenny Bruce." Vawter delivers the opening lines of Flaubert's *Saint Antony*: "One more day! one more day gone! Surely I used to be less miserable!"[55] In this rehearsal, but not in the final version of the piece, Vawter repeats these lines as a kind of refrain whenever Kate Valk, sitting on the bed to his right, taps his arm during his opening "Lenny Bruce" patter. Vawter is standing in the downstage trough, his head sticking up through a hole in the center stage bed, speaking into a hand mike. Jeff Webster, also standing in the trough, shakes the bed slightly. Willem Dafoe stands by an upright microphone, far right, reading his lines aloud as he eats. Anna Kohler and Nancy Reilly sit on the upper platform to the right and left of the bed, respectively. Peyton Smith stands or sits by an upright microphone far left. The "Channel J" tape runs throughout. Assistant to the director James Johnson reads aloud the lines of an absent actor. LeCompte tells Vawter "to link up" with Bruce's words, recorded on tape, whenever possible, "like a crazy person picking up signals everywhere." As rehearsal continues, she says, "Much better, much simpler too." Her note to Valk, who reads passages verbatim from the opening of *Saint Antony*, is, "Kate, read it more presentational. . . . Just read it."

At LeCompte's small director's table, books proliferate. Today I see seven books, several with bookmarks in them, piled on top of each other, and five more on the floor by her chair. There is another pause for technical reasons and again LeCompte reads aloud to the cast, this time from *Saint Antony*, editorializing as she reads: "Each paragraph is an entity in itself. It doesn't lead to anything else." She asks Vawter to add another line from Flaubert to his script; her phrasing is characteristic: "Ron, *try* this." An actress suggests a change in the script. LeCompte considers it briefly but does not accept it.

Part of Dafoe's role in this version of the piece is to paint, or pretend to paint, using as a prop a small painting LeCompte bought on the street several weeks ago. The director's instructions are to mime the painting unless Dafoe really wishes to paint. During a break in rehearsal I observe Dafoe quietly painting a canvas on the stage. A pink blob is shaded over by black paint quickly turning to gray as it meets the pink. I notice how seemingly exposed the process of painting is: one sees clearly what color comes first, how each new color affects the previous ones. Now Dafoe paints white over the remaining visible pink and pauses briefly to come down into the auditorium to add colors to his palette. Suddenly LeCompte glances up at Dafoe's painting hanging on the upstage wall: "That's perfect. Don't do any more. I want to use it [in the theatre piece]." Brush poised, Dafoe asks, "Can't I for myself?" The director replies, "No, I want to use it." The painting stops. Even as I am gazing at this work-in-progress in the theatre, it is coopted by the director's gaze for "use" in another work-in-progress, the mystery of its making no more revealed in the one than in the other.

During this afternoon's rehearsal LeCompte uncharacteristically discourages improvisation and inspired foolery. What previously delighted her is now a distraction, e.g., an actor writing *cabbaleros* in white chalk over an upstage door. She carefully, meticulously, stages the physical details of an upstage entrance by Michael Stumm. She establishes the loudness and softness of two knocks at the door, the exact length of the pause between knocks, the exact angle of Jeff Webster's body as he pushes Stumm back out the door, the precise position of Dafoe's gun as he points it toward the door and shoots through the keyhole. When she runs the scene a second time, an actress appears too soon. LeCompte says, "Wait for the beat. Do you all know what beats are?" Someone says, "Yeah, you put them in borscht," but the tension is not diffused.

A few minutes later Dafoe, in response to a directorial note, says, "I can't do it any better." The director, looking over her shoulder for a substitute, says, "Willy, I'd like you to step out and let someone stand in for you today." Dafoe takes the prop pistol he is holding, points it at LeCompte, and fires. The extra-loud, smoking caps procured for it make an ear-deafening sound. The director falls to the floor and rolls over, "playing dead." An actress who has come to rehearsal with a headache remarks, "Doing that without warning and so close to others' ears!" Le-Compte sits up, asks Dafoe to leave the stage. He removes his rehearsal costume, a bathrobe, and begins to leave the theatre. LeCompte says, "No, Willy, I don't want you to leave the theatre. I want you to stay in the theatre and watch. We have to go on. We have to work things out." The cast is silent. LeCompte turns and looks over her shoulder at me, says in a quiet voice, "Susan, would you mind leaving now?" As I walk through the door, I hear her voice, full of pain, "We have to work this out."

Outside on the street in the bright sunshine is a member of the tech crew who has been going in and out of the theatre carrying his tools. Unaware of what has just occurred, he smiles broadly and says, "You're really finding a lot to write about, aren't you?" I smile and nod. LeCompte's words echo in my mind: "We have to work this out." Shooting the director is a violently staged metaphor for closing down the directorial gaze. Asking Dafoe to leave the stage but "to stay in the theatre and watch" is both an affront to him as an actor and an invitation to join the director in her role as observer. It is an exercise of power and a sharing of its site: "watching" *is* the director's way of "work[ing] things out" in the theatre.

When I return to rehearsal almost two weeks later, LeCompte says, "I thought we'd scared you off forever. You're very brave." But, of course, it is the company that is very brave. This production is perhaps the most stressful the Wooster Group has attempted to mount, and the strains and tensions will continue. Eventually, in the winter of 1986–1987, after the return of the company from its European tour, rehearsals will be closed even to staff at The Performing Garage.

Today the company is creating a working script based on the opening dialogue between Antony and Hilarion in section three of Flaubert's *Saint Antony*.[56] LeCompte asks the actors to do verbal improvisations on the dialogue, spontaneously creating their own versions of the translation by Mrosovsky. As Vawter (Antony) and Dafoe (Hilarion) improvise, Valk and Smith listen and make suggestions along with LeCompte. Both the improvisation and intervening discussion are recorded on audio tape. The company's first readthrough of Bergman's screenplay, seated around a table upstairs, occurred on September 20, 1985. It is

June 23, 1986 and LeCompte is still creating the script in the midst of the company: "No, no, it needs to be more specific and we need to put in plot information, connect it to what we've been doing. . . . Let's just try it. We can go back over it later and [interlayer the text]. . . . This is the center of the play. We have to go back and then forward." As in the first readthrough there are protracted pauses while director and cast do close readings of Mrosovsky's translation of Flaubert.[57] After detailed discussion of one of Hilarion's arguments, two improvisations are offered: Dafoe's "Suffering ain't suffering if it feels too good" and Vawter's "Suffering too is a temptation." The company chooses the latter. When the line is repeated half an hour later, it sounds less like a spontaneous paraphrase than a studied and elegant translation.

Improvisation in this rehearsal functions not as work *on* a script but as a means of creating it. Here is a sample of the dialogue first as it appears in Mrosovsky and then as it occurs in the Group's improvisatory work:

> ANTONY: It must be one of the Queen's servants.
> VAWTER: Is that Mario Lanza?
>
> ANTONY: Who are you?
> VAWTER: Who are you?
>
> HILARION: Your old disciple Hilarion!
> DAFOE: An old student of yours, Hilarion.
>
> ANTONY: You're lying. For many years now Hilarion has been living in Palestine.
> VAWTER: That's a lie. For some years now Hilarion has been living in Pasadena.
>
> HILARION: I've come back! It is I!
> DAFOE: I've come back. It's me alright.
>
> ANTONY: But his face was as bright as dawn, open, happy. This other looks quite dull and aged.
> VAWTER: (to be improvised; a possible version: But you don't look like Hilarion)
>
> HILARION: Long labours have tired me out!
> DAFOE: I've been workin' hard and I'm fagged.[58]

As rehearsal continues LeCompte begins to revise certain lines so as to pick up and continue the Del Fuego subtext of Bergman's

The Magician.[59] When an actor, trying to make a clean copy of the script, complains that the director keeps "changing it," LeCompte simply replies, "That's right. That's what we're doing."[60] LeCompte's repeated, "Let me hear you say," replaces her characteristic refrain, "Let me see it"; the ear, as already suggested in my account of Akalaitis' rehearsal, takes on some of the functions of the directorial gaze.

As voice takes center stage in the company's collaborative creation of a working text, LeCompte says, in response to the improvisation of one actor, "I like what I said better. I can't remember what I said. But fortunately it's on tape." Unlike Renfield, who remembers the physical improvisations her actors cannot recall in rehearsal of *The Cherry Orchard*, LeCompte is herself a participant in the improvisatory inscription of the text. Later Kate Valk, trying to recover LeCompte's forgotten phrasing, sits silently listening to headphones attached to a tiny Sony tape recorder in her lap as the company continues work. Suddenly the actress eerily begins to speak aloud LeCompte's words, which turn out to be fragments. After a short pause Valk says, "That's all." The director's own words, like the other ghostly source-texts, now require intervention from the site of ongoing rehearsal.

Once completed, the transcribed working text of the dialogue between Antony and Hilarion is intertwined with a dialogue between Albert Vogler and Ottilia Egerman, two characters from *The Magician.* LeCompte now directs the staging of the intertextual creation, establishing the placement and pacing of the "Flaubert" and Bergman lines. Reilly, upstage far right, delivers the lines of Ottilia Egerman propositioning Vogler. Vawter, standing in the downstage trough with his head and part of his upper torso sticking through the hole in the bed downstage center, is both a mute Vogler and a speaking Antony. Dafoe, seated with a hand mike on a stepladder, reads aloud the lines of Hilarion. Smith, substituting for Michael Kirby, is lying in bed under a sheet, impersonating a variously identified puppet-like figure[61] eventually replaced in performance by a dummy made of a red packing blanket and old pillows rolled into a cylindrical shape. LeCompte, listening to and watching the interweaving of voices, situations, texts, and subtexts, makes interactive adjustments in pacing, blocking, and delivery of lines,[62] as well as minute alterations in the working script.

On the next day, June 24, 1986, LeCompte begins rehearsal by saying: "I'd like to try something. I'd like to take the actions from what we were doing yesterday and put the Brahms [Piano Concerto #1] on top of it. I've been thinking about [this section of *Temptation*] . . . last night. . . . I want to combine what you're doing with Peter Sellars's [adaptation of Flaubert] . . . with the Bergman. You're performing the Peter Sellars piece *through* the Bergman. I *think* it will work. . . . Do Peter's piece to the Brahms. . . . You're in two plays at the same time." During improvisatory work on the preceding day, Vawter says of a passage transcribed almost verbatim from *Saint Antony*: "Who would have thought that the Flaubert as written would serve to reinforce the subtext of *The Magician*?"[63] LeCompte's "You're in two plays at the same time" is an appropriate theatricalist expression of the nature and difficulty of *Frank Dell's The Temptation of Saint Antony*; eventually, it will incorporate four or more different "scripts" (the texts of Flaubert, Bergman, Bruce, and Strahs, along with quotations from Geraldine Cummins's book which haunts the piece throughout).

That the process is no less arduous for the actors than for the audience is suggested in Peyton Smith's remark during rehearsal: "This is interlayering with a vengeance." Despite the director's reassurance, "I know it will work. It's just a matter of how long it will take to find where it meshes," the cast is at first uncertain about the mesh of Flaubert, Bergman, and Brahms. LeCompte decides to shorten the Devil Dance "to fit *what I see* is really happening" (emphasis added). As she asks the actors to set up the stage for the end of the dance, the director says quietly, "I think this is right. . . . I had this vision that this is where those things come together. I know it's right."

By herself the director has "seen" a fit, a possible theatrical resolution, formulated with confidence and clarity: "You're in two plays at the same time." Her private vision follows and will be followed by weeks of troubled struggle, even bafflement. The successful interlayering of texts (Bergman, Flaubert), subtexts (a theatrical troupe on the lam: the Del Fuegos, the Wooster Group), and directorial styles (Sellars, LeCompte) is not a reality, as the director knows, until the company, still a little stunned by her sudden announcement, gives it reality.

As the rehearsal begins, I too have the impression that two dramas unfold at the same time. I sense with a real shiver that something extraordinary is happening. There is a new fullness and richness of texture. I glance at LeCompte to my right. On her face is a look I have not seen before. Her eyes are bright and wet. She says, under her breath, nearly inaudibly, "It's working. I could almost cry." A tape of Brahms's Piano Concerto #1 plays, bridging Sellars's adaptation of Flaubert's text and the storyline of *The Magician*. After the runthrough the director says, in an uncannily calm voice, "Okay . . . that's going to work." She inter- rupts subsequent rehearsals to readjust the timing and place- ment of lines based on Bergman's screenplay as they punctuate the actors' "Channel J" taped voices improvising the dialogue, read off-camera by Reilly, between Lust and Death, between the Sphinx and the Chimera, in section seven of *Saint Antony*. She reblocks the scene, moving more actors downstage, and experi- ments with the absence of artificial amplification. This section of the piece is rehearsed over and over, with further modifica- tions in staging, later rejected. Eventually the taped voices will be eliminated. In the final version of the piece Vawter will ven- triloquize the voices of the actors who appear soundlessly on the "Channel J" videotape.[64]

That evening in rehearsal, after the dinner break, there occurs a new problem. The envisioned interlayering is working and not working. The competing sounds are disorienting for the actors. Peyton Smith remarks, "Too much language overlaps." The di- rector insists, "No, it's not [even] enough." From the auditorium the sound of the actors' live voices, the taped voices, the knocks on the door, the Brahms score are clear and distinct. But, as in Akalaitis' rehearsal of *Voyage of the Beagle*, the actors on the stage experience a kind of aural vertigo. They complain variously that they cannot hear their own taped voices, or the Brahms, or both. LeCompte, from her vantage point in the auditorium, where all sounds are audible, says to Vawter, seated next to her, "Ronnie, it is perfect. It's just perfect." The actor replies, "I wouldn't have believed it if you'd told me." The actors' difficult- ies are real, but so is the vision, at last. And yet even as this conversation takes place in the auditorium, Dafoe calls down from the stage:

> It's a different world up here.
> We can't hear.

In just such an experience, as in so many other concrete and pragmatic ways, the different worlds of actor and audience are defined in rehearsal. The director, who bridges the two realms, is associated with the non-actor world and yet is appealed to, solicited by, the "different world" of actors acting on stage.

A little later LeCompte asks the cast to join her in the audience section of the theatre and to remain there as they mark the score. I am reminded of Antony Sher's description of rehearsal in the theatre when the actor is "without an audience or the need to perform": "the holy magic this place has in repose."[65] The cast has come down from the heat and humidity of the airless stage to sit or stand in a semi-circle around the director underneath four overhead fans in the cool, semi-darkened auditorium. The Brahms piano concerto begins. One actor, Jeff Webster, places his script on a music stand. Willem Dafoe joins him beside it. The other actors sit on tan aluminum chairs, like my own, delivering their lines in natural sounding, low-speaking voices "under" the music and their own taped voices. The effect, even though it gives prominence to the Brahms, is to render all the sounds as part of a musical composition. The human voice becomes just one more component in the total score. Sound, not sense, gives its own kind of pleasing coherence and texture. In this moment, and it is but a moment, there is an almost hallowed feeling of reconciliation of disparate materials no longer seeming disparate.

Rehearsal continues. The Brahms tape is played again. Certain actors are more adept than others at taking cues from the music. LeCompte proposes establishing some other cuing device for those who need it but the actors in question press for more time to learn the musical score. Rehearsal ends at 9 p.m.

On June 25, 1986, my last day of observing the Wooster Group, LeCompte again rehearses the troublesome Devil Dance. There is the classic conflict between how the staging feels (actor: "It *feels* good") and how it looks (director: "It's almost there but it still doesn't work"). The dance is performed on stage. Adjustments in blocking are suggested, discussed, revised. The dance is run again. LeCompte comments afterward, "It's a real conundrum. It's almost as if we have to see it done and then destroyed." To several actors' rejoinder, "This feels a lot better," the director replies: "Oh, it's definitely better. . . . [but] it's like a little kink here somewhere. . . . It has to do with . . . It's so easy to dissuade me from thinking. . . . but I don't want to do it. It looks like . . . [the staging] is confusing. . . ." The actors protest, offering tenable interpretations: "But this is *performance* within the Bergman script. This is part of Bergman" (Smith); "Using *our* subtext, this would be like the company [theatre troupe impersonating the Del Fuegos] was actually in performance in the lounge down-stairs" (Vawter). LeCompte is firm: "It doesn't have enough of the *Saint Antony* text to make it clear. . . . It's too monochromatic. That's all I can say. This is how *we*, the Wooster Group, would perform it. It doesn't have . . . distance. . . ."

Once more LeCompte returns to rejected material. She asks the actors to perform the original version of the Devil Dance, rehearsed by Peter Sellars and presented in Washington, D.C., six months earlier. Now she restages the scene so that Nancy Reilly is standing upstage right and Michael Stumm is seated upstage center. She then asks the other actors to perform with their backs to the auditorium. The removal of the usual perspective is also the addition of another: the theatre troupe seems, is *seen*, to be performing for an onstage audience. Vawter immediately begins to experiment with the reversed perspective. He visibly pants "behind the curtain" in between acts, slicks his hair back in a mirror.

LeCompte, watching the perspectival shift conceived and explored in rehearsal, seems elated: "This is it. You're not facing out. What a relief." The actors agree. This restaging of the show-within-the-show is retained in performance, though the upstage audience is removed and the actors eventually play to an invisible backstage audience. The problem the director had difficulty defining is resolved. It is as if a painter were to try to speak her vision in words as she paints or a poet were to paint with the left hand as she writes with the right hand. The director's earlier elliptical language reveals her struggle to hold onto what she sees in rehearsal as against a private vision of her solitary creating. She knows the dance is working on some level, as the actors say and feel. She sees it work ("Oh, it's definitely better") but she sees something wrong ("a little kink here somewhere") and she communicates her struggle to trust her sense of the situation in rehearsal ("It's so easy to dissuade me from thinking [that there is a kink somewhere] . . . but I don't want to do it. It looks like . . ."). The company's willingness to privilege, even without fully sharing or understanding, the director's sense of dissatisfaction, the vision under revision, and the emergent new direction makes possible a resolution in rehearsal of a crisis in the collaborative process.

That this process is not without its tensions and strains is reinforced by the remarks of dramaturg Norman Frisch the previous evening:

> Rehearsals are about the play that Liz [LeCompte] is trying
> to see in front of her. . . . She has to see things before going on
> to the next thing. . . . One of the huge tensions of the Group
> has to do with people's ability to enact visions which only
> make sense to her. . . . Often others can't enact her visions or
> help because she can't say what the problem is. They have to
> do what she says, trusting that it's for the best. That is difficult
> for some of the cast.[66]

Frisch adds that what is "right," or "wrong," seems at times to
be "in her head." The power of directorial seeing is based on this
problematic: What the director sees in rehearsal, no less than
what the audience or critic sees in performance, is both "in her
head" and, at the same time, the primary mode of vision for
actors who are always seeing themselves being seen.

Interviewed during a break in rehearsal, LeCompte offers the
following distinction: "I can't make it *not* work in my head. I
have to come in here [The Performing Garage] and *see* it not
work in rehearsal. That's the danger of the way I work. . . . That's
why the work is so broad. There's no solipsism." Her description
of her role, with its dangers, is suggestive of that of every director
I observe: "I have to come in here and *see* it not work in rehearsal." Asked what it is, in a given moment, that precipitates
or allows a resolution of crisis in rehearsal, LeCompte nods her
head, indicating the impossibility of fully answering a question
she fully appreciates: "It's hard to trace the process." She speaks
about the layering of the piece, with its necessary ambiguity,
and yet the need for clarity about what is happening. She acknowledges that she does a great deal of reading and thinking at
home privately before coming to rehearsals but that she did not
have in mind the reversed perspective—though she has used it
before in other productions—when she arrived at rehearsal today. "But I knew something was wrong when I saw it. I realized
that it had to be clear who they were and what they were doing.
They are the Bergman troupe, also the fake Del Fuegos, performing the Flaubert dance piece, and they are performing for
the Critic, not for the theatre audience."[67] The lucidity of her
speech seems partly a result of the light cast on the problem
by the staging of its resolution, as if the breakthrough itself
illuminates the nature of the impasse.

As rehearsal resumes LeCompte remarks, "I'm in heaven." She
makes technical adjustments as she reblocks the Devil Dance

and magic show for a double audience, exploring three or four different stagings of the levitation scene so as to conceal from the upstage audience what is fully exposed to the theatre audience: the raising of a prone figure, later a dummy, with strings visibly operated by three actors.[68] Finally, the cast invites the director to view rehearsal from the "audience" perspective onstage. LeCompte temporarily joins the actors on the stage as she redirects the scene. After she returns to her usual seat in the auditorium, Michael Stumm begins to make frequent directorial suggestions from upstage. The actor prefaces his comments by saying, "As an active audience-participant, I think. . . ." Momentarily he shadows the director's role. As an actor impersonating the audience, he straddles two worlds, the world up there and the world down here. These different worlds, straddled by a director who stages a theatre piece about the staging of a theatre piece, are the substance of LeCompte's *Temptation* as a theatrical event, a medium that evokes hidden passages and passageways between and among musical, visual, and literary texts as well as visible and invisible realms.

The title of the trilogy, *The Road to Immortality*, suggests that the Wooster Group is after bigger game than texts. David Savran may be right when he says that *Frank Dell's The Temptation of Saint Antony* seeks to recover "the magical power of theater to cheat death, to commemorate what is no longer there," that it "performs a kind of high-tech séance, listening to and broadcasting the voices of the dead."[69] Or he may not. But it is no surprise that LeCompte's *Temptation* retains, with slight alterations, the following lines from Flaubert's *Saint Antony*:

> Form is perhaps an error of your senses, and substance an image in your mind.
> Unless—the world being a perpetual flux of things—appearance on the contrary were to be all that is truest, and illusion the one reality.
> But are you sure of seeing? Are you even sure of being alive?[70]

These are the words of Flaubert's Devil and they are perhaps the final temptation, the final danger, of any theatrical making.

Fig. 7.1. Scene from The Birth of the Poet. *Left to right: Max Jacobs (Propertius); Jan Leslie Harding (Cynthia). Photograph by Beatriz Schiller.*

7

Richard Foreman Directs
The Birth of the Poet

A Reverberation Box

Richard Foreman has written, designed, directed, and at times musically scored more than forty productions since 1968 in New York and in Europe. His own Ontological-Hysteric Theatre[1] is regarded as one of the major innovative voices in Western theatre of the last twenty years. He has directed one feature film (*Strong Medicine*), received five Obie awards as well as Rockefeller and Guggenheim grants, and is one of the few American directors to have received a yearly French subsidy. His range is suggested by his having directed *Threepenny Opera* at Lincoln Center, at least half a dozen productions at the Public Theater, *Don Juan* and *The Golem* in Central Park's Delacorte Theatre, and *Die Fledermaus* at the Paris Opera, as well as over twenty plays for his own Ontological-Hysteric Theatre.

Foreman's production of *The Birth of the Poet*, presented at the Brooklyn Academy of Music's Opera House December 3–8, 1985, with libretto by Kathy Acker, music by Peter Gordon, scenery and costume design by painter David Salle, deconstructs the distinction between collaboration and non-collaboration. Descriptive copy written by the director states that "*The Birth of the Poet* represents a unique collaboration."[2] Interviewed in BAM's Next Wave magazine, Foreman uses the word "collaboration" but carefully redefines it: "It was a collaboration in which none of the collaborators discussed things with the others, something unique in my career. I did not tell Peter [Gordon] what kind of music I thought I needed for the text, and I didn't say a word to David [Salle] about what he should provide for the decor."[3]

Reviewing *Birth of the Poet* in the *Village Voice*, Michael Feingold does not mince words: "The phenomenon of a large-scale production in which the four key elements have been allowed to go off, more or less randomly, in their own directions, suggests decadence at work." He concludes, "This non-connection, which reaches out to embrace all four artists in their noninterrelationship, is the central failure, or maybe triumph, of *Birth of the Poet*. It lives in that new world where all the old definitions and conventions have been gotten rid of. It asks the question, essentially, whether art as we know it can continue to exist."[4] Erika Munk, writing in the same issue of the *Village Voice*, directly to the left of Feingold's column, demurs: "Michael's right that the directing, design, and text fought each other, sometimes to make a point, sometimes to kill one. Where he sees purposeful, deliberate noncoherence, however, I see a failed attempt at resonance among parts." But for Munk there is another problem: "While I admire Foreman—whose previous work has personified a direly manipulative use of women—for taking on a woman's words, there seems no way he could help slightly subverting them. Still: something serious was being attempted." Munk attributes the audience's "fury" at the piece not to its problematic form and putative decadence but to the "*blatant* content . . . [of] Kathy Acker's libretto. . . . A woman writes loudly and dirtily about woman's desire hurling itself against man's contempt. How dare she? The subject becomes a nonsubject."[5]

Foreman, who repeatedly praises Elizabeth LeCompte's work and who has several times directed the members of the Wooster Group, including LeCompte herself, in his own plays, has said: "My task is to try to resist everything spiritually deadening about the eighties and to keep something else alive. This is why I did [*Miss Universal Happiness*] with the Wooster Group. . . . And the one group that I respect in New York, that I think is as interested in getting into trouble as I am, is the Wooster Group."[6] Critics may, and do, disagree on the kind of trouble Foreman gets into, but not on the provocatively troubling nature of his work.

In an admiring review of Foreman's *Symphony of Rats*, presented by the Ontological-Hysteric Theatre and the Wooster Group at The Performing Garage, Feingold remarks that "his wonderful works remain as elusive, as dazzling and maddening, as ever. . . . No theater in New York, maybe even in the world, contains as much concentrated intellect as Foreman's. Every theater artist puts on stage a vision of his own mental or spiritual state, but Foreman is the only one I can think of who concentrates on doing that, purposively and exclusively, in an active, dramatic way."[7] Feingold is writing of Foreman as author-director-designer, and Foreman has said, "Even as a director, as a person who makes his scenery, makes his music, I think of myself as a writer making texts."[8] What, then, can be learned of such an auteur-director working in the context of "a unique collaboration" in which he neither controls nor influences the writing of the text, the designing of the set and costumes, the scoring of the music? The account that follows will not take issue with Gordon Rogoff's comment on Foreman's work: "While there may be a temptation to cast interpretive veils over his signals and images, it is sufficient to take the journey as given—no more, no less than what it looks like or seems to be at any passing moment."[9]

In the tiny Attic Theater on the sixth floor of the Brooklyn Academy of Music, the cast of *Birth of the Poet*—six women and six men, some dancers as well as actors—rehearse rigorously, six days a week, from 10 a.m. to 6 p.m., with a one-hour break for lunch from 1 to 2 p.m. When I arrive at 9:40 a.m. on October 18, 1985, the fourth day of rehearsal, most of the cast is present, the actors mainly studying scripts over styrofoam cups of coffee or tea. Foreman, dressed in his characteristic dark attire—dark pants, black short-sleeved jersey, black vest and suspenders—stands apart from the actors leaning against a wall at the very edge of the playing area, what I first take to be far stage left. It turns out that, because of the shape of the rehearsal space, the playing area has been arranged so that its downstage portion abuts on a wall, against which Foreman is squeezed. After the lunch break Foreman alters the sense of the stage space so that he can simulate a more reasonable audience point of view. From this point on he sits on a chair in front of the fifth riser in the audience section of the Attic Theater, next to a small elevated model of the set to his right. The stage managers continue to sit behind a table in front of the third riser; the sound equipment and production soundman occupy the sixth riser. Foreman has no director's table but instead occasionally makes use of a music stand on which he props his over-sized copy of the script, at times pointing his pen toward various members of the cast as if it were a baton. I generally sit on the padded area of the riser about five feet to the left of the director.

Foreman characteristically works quickly, arranging the placement of performers, who are all still on book, and objects in the playing area.[10] Rehearsal begins promptly at 10 a.m. Foreman addresses the cast briefly, uses the model of the set to illustrate a point about blocking, himself moves certain rehearsal

Fig. 7.2. Richard Foreman in rehearsal of The Birth of the Poet. *Photograph by Beatriz Schiller.*

props into the playing area to simulate the placement of objects on the stage itself, then says, "All set. Let's go." The prerecorded music of Peter Gordon which plays continuously throughout the piece begins and the cast goes into motion. I see many varied stage actions, hear very little spoken text. Foreman watches intently, occasionally yells, "Cue."[11] He makes no comment on or correction of line readings in this blocking rehearsal. The actors are fairly loose, physically agile, though a bit joyless. Foreman answers all questions clearly, quickly, sometimes in telegraphic style. After a brief run of part of act two, he gives extended notes in lucid straightforward terms, e.g., "You need to flair out toward the audience; you tend to bunch up right now." There is no talk of psychological motivation or "inner life," just clear visual portrayals of the patterns he wants to create. Foreman says that he does not expect the cast to be able to perfect this blocking for about five days, that he knows he is asking for the impossible now but wants them to begin to get the movements in their heads. Once he demonstrates the action of simply taking off a jacket but in such a way as to make evident that he does not want that gesture imitated exactly. At times the director pauses without interfering while the actors clarify or rephrase aspects of the blocking directions for and among themselves. Foreman's unembarrassed approach to using utterly conventional language for what is clearly not conventional theatre work demystifies the creative process in the midst of the process itself.

Working with a group of six actresses standing in a horizontal line practicing a routine, Foreman demonstrates movements occasionally with his own agile body. Working less successfully with a group of five actors, Foreman asks them several times simply to walk rather quickly across the stage. "On a diagonal?" asks one actor. "No, straight across." Later, during a break in rehearsal, when I mention the prevalence of horizontal crosses in his blocking, Foreman remarks, "I know I don't like diagonals. . . . I like to know where you are. I don't like crosses and movements that render the space ambiguous. It keeps the shell in which you are operating 'real.' It reinforces the sense of the shape of the space. The shape of the container should naturally invoke what arises within it and the movements on stage should reinforce the shape of what 'contains' them."

In this morning's blocking rehearsal, Foreman demonstrates very effectively a horizontal cross while holding a giant comb poised just at the right ear as if in readiness for use in arranging his hair. Five actors attempt this over and over and over again, perhaps seven or eight times. The pace of the director's requested repetitions of group action is so brisk that one loses count of the number. Foreman's crisply articulated blocking directions, fairly rapid speech, swift decision-making, allow him to move his groups of actors in and out of positions with great dispatch. At times, if one were not paying close attention, it might seem as if Foreman were choreographing a chorus line in an avant-garde version of a Broadway play.

And yet there are, throughout the rehearsals, distinct and characteristic moments in which the director talks more slowly and hesitantly, pauses, stops altogether for up to five full minutes while he thinks on his feet, often with a prop in his hand. This morning, for example, after directing the actresses to move rehearsal props—substituting for David Salle's over-sized constructed "head," "torso," and "hips" of a human figure—from upstage center to far stage left, Foreman walks through the blocking himself, sees problems with it, and begins revising. His speech rhythms become more meditative, more reflective of an ongoing process rather than a clipped summary of its result.

Ironically, once the director's voice and manner seem to indicate that he is in the midst of rehearsal exploration, the cast seems slightly uneasy, fidgety. There is an uncomfortable pause. The actors begin to look bored. The director is thinking out a problem he sees and they don't; this is often in fact the subtext of the rehearsal. Finally, Foreman smiles to himself, and rearranges the position of a major prop (a chariot) as well as an actress whom he now places within that prop as she delivers her lines.

Foreman tells me, "Theatre starts with the word for me. . . . For me the word is the center because in the rehearsal blocking is always an attempt to clarify what is said. Blocking is for me not the truth of what is going on between two actors. [That kind of blocking] . . . is what naturalistic directors may be interested in but it doesn't interest me at all. . . . What I need to do is set the stage so that the weight of [each] particular phrase reverberates best—like cutting a diamond to reflect the light. In my staging I try to set up the maximum possible number of things for reverberation."[12] An example of this, a strikingly appropriate exception to the avoidance of diagonals, occurs the next day when Foreman directs Jan Leslie Harding, playing Cynthia, to move on the line, " 'Propertius is no more' "[13]: "As the reality hits you, it backs you onto a diagonal." He then shows the actress a simple change of hand position, an eloquent accompaniment to the line, and comments, "It's an earthquake. The whole world is no more."

In today's rehearsal Foreman's attention is caught by the placement of a prop, a trash can, upstage right. He walks first to the onstage object and then, spying another prop, a basketball, just outside the playing area, picks it up and says to actress-dancer Valda Setterfield, "I wonder . . . a little aesthetic foreshadowing. What would it be like to have you bounce the basketball?" She delivers her lines while bouncing the ball. He does the same, then says, "Let's try it." This is the first of many examples of Foreman's rhetoric of exploration, poised midway between address to the actress and audible self-address.[14]

During a break in rehearsal a month later, Foreman remarks, "The actors have to enter the world of the director's philosophy and vision as an experiment during rehearsal. . . . The actors are getting the play through me, not directly from Kathy [Acker] or Peter [Gordon], though I hope I'm respecting them [the author and the composer]." There is almost no unstructured improvisation in Foreman's rehearsal, in contrast to LeCompte's explorations with the Wooster Group. For example, on the last day of rehearsal in the Attic Theater, Foreman devotes fifteen to twenty minutes of detailed work establishing a particular physicalization whose duration will be about half a minute in performance. He begins by asking the actresses, "On 'thumb,' can you swing your disc to the floor?" (the actresses have been rhythmically revolving large white discs behind their heads). Valda Setterfield replies, "Depends on where we are in the sequence." Foreman's comment, "That's true. Let's see what else *we* can do" (emphasis added), is followed by his entry into the playing area where he takes one of the actresses' discs and rolls it back and forth on the floor in rhythm with the prerecorded music. He first asks the actresses to throw one leg over the top of the disc as Cynthia says, "thumb" (II.3, p. 21), then asks them to raise the discs over their heads on the word "thumb." (The line being "illustrated" here is, "Thumb, your two fingers pinch my nipples while your master bears down on me.") He stands in the playing area silently thinking for a moment, then asks the men to kneel in profile in front of the women and to move their left hands sensuously across the large white circular discs held by the women.[15] Again Foreman asks the women to raise the discs above their heads on the word "thumb" and then, as a second option, to raise the discs and shuffle backwards. Now he takes one of the discs himself, lifts it and holds it daintily to the left side of his head. Returning the disc, he asks the actresses to lift their discs daintily to the left side of their heads on the word "thumb" and move *forward*. He again takes one of the discs and demonstrates rolling, rather than lifting, it as he moves stage left. The actresses rehearse this blocking several times. Foreman now runs part of Cynthia's sexually explicit speech in II.3, beginning with the line, "Sex is public."[16] Five actresses enter with hands pressed to their foreheads, give a slight groan, exit. As Cynthia continues her speech, the men enter as if sowing the ground. The women reenter, rhythmically rolling their white discs from right to left. At the word "thumb," they roll the discs stage left and exit in this fashion. The director seems pleased with this resolution of the blocking accompanying the word "thumb."

During a break in a technical rehearsal without actors at the Opera House, Foreman describes "the center of . . . [his] lust for the theatre" as the "manipulation of three-dimensional space," the "desire to have moving three-dimensional objects and three-dimensional space in relation to the objects. . . . I'm interested in the different ways people can be arranged in time in a particular space." He does not define himself primarily as a visual artist: "Things that impinge on my visual field immediately get translated kinetically into my body. I have a kinetic sense of how things look." It is this "kinetic sense of how things look" that defines Foreman's directorial style. Demonstrating a certain action in the playing area, he says to actress-dancer Brooke Myers as she is about to make the next move, "I don't know. How are we going to do that?" He is far upstage, about fifty feet from me and the rest of the cast. In this overheard "we," I feel a sense of paradox: a firm, controlled, controlling director whose plural of majesty may always be referring to his own "philosophy and vision" appears to be in tentative, shared, physicalized exploration with the actress.

Throughout rehearsal work Foreman is meticulously clear, decisively precise, but openly and, at times, tediously exploratory. He has said that his "technique in the theatre is to feel the impulse, not knowing yet what it means or how it wants to work, but to let the impulse lead me. Then it takes on a three-dimensional, actorly, proplike form—but I always remember to keep present for the spectator a kind of interplay between the original thrust, the place that it came from, and the real three-dimensional human, physical manifestation that it takes on at this particular historical moment. This impulse leads to another impulse, which leads to another impulse."[17] Foreman's physical demonstrations in rehearsal seem to function first as his own kinetic translations of visual impulses and then as clues, or stimuli, to actors who, no matter how detailed the rehearsal work becomes, do not precisely reproduce the director's gesture or movement. This may seem an untenable claim, given Foreman's reputation, but close observation of his rehearsal work will confirm, I think, that his "demonstrations" are a bodily language—even at times a kind of physicalized abstraction—in response to which an actress will find her own conceptual-physical equivalent.

In early November, Foreman, working with Brooke Myers, demonstrates a gesture of recoil. As Myers rehearses it, she pretties up the gesture. Foreman repeats his demonstration several times, describing the blocking as he enacts it. He is relaxed, even smiling at himself, as she watches. Of his rehearsal "demonstrations," Foreman says, "It's the only way I can think at that moment—acting out some physicalization. . . . [I'm] not showing the actor so much as feeling on stage what that [moment] is."

If, after they have been given blocking directions, the actors do not quite reproduce what the director has in mind, Foreman often has them do a variation on the original blocking, sometimes suggested inadvertently by the actors. In this way the actors' variants on the director's initial vision become part of the final creative conception and staging of the theatre piece. What I am describing occurs throughout Foreman's rehearsals, as in those of other directors, and is usually not remarked upon. An explicit example of actors' variants replacing the initial directorial blocking occurs fairly late in rehearsal, in mid-November, when Foreman, running II. 3, stops the scene abruptly and says, "Stuart [Hodes, a dancer] just made a mistake and I think it's better." The contribution of the actor is clearly not a solicited offering and it is hedged by the pejorative implications of the category in which it is placed (error),[18] yet it is still fully accepted as correcting the directorial design.

At one point during the morning of my first day of observing rehearsals, Foreman gives a fairly unstructured direction to the entire cast. Speaking of II. 2, which opens, "During the night, these streets very narrow dirty uneven rocks no way to be sure of your footing much less direction as for safety all sorts of criminals or rather people who have to survive hiding,"[19] the director says to the actors: "A naturalistic moment, life in the urine-filled streets of Rome. Do whatever you want: examine your scabs, clean yourselves, take provocative positions on the floor." But in the runthrough after the lunch break the results are rather pale, uninteresting movements. In a later rehearsal on November 1, I hear Foreman say in response to a question from Jan Leslie Harding, "I don't know yet. Whatever feels right to you."

The director continues to work out the staging in the midst of the actors, despite the fact that *The Birth of the Poet* has had a prior production, its world première, at the Ro theatre in Rotterdam, in April, 1984. Foreman finds it "very difficult to produce again something I've already done. . . . It's about 80 percent staged differently. I like to think I'm completely redoing it. . . . I want to feed out of the energies that are in me now as I'm reading the text and sitting here in New York City at this moment in my life and *looking at* these actors" (emphasis added).

Blocking in *The Birth of the Poet* is often presented to groups rather than to individual actors. At one point in the morning rehearsal on October 18, Foreman asks the entire cast to hum as they move in a "séance circle." When the cast begins to hum, the director comments, "I don't mean [for you] to make noise. I'm suggesting that you hum within your bodies in the rhythm of your moving in a circle." The cast responds to the clarification with pleasure. Whether fortuitous or intentional, it is effective to have allowed the conventional interpretation to be enacted first in the process of finding the less literal "hum" of the moving circle.

A revealing example of Foreman's use and deflection of literalistic blocking directions is his staging of an unanswered question posed to Cynthia in act two. At the funeral of her mother, the family lawyer asks, "Where are the 800 IBM shares?" and Cynthia responds, "What 800 IBM shares?"[20] On the phrase, "IBM shares," Foreman suggests a group physicalization which he describes as "like brushing your wind-swept hair with your hand as you ride in the convertible you bought with your IBM shares." Foreman seems to be staging an "illustration" of an episode in an unwritten narrative suggested by a single phrase in the playtext. A clear, simple, unambiguous direction is presented to the actors as a group, all of whom are invited to share and enact the same impulse, as in the request to "hum" in the rhythm of their bodily circular movement. The 800 IBM shares in the text are, and remain, missing; the ride in the convertible is also missing, neither written by the playwright nor staged by the director. To an audience intent on locating meanings in the context of a storyline, the blocking is no doubt unclear and unreadable. For Foreman it is perhaps a staging of what he calls "Duo-consciousness," in which "You are in two places at once (and ecstatic)."[21]

In an early manifesto, Foreman has said, "Art should awaken a hunger for an immersion in being-conscious-of-process. . . ."[22] He repeatedly insists that he is interested in clarity—"Despite what people say about the obscurity of my work, the only thing I'm interested in is clarity"—but it is the clarity that comes from understanding the processes of perception. He himself understands the "real part" of the event on stage to be the author's or director's "Act of MAKING the thing we/ are looking at. . . . It's the only subject/ (the making of this as it is made)/ that avoids the built-in/ deadness of the language in which it articulates itself . . . because language . . . doesn't have to be something that/ 'refers to'/ . . . but only spins out itself—web-like—as/ its own evidence of what it is, in collision/ with what one would make. . . . Creativity (the effort at it) as the subject."[23]

In the midst of rehearsing a long monologue containing Acker's most provocative sexual language, Foreman repeatedly interrupts the actress delivering Cynthia's lines to make detailed revisions of the placement and movement of performers and inanimate objects. The actress at first has difficulty delivering some of these lines. There is one line, for example, on which she says she always stutters.[24] Foreman's continual interruptions of Cynthia's speech at the beginning of II.3 at first seem to dilute its strength and disorient its speaker, but eventually the speech, which I myself find as upsetting in rehearsal as critic Erika Munk does in performance,[25] seems galvanized by the work that comes about as a result of these interruptions.

Foreman remarks, during a break in rehearsals,

> The hardest thing when you see runthroughs . . . the disappointment you feel in seeing runthroughs is because the play is lacking the counter-rhythm of my own interruptions into the rehearsal process, so that as you refine the piece, some of the things you're adding are intended to recreate the actual physical experience of the interruptions. . . . The actual texture of the actual fact of the interruption [has to be recreated by other means].

As examples of the means by which the felt experience or effect of interruption might be recreated, he suggests "a certain change of light; a certain cross that interferes with the action; a different kind of music coming in; and, in this piece, for example, people running and hitting against the wall and going 'owww'. . . . The tendency in rehearsal is to try to make things as smooth as possible so you have to keep putting the jaggedness back in. . . . Why did drips start appearing in painting? Similar reason."[26]

On the afternoon of my first day of observing rehearsals, Foreman spends nearly three hours blocking four pages of the script. Most of this time is devoted to Cynthia's two-page monologue in II. 3. At times Foreman stops the actress' delivery of the lines to give excruciatingly detailed blocking directions. At one point there is a pause while nearly the entire cast offers suggestions to an actress on how to sit in a chair so that when she is removed from it by two actors she will end up being dragged *backward*. At other times Foreman directs "over" Cynthia's ongoing speech, e.g., asking four actors to carry a table in and out quickly and four actresses to sit in a semi-circle at Cynthia's feet, then rise, and while holding hands take a giant step into "the house" where they sit on a "pillow" (the set and stage properties referred to are not literally present in rehearsal or performance).

After the first hour of such detailed blocking of the speech, the actress' voice becomes more and more affectless, not at the director's request but simply as a natural consequence of repeated interruptions. Foreman does not give elaborate, or at times any, explanations of the physicalizations he establishes in this blocking rehearsal, and yet many of the odd gestures and movements seem to establish a clarifying context for the language of the text, though never a literal one. For example, on Cynthia's line, "Legs lie against legs," Jan Leslie Harding lies supine on the floor of the playing area, one knee raised against a table leg, as if pressed against another, absent body. After an hour and a half, still working on the second page of Cynthia's opening monologue, Foreman blocks the line, "In the other case, there's a 1 percent chance you'll keep touching his flesh." Behind Cynthia's back two actors and two actresses run into the playing area and sit on chairs while three actors on the other side of the stage perform a kind of caterpillar walk with three actresses. The director gives no explanation that I can hear but the unexpected staging gives an edge of jagged excitement to an otherwise unexceptional line.

As the actress playing Cynthia reads aloud the stage direction, "Cynthia, sitting . . . in her little apartment overlooking the middle-class Roman whores' section, is dressing her hair,"[27] Foreman interrupts her to arrange three couples dancing upstage of Cynthia who sits on a sofa with four other actors. He then asks three actresses to stand to the side of the sofa and to mime punching a punching bag or boxing. From behind the actresses three actors enter the playing area rubbing their crotches. As Cynthia continues with her own lines, "wild city DOGS should drive their thousands of TEETH-FANGS through his flesh," Foreman asks the actors on the sofa to begin rubbing their crotches. On the next lines[28] he asks Cynthia to spray her hair. As she says, "I want his lips to dry up in Grand Canyon gulfs," Foreman interjects, "You're now doing a sort of Shakespearean curse. . . . Get up, walk, continue spraying your hair."

There is an unexpected pause. The director stands in front of the actors seated on the sofa, facing them, totally still as he thinks in their presence. Finally, Foreman asks the four seated actors to rise and gingerly "[dip] a foot in water and bite one hand in order not to scream at the coldness of the water." What seems a moment of naturalistic miming, even an acting class exercise, is offered without explanation or contextual support other than possibly the following passage in Cynthia's "Shake-spearean" curse: "the driest and coldest dry ice: the top of your head will burn and the rest of your body will freeze. . . ." Certainly the director does not explain why there is suddenly water in front of the sofa or why at this moment the actors rise and dip their feet in it.

Four weeks later, as the line, " 'There's a car wreck,' "[29] is sung by a voice prerecorded on tape, actors in the playing area are rattling chairs. Suddenly Foreman stops the scene and says, "Protect your chair. Protect it from other chairs." The scene, rehearsed again, is much more effective.

Foreman's kinetic visualizations take off from the text, often respond to words or phrases as disassociated verbal cues.[30] His instructions to the cast at times make use of psychological moti-vation or conventional acting objectives ("bite one hand in order not to scream at the coldness of the water"; "protect your chair") but create for the audience what will be perceived as a stylization of human experience (e.g., fear and trembling). These recreations of the playtext (his own as well as other authors') are startling, brilliant, theatrically provocative.

In rehearsal, Foreman's blocking directions create a tenuous, momentary connection between a verbal text and an expression-istic stage enactment with roots in human experience. The rehearsal process is revealed as a kind of slow-motion representa-tion of the clarifying impulse in the creative/recreative imagi-nation.

About two weeks after rehearsals begin, Foreman schedules a runthrough in the performance space itself. An actress, entering the BAM Opera House, says, "Gee whiz . . . the real thing!" Fore-man shows the cast where the sight lines are and describes what the set will be like. He runs the piece from beginning to end without interruption except when there are technical problems with the taped music and the artificial amplification of the actors' voices. While their performance is initially impressive, the actors in their rehearsal clothes seem a bit dwarfed as they perform in the magnificent historic house. (When Robert Wilson first brings his actors into BAM's Carey Playhouse this fall for extended lighting rehearsals of *Golden Windows*, they are in full make-up and costume.) During the runthrough in the Opera

House, the director is separated from the actors he observes by the deep hole of the orchestra pit. In the physical layout of the performance space I feel the symbolic distancing and ultimate severing of the director from the collaborative creative process. The actors, cut off physically—and, to some extent, audibly—from the director, cue each other as they begin to form that self-contained, self-helping unit they will become in performance.

When, after a short break, the cast reconvenes in the Attic Theater, Foreman rigorously rehearses line readings in III. 6: "We need to go through it line by line and coordinate it with the music." The lines in this section of the play have no speech-tags. They are individually assigned to different actors and must be spoken in the setting of taped voices singing the lines to music composed by Peter Gordon. Here, clearly, the voicing of the word is the center of Foreman's "reverberation box."[31]

As the cast sits in the playing area, each actor delivers her or his line, and the director comments on each individual rendering. He asks Zach Grenier to move into a higher register; he asks Ingrid Reffert not to speed up her pauses and to give a different emphasis to the word "door" in the line, "Ali knocked on the door of the mosque"[32]; he asks two actors to pronounce "mosque" with a clearer enunciation of the "k" sound; he asks Anne Lange to speak more softly and "conducts" several repetitions of one of her lines, setting low and high "notes" as well as pacing and volume. He tells Max Jacobs to give equal emphasis to the words "tea" and "sweet" (The line is, "In the mosque they drink tea and sweets.").[33] He gives a group direction: "[There] has to be a kind of artificial sing-song range for all of you. . . . The higher notes should be little rapier-like thrusts, for all of you." As he rehearses, he "conducts" sharp staccato notes and long drawn-out notes with his right hand, pointing upward for higher notes, indicating by gesture the rhythmic punctuation of particular lines. "On the high notes, whenever possible there should be two notes. . . . [How to do] those high notes: think of your favorite food—mine is chocolate—smell your chocolate, feel it on your tongue." Jan Leslie Harding delivers a line, and Foreman responds, "No, . . . you're not *tasting* [the word] 'anything.' "

In this session, as contrasted with his earlier blocking rehearsals, Foreman is intent on making the actor's voice a finely-tuned instrument. For thirty minutes the word is tortuously considered, "tasted," deconstructed into rhythmic yet surprising sound. Then there is a seated readthrough followed by a runthrough of the entire four-and-a-half page scene "on its feet." Now Foreman asks that the cast do the scene again, this time delivering their lines quickly and keeping their voices "in a low register." He interrupts the revised run to say, "I think I prefer this. It's less arty. Let's do the scene again this way . . . low voice, precise, quickly." It is a significant, and barely explained, change from the preceding half-hour's work. Acknowledging this difference at the end of the new low-voiced, quickly-paced version of the scene, Foreman remarks, "After all that, I prefer this." The revised voicings, however, retain some vestige of the previous care taken with emphasis, precision and clarity of expression, pacing.

The rehearsal process inevitably seems to consist of trying out approaches that will be rejected, making false starts and only by that means arriving at one's final destination. Foreman's previously quoted statement bears repetition: "But! It is those continually REJECTED choices of the backdrop, never articulated yet always present as the un-thought 'possible' which give plasticity and depth and aliveness to what is chosen."[34]

When I enter the rehearsal room the next afternoon, Foreman is reblocking II.4. I am struck by the disparity between the inflammatory misogyny of the speech being rehearsed[35] and the coolly technical character of the comments and corrections made by the director. Perhaps this is the way students, including my own, feel when English professors talk about rhyme and rhythm, caesuras and oxymorons, in certain Shakespearean speeches. In this rehearsal Foreman is initially concerned with the physical positions of the actors, their distance from each other, the particular placement of their arms on other bodies or objects. For over twenty-five minutes the company works in detail on the staging of one page of Propertius' monologue in II. 4, with only a few corrections of line deliveries. Finally, the play is rehearsed from this scene to the very end. Watching the runthrough in the rehearsal room, I see a verbal text in the process of becoming a sequence of enacted configurations under the pressure of innumerable directorial choices. If it first seemed perhaps tedious to remember whether to walk in a large circle or a quarter-circle and when to turn one's face briefly toward the audience during such a walk, and how to bounce a basketball as you speak, now these hundreds and hundreds of individual blockings have become part of a process that at its best seems to energize the actors and the written text simultaneously. Eerily I have the feeling that I am watching a single human consciousness at work.

I see, or seem to see, "a drift toward coherence"[36] in a series of decisions that, taken by themselves, often appear arbitrary, eccentric, playfully puzzling.

Now Foreman asks the cast to deliver their Persian lines in act three as if they were revolutionaries. The effect is striking and the style is retained. In Elizabeth LeCompte's or Lee Breuer's improvisatory rehearsals, the actors might hit upon this choice by trying out, experimenting with, certain tones on their own. In Foreman's rehearsals, acting choices seem explicitly subsumed in directorial choices. Once, however, the director identifies the cast as "revolutionaries," each actor finds her or his own voice within the possible range of "revolutionary" voices. As for the imposition of the director's choreography on the actors, there is leeway for variation.

Foreman, watching the actors rehearse a skipping motion over and over in act three, suddenly says, "I don't like that skip [one of the hallmarks of the rehearsal at this point]." Entering the playing area, he tells the cast, "Just come on stage and walk around." They do. Foreman, no longer standing in the playing area, interrupts the actors, "Hold it. That looks . . . too easy. What else could you do?" The "you" functions as does the "we" in Foreman's rhetoric of exploration. The director reenters the playing area, delivers the lines slowly as he walks, pauses, experiments with some hand gestures, asks the actors to follow suit, then watches as they experiment with hand gestures similar but not identical to his own. I hear an actor say, playfully, "That's external, Valda," and the serious reply, "But it makes the internal function."

When the scene is run again, the skipping is replaced by walking and the hand movements have evolved from competitive game-playing gestures to tentative, slightly stylized head-scratching. Foreman begins to rehearse the following scene, III. 2, and suddenly stops it: "No skipping. I'm sick of the skipping." He asks the actors to stand still, bounce, pound their fists, squat as they recite their lines. As the cast enacts this series of physicalizations, I seem to see the director's eye almost instantaneously reject or give provisional assent to what impinges on his visual/kinetic field, as if his evaluation of what he envisions is just barely completed before the next envisioning occurs. The actors seem to play to and for him. As he "conducts," their bodily movements continually expose further possibilities, refinements, limitations, wrong "notes" in his ongoing composition.

Peter Sellars, rehearsing the Wooster Group, worked with and in some ways resisted the particular style of a talented theatre collective. Richard Foreman in rehearsing *The Birth of the Poet* is in the more usual situation of creating a group style in a temporary collocation of actors. Each of these directors has an underground affinity with the actor, a startling kinetic energy that at times materializes in the form of inspired physical improvisations. But neither director encourages in the actors a kind of presence or prominence that does not have the directorial design as its controlling context.[37]

Foreman's rehearsal of the prologue to act three may serve as a paradigm of his directorial style. Like Sellars rehearsing Flaubert's *Saint Antony* with the Wooster Group, Foreman assigns to individual actors lines that are narrative descriptions or stage directions. The director allocates a series of statements in the prologue to certain actors whose verbal intonations, emphases, and pacing he carefully establishes. He experiments with, clarifies, and precisely establishes physical movements and gestures that clash with the portentousness of the language.

It is sometimes Foreman's habit, as already suggested, to hold in his hand a relevant prop while he directs a scene. For example, when he rehearses a scene in act two, he holds a plastic plate while he directs the cast to grip their plastic plates as if they are discus throwers. I see him standing in the playing area with a brown miniature baseball-bat-like club in his right hand, the plastic plate still in his left hand, as he directs the final scene in act two and the prologue to act three. He uses the bat to point, to slap his thigh, to tap his chest, then swings it slightly at his side as if to release excess energy. Finally, he uses it to demonstrate what is to be done with it and then hands the "little stick" to the actress standing next to him. Still holding the plastic plate in his left hand, he continues to direct and redirect two actresses who fence and occasionally hit each other on the top of their heads while they deliver lines from the prologue to act three. He remains in the playing area during the rehearsal of the prologue, sometimes enacting the gestures of one of the two actresses as she delivers her lines. Sometimes he corrects and demonstrates line readings. Several times he corrects the delivery of the line, "All languages, finally, are ornaments,"[38] delivering it himself in such a way as to hold off, delay, and stress the word "ornaments." He then adds two actors who speak the final lines of the prologue.

Resuming work on act three, after a short break, Foreman

redirects an "individually fascistic" walk by the actors, physically demonstrating a stylized goose-step with arms high. He tells the actresses that they are not "romantic" enough and asks for a "clichéd contrast between macho men" and romantic, wilting ladies. The clichéd contrast he wants is not a succession of images limply left in the minds of the audience but a false opposition created by overused postures. He seems to be finding stage equivalents for a society whose tensions are partly created by such juxtapositions.

A play rehearsed is an interrupted text. By observing the slowed down, stop-and-start process of rehearsal work, I am able to "see" in a way that shadows the director's way of seeing. The kind of seeing that the interrupted rhythms of rehearsal make possible is not transferable to any viewing of performance. Rehearsal is behind-the-scene work: it is also behind-the-seen work. Foreman tells me that at the age of 26 or 27,

> I said to myself, "What do I want to see up there on that stage?" And I began writing the kind of plays that made me want to become a director. When I answered that question, I saw two people up there in a moment of tension. In the plays I began to write, I tried to remove everything that would distract from that tension. There were no narrative or psychological elements. It was like a physiological study, e.g., this is Rhoda's leg. What I was doing could be looked at psychologically as trying to start from birth again.[39]

One might speculate that the director's hidden agenda is to see and interrupt the primal scene, symbolically revisiting the site of one's own creation.

Kate Davy writes of the early work of Foreman, "While the traditional process of theatrical production usually involves collaboration among producers, directors, set and costume designers, there is no collaboration in Ontological-Hysteric Theatre— every aspect of Foreman's art is done for and by himself."[40] That this statement must now be qualified is, I hope, suggested in the preceding observations. Under the shaping power and pressure of distinct directorial decisions, a verbal text becomes a sequence of enacted configurations, individual and choric voicings. In this most dissonant "collaboration" of designer, composer, author, and director who explicitly refuse unity of vision or even sustained discussion of differences, there is in the rehearsal work some kind of collective creation by actors and director.

It has been suggested that when we watch a flock of migrating birds in the sky overhead, we project onto them a flight pattern which we mistakenly attribute to the birds themselves. We attribute patterns to moving groups when in fact what we see may be massed random movements. Although I am aware of this healthy antidote to my own way of seeing in rehearsal, it nonetheless seems that, as the days and weeks pass, choices which in themselves appear arbitrary eventually attract other choices and eventually culminate in a vocal, visual, and physical collocation whose history of revisions, rejections, and happy accidents is recorded only in these pages, and only partially. What patterns the birds are actually making above our heads we may never know. But the patterns of human actors, particular bodies and voices in rehearsal, can at times be apprehended. In describing the rehearsal process I must shift back and forth from what is "given" to what is achieved, from what is controllable to what is not, from what is there to be taken in to what in us wants to give back, from what is fashioned for the observing world to what intrudes on that fashioning; finally, from a world where consciousness is action to a world where acting is a performance of consciousness.[41]

Fig. 8.1. Robert Wilson and David Warrilow rehearsing The Golden Windows. *Photograph by Johan Elbers.*

8

Robert Wilson Directs
The Golden Windows and
Hamletmachine

"get in a position what else is there"

Analyzing Elizabeth Bishop's poem, "The Monument," David Bromwich writes: "An active mind alone makes the world cohere."[1] This declaration may be the best brief introduction to the work of Robert Wilson. Writing of him in the fall of 1986, Alan M. Kriegsman says, "Wilson may be, as Eugène Ionesco has called him, the most important figure in American theatre—he's certainly the most daring and visionary—but the plain fact is that relatively few American theatregoers have ever seen his work and many don't know the name."[2] Two years later Kriegsman concludes, "Wilson remains the most preposterously underappreciated American artist of his era."[3]

Author, designer, and director of nearly 100 theatre, opera, dance, film, and video works, Robert Wilson is probably best known for *Einstein on the Beach*, his 1976 collaboration with composer Philip Glass, revived at the Brooklyn Academy of Music in 1984. In 1986 Wilson was the unanimous choice of the Drama Jury to receive the Pulitzer Prize in Drama for his international opera, *the CIVIL warS: a tree is best measured when it is down*. The Pulitzer Board declined to give the award. In 1988 Wilson directed, designed, and choreographed a production of Debussy's *Le Martyre de Saint-Sébastien* for the Paris Opera Ballet, later performed at the Metropolitan Opera House in New York as part of the Paris Opera Ballet's United States tour. In this same year he also directed and designed Heiner Müller's *Quartet* for the American Repertory Theatre in Cambridge, Massachusetts, where he had previously directed a production of Euripides' *Alcestis* in the winter of 1986. In addition to Guggenheim Fellowships and grants from the Rockefeller Foundation and the National Endowment for the Arts, Wilson has received numerous awards, including the Drama Desk Award for Direction (*Deafman Glance*); an Obie Special Citation Award for Direction (*The Life and Times of Joseph Stalin*); and an Obie Award for Direction of *Hamletmachine* in 1986. His drawings and sculptures are held in private collections and museums throughout the world.

In the summer and fall of 1985 I observe extended rehearsals of Robert Wilson's own theatre piece, *The Golden Windows*, beginning in mid-July and continuing until the first preview performance on October 22 in the Carey Playhouse at the Brooklyn Academy of Music. Between mid-August and mid-September there is a month-long break in rehearsal while the director begins preparations for his production of *Alcestis* at the American Repertory Theatre in Cambridge. In the spring of the following year I observe Wilson direct Heiner Müller's *Hamletmachine*, with the German playwright in attendance, in a 74-seat theatre, Mainstage Two, at New York University's Tisch School of the Arts where the piece was performed from May 7 through June 7, 1986. Reviewing *Hamletmachine* in the *New York Times*, Mel Gussow notes, "Wilson, who has presented epics on the stages of the world's great opera houses . . . , is equally adept in these confined quarters."[4] The following pages will track Wilson's artistry in rehearsals of *The Golden Windows* at the Brooklyn Academy of Music and his Obie-winning direction of student actors rehearsing *Hamletmachine*, described by its translator, Carl Weber, as "probably Müller's most complicated text, and the most difficult to decode."[5]

The title of Robert Wilson's theatre piece, *The Golden Windows*, is taken from a children's story by Laura Shapiro. Asked by an actress late in the rehearsal period to tell the story, which he had heard as a child, the director gives this abbreviated account: "A boy lives in a house with his father. Always he looked at the house across the valley with golden windows and wished he lived in it. Finally he went across the valley and climbed up to the house at sunset. As he looked back to his house across the valley, he saw it had golden windows."[6]

Wilson's *Golden Windows* is a child's vision of deep blue starspangled sky, of statuesque, radiant, slightly mysterious female figures, of comic-book-like jagged apocalyptic earthquakes, of endlessly smoking guns, of small dark houses suddenly lit with brilliant golden light, of hanging men who talk; but its text is filled with the fragmentary, clichéd, banal, allusive language of adult consciousness. Throughout there is a tension between the visual clarity and beauty of the child's fable and the complicated ambiguities, violence, danger, and dissonance of contemporary experience.[7] Writing of the production Robert Coe says, "Departing from this simple children's story by Laura Shapiro, Robert Wilson's *The Golden Windows* has no subject or story to tell."[8] But Wilson's theatre work clearly has a subject and it is the subject of the not-so-simple Shapiro story: it is the subject of the relativizing of time and space, the post-Kantian subject of all our stories.

When I first enter the Lepercq Space on July 21, 1985, fifteen minutes before rehearsal is to begin, I see a single actor seated on a wooden bench by a black music stand, right hand on cheek, left arm on left knee. Soundlessly David Warrilow rehearses, moving his arms and hands slowly with great concentration. The right hand lowers, joining the left hand just inside the left knee. The face is placed in right profile and then looks up suddenly. The right arm is flung upward, then is lowered very slowly to its former position. The head slowly moves back to center, facing the audience directly. The right arm lengthens and stiffens, the right hand still holding the left hand. What I observe is baffling and mesmerizing. At the end of this first day of observing rehearsal, en route back to Manhattan, David Warrilow says to me, "I think this is the most demanding role of my life." Later I will read the simple spatial and temporal stage direction: "1 on the bench (five minutes)."[9]

Exactly at 1 p.m. the air conditioning and an impressive array of overhead lights turn on in the large rehearsal space on the third floor of the Brooklyn Academy of Music. The staff and actors are present but there is no sign of the director. At 1:15 p.m. Ann-Christin Rommen, assistant to the director, and production stage manager Charlie Otte, along with composer and sound designer Hans Peter Kuhn, accompany actors Kimberly Farr and Charles Whiteside to a small room on the floor above the Lepercq Space. There they watch together a videotape of a rehearsal of *Golden Windows* in Munich, where the play, translated into German, was given its world première in 1982.[10]

All the "characters" in *The Golden Windows* are referred to by number, with a brief description of each. Of the four roles, three are double-cast. "2, woman in black dress," will be played on alternate nights by Jane Hoffman and Gaby Rodgers; "3, man on the rope," will be performed by Charles Whiteside and John

Bowman; "4, woman in white dress," will be performed by Cynthia Babak and Kimberly Farr. Only David Warrilow, playing "1, man on the bench,"[11] will appear in every performance. While the actors wait for the director to arrive, Charles Whiteside watches a German actor rehearse the role of "3" on the videotape which Hans Peter Kuhn occasionally supplements with his personal recollections of the Munich rehearsals. The eyes of the German actor open and close at specified intervals. There are isolated shots of small finger and hand movements; the videotape is stopped several times while the American actor watches and at times imitates the hand gestures of his German counterpart. At 1:25 p.m. the director arrives and we return to Lepercq.

Dark rose curtains have been drawn over thirty-foot-high windows, as they will be throughout Wilson's rehearsals, obliterating all sources of natural light. Today there are more staff members than actors. Behind or near two rectangular tables facing the marked playing area sit assistant director Julia Gillet, production stage manager Charlie Otte, assistant to the director Ann-Christin Rommen, stage manager Susan West, sound designer Hans Peter Kuhn, lighting designer Markus Bönzli, production soundman Thomas Paulucci. Actors David Warrilow, Gaby Rodgers, Kimberly Farr, and Charles Whiteside sit to the side of the playing area or on risers in the audience section of the rehearsal space. In general, the seating arrangement remains the same throughout rehearsal in Lepercq, the director always returning to the same table, and the same chair, while the actors tend to seek out and return to their individually chosen seats.

In contrast, when the company moves into the auditorium of the Carey Playhouse during lighting rehearsals in the fall, one rarely knows for certain who is present. Except for the production stage manager and the lighting personnel, who must sit at specific locations in the theatre, everyone seems in continual flux, sitting here, then there, standing, moving about in the house. In the Playhouse the air is filled with names called out in the darkness, names at times echoing those in the dialogue of the script: "Michael? Richard? Jim? Bob? Are you here?" (Jim is a member of the work crew; Bob is Robert Wilson.)

The lighting rehearsals in the theatre make palpable the actors' experience of the play itself. "Characters" in *Golden Windows* are not fixed, not really delineated at all. Often they are positioned on stage so that they cannot see each other. With regard to conventional meanings of theatrical discourse and conventional understanding of human relationships, the characters in *Golden Windows* are largely blanks, and Wilson as director does not really care or control what identities, motivations, justifications, "inner life" the actors give the roles they play.

Being "in the dark" is something the actors experience from their first day in Lepercq; in the October rehearsals at the Carey Playhouse it becomes literally true. We in the theatre auditorium are also in the dark, a literalization of our own experience in trying to make discursive sense out of these actors' presence on stage before us. They are always illuminated in part, never entirely. That is their condition and ours, watching them. The back of a head, a right hand with outstretched finger, a beautiful line curving from neck to left shoulder, are visible, highlighted. The whole figure is not: it remains ultimately unknowable, as it is, Wilson seems to believe, in our daily experience outside the theatre.[12]

On July 21, in Lepercq, Wilson starts the second day of blocking rehearsal by saying in a quiet voice, "Places, everyone." Rehearsals began formally only a few days ago, with one of the two casts seated at table reading the text aloud and pausing to discuss its possible meanings. In rehearsal the director neither imposes nor privileges any particular interpretation of the situation, relationships, implications of his own text. For example, in Part A of *Golden Windows*, character "2" refers to "jim bob."[13] The unpunctuated script does not make clear whether this is one name or two. In fact, the two actresses alternating in the role make different choices: one pauses to indicate separate identities for "jim" and "bob," and the other delivers the line so as to ensure that "jim bob" designates a single person. Wilson never comments on these differing interpretations and they remain distinct in performance.

While Hans Peter Kuhn makes arrangements to play the prerecorded music of the overture, Wilson walks over to Charles Whiteside, who is lying on his back on the floor, picks up his legs and moves them slightly, then slightly rearranges the position of the actor's hands. Suddenly the director himself lies down next to the actor, remains silent. He walks back to his director's table, looks at the actor, returns, rearranges slightly the actor's head and body. Meanwhile production stage manager Charlie Otte marks with tape on the floor the revised position of the top of the actor's head. Returning to his table, Wilson looks again at the actor on the floor and returns to rearrange his hands and arms slightly.

The director walks back to his table, stands silently, looking. There is a moment of total stillness in the room. Still standing by the side of his chair in what would be first row center, orchestra, the director makes a small clicking sound with two thick wooden sticks and Hans Peter Kuhn plays the prerecorded music of the overture. After a few minutes the director says, "Lights are coming up," then "Lights complete." The actor begins to whistle. Wilson comments, "Too fast. Eyes closed." He walks toward the stage right edge of the playing area to stand near assistant director Julia Gillett, looks at the actor, returns to his former position, says, "Eyes open." Charlie Otte reads aloud a stage direction to Kimberly Farr, who will enter the playing area from a small sentry-like house upstage, "Four short laughs." Otte tells the actress when to stop laughing and tells the actor to stop whistling. Wilson adds, "I think the eyes should close when the whistling stops." Otte now says, "Open door, 24 seconds." This is the precise timing of the stage direction, "[the] door opens slowly," followed by the further direction, "a shadow grows slowly from doorway of house."[14]

Only in the October lighting rehearsals is this staging fully rendered. In the darkened Carey Playhouse the door of the little house is opened slowly by an invisible member of the stage crew[15] and a diagonal shaft of light emerges in the shape of a funnel; then a shadow appears in the shape of a human figure. There is a temporary blackout and "4" appears outside the house on the same downstage diagonal.

What is merely an arbitrary pause in the Lepercq rehearsal is a stunning moment in performance, an explicit dramatization of the role of light in Wilson's theatre. Speaking of *Golden Windows*, Wilson says: "Light plays an integral role in the work. It's like an actor."[16] During rehearsals in the Carey Playhouse, the director tells me, "Lights are to me an essential element, as essential as anything else. . . . Lighting that glass [points to a glass lit near the edge of the stage] is as important as anything else."[17] At one point, just before midnight, near the end of a long lighting rehearsal, Wilson says, "David, your sleeve is getting in John . . . [Bowman's] light!" David Warrilow shivers slightly, says to me later:

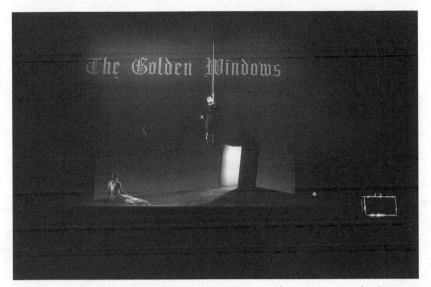

Fig. 8.2. Scene from The Golden Windows. *Left to right: Kimberly Farr, John Bowman. Photograph by Johan Elbers.*

> Yes, that was a violation. . . . Light is like a three-dimensional object. It has presence, weight, power. It takes up space and it demands respect. . . . If an actor doesn't find his light properly, he won't create properly and fully a sense of theatrical presence. It's *not* just a matter of vanity.[18]

Shortly before *The Golden Windows* opens, while the stage of the Carey Playhouse is unexpectedly empty in preparation for a runthrough, I ask associate lighting designer Ken Tabachnik if I might be allowed to experience the effects of the lighting Wilson has established. He says, "Sure," and immediately calls for #87, the strongest light in the production, one which is focused on Warrilow as he opens the play seated on his bench downstage right. I kneel, just as the lighting designer demonstrates, so that I can feel the light in exactly the position the actor does. I ask if David Warrilow must look directly into the light at any point and the designer says, "Yes." I do. It is a surprisingly strong, warm, palpable presence. It seems both an obstacle to concentration and a focus for it, disorienting and yet orienting. It is something that draws and attracts me, makes me (though I am not

an actress) want to play to or with or against it. It is something
that must be acknowledged, that cannot be ignored.

On July 21 in Lepercq, after an appropriate pause for the
gradual entrance of the light—the as yet missing member of the
company—"4" emerges from the house as "3" reads aloud his
lines from his position lying on the floor. Wilson stands up, his
arms and hands seemingly involuntarily taking on the silent
gestures of the actress playing "4." Then he physically moves
Kimberly Farr's arms and hands into the positions he wants; the
actress makes notes in her script. To Charles Whiteside playing
"3," he says, "Give a loud shout, 'No!' " ("NO" is in capital letters
in the script) and shouts the word himself. The air conditioning
is now turned down and the actors' microphones are turned
on. As the actress begins her silent arm and hand gestures, the
director makes seemingly exploratory movements with his own
hands, then walks into the playing area to adjust the position of
the actress' left arm and hand. He remains standing by her side,
demonstrating gestures as she moves her arm and hand, then
again physically repositions her left arm and hand. There is utter
stillness in the rehearsal room. The director returns to his seat,
and the production stage manager says, "Stand by." Then Wilson
walks back into the playing area, readjusts the position of the
actress' left arm and hand, and remains by her side, demonstrating with his own arm and hand as she moves hers. He then
moves downstage on a diagonal to look at her. Finally he returns
to his director's table. Standing behind it, he says to the actress:
"A little more space under the right arm, just a bit."

In his blocking directions Wilson is characteristically concerned with "the space around the movement" : "the space under
the arm." It is part of his concern with ways of seeing: "In the
theatre you have to always fill the auditorium with a presence.
. . . The weight of that gesture has to get to the exit signs. And
the space around it helps us to see it. . . . as I've said many times
. . . a small dot in a large room . . . will fill the room simply
because of the space around it. Like Sheryl . . . [Sutton's] tiny
little hand gesture in *Einstein [on the Beach]*."[19]

The blocking rehearsal continues. Now the actor playing "3"
has difficulty with a particularly intricate physical turn and re-
balancing of the body. Wilson walks into the playing area and
tries, with hesitation, to perform the movement while the assistant director reads him her notes on the position. As he finally
executes the complicated choreography, the director for a mo-

ment seems almost to have forgotten the actor. He seems intently in touch with some other dimension in which this work, his theatre, lives fully. Then quickly turning toward the actor, he watches him, saying, "We'll work on it. . . . We'll get it. . . . It's difficult. . . . It shouldn't look too ballet [sic]." The actor continues to move across the stage and the director, unseen by the actor, makes the same movements standing in place behind his table. The actor sits on a bench, downstage left, as indicated in the script, making notes on his blocking. The director returns to the actor's earlier position, downstage right, again executes the intricate turn and moves across the playing area toward the actor. Neither seems aware of the other, yet director and actor are both in the playing area working with intense concentration on the same moment in the visual script.

Shortly after this, as Kimberly Farr performs a kind of aria of silent gestures, Wilson stands in front of his director's table just outside the tape mark indicating the edge of the playing area, enacting her gestures in a kind of liminal space neither quite the director's nor the actress'. Farr, head down, focused on her own choreography, does not notice the director, who continues nonetheless to "perform" her gestures, sometimes pausing to watch her. There is no role reversal (actress demonstrates; director imitates). In fact, there is no obvious exchange or interchange at all, and yet director and actress seem somehow "joined" in an unexpected way, a way that replicates the relationships of "characters" in the play. Now the actress stands with her left hand raised, her back to the audience; the director stands behind her in the same position downstage. Neither seemingly relates to the other: together they create whatever lines of force exist on the "stage" of the Lepercq Space.

In designating subcategories of Wilson's blocking technique, more various than those of any other director I observe, I find myself resorting to the following system which of necessity allows some overlap.

> Bp: physically positioning or repositioning the body or parts of the body of the actor
>
> Be: experiencing the blocking with the actor, usually in the playing area[20]
>
> Bes: exploring blocking for himself[21]
>
> Bd: demonstrating blocking for a watching actor

Bde: demonstrating blocking for an actor who does not or cannot see the demonstration

Bc: verbal blocking directions conveyed, at times collaboratively, without interrupting the scene[22]

Bdda: blocking as a dance of director and actor[23]

Bim: blocking as implicit metaphor for the actor's situation and the director's role in rehearsal[24]

Movement in *Golden Windows* is timed to the millisecond. Charlie Otte, rehearsing the cast one morning in the absence of the director, tells an actress with deadly seriousness that her gesture is "about a half millisecond behind [another actor's gesture]." The exact trajectory and resting points of diagonal crosses are marked with tape on the floor of the playing area. Flashlights are used to signal when the actress playing "2" has completed a precisely timed laugh. Gestures which might naturally occur simultaneously are made sequential: "Gaby, break it down so we have time to register each thing. Hold everything at least four seconds. Just open the eyes. Hold four seconds. Don't also move the head. It's too complicated." At the same time Wilson says, as he enters the playing area, "I walk and I stop, but still with a sense of movement. . . . Usually it takes about thirty seconds for an audience to get a mental register [of the actor's movement]. . . . If you're speaking a line, especially in a text as fragmented as this one, the silence is a continuation of sound. . . . Whether you're speaking or not speaking, it's the same thing. John Cage says there's no such thing as silence. . . . When you stop speaking, you're still always aware of sound. It's one continuous movement. It's not stop and start. And the same with [physical] movement [as with sound]." The effect Wilson creates is most accurately described by dance critic Anna Kisselgoff reviewing his production of *Le Martyre de Saint-Sébastien:* it is "slowed-down stage time with activity occurring within stillness."[25]

But how is the actor to inhabit an unnamed "character" whose movements and gestures have not in any single case been generated by the performer in rehearsal? Many speeches in the play are delivered with the actors' backs to the audience.[26] Lines alluding to love, fear of loss, murder, mourning receive no interpretive comment from the director. The verbal text of *Golden Windows* itself performs the directorial function of interrupter: its dissociated language repeatedly disrupts an actor's attempt to sustain an objective or through-line. An example is the following unpunctuated speech of "2" at the end of Part Two: "there is nothing wrong there will be the fog is in here everywhere it is not necessary for you to be anything do you think my children will know me oh yes in a moment . . . now what is that so many many 430 stars so so here is what happening."[27] In a way that recalls Peter Quince's redistributed punctuation in his Prologue to the Pyramus and Thisby play at the end of *A Midsummer Night's Dream*, the actress in determining her own placement of pauses and full stops shapes the way the speech is heard by the audience. Rendered quite differently by Jane Hoffman and Gaby Rodgers, this passage is inexplicably poignant in performance.

Wilson avoids words like "objective," "motivate," "justify," "inner life." Speaking more in painterly than in psychological terms, the director tells John Bowman ("3") to deliver one line with a very "hot texture," the next line with a "cold texture." Early in rehearsal my ears perk up when I hear Wilson say to the production stage manager, "Charlie, something is not right in this relationship," only to add, "Kimberly should be more in this diagonal. David should be seated here."

Stefan Brecht writes of his experience as an actor in Wilson's production of *A Letter for Queen Victoria* (1974–75), "The mind is immersed in the body, at its service. . . . The very precise choreography, a lengthily developed sense of what the others are doing at any given moment—body awareness—facilitate timing even more than in any other theatre. . . . The actions required are . . . so slow that the performer finds himself engaging in them for their own sake."[28] As rehearsals of *The Golden Windows* continue, precise hand and arm gestures, like the slowed-down movement through space, become more and more an essential part of the theatrical expression, not as physical enactments or representations of the perceived significance of the spoken text but as visual components that speak for themselves.[29]

In rehearsing choreographed gestures and movements with extraordinary discipline and utter concentration, the actors seem to appropriate a new vocabulary. As David Warrilow says to me after rehearsal on July 21, "At first the gestures which we were given and not invited to create or individually modify seemed arbitrary but we're in the process of making them . . . our own 'other' vocabulary." Actors in Wilson's rehearsals enter a process of precisely nuanced articulations in which a gesture caught for a moment in warm or cold light is no more and no less important than a voice shaded by a warm or cold tone. The actors "get into a position" whose expressivity, in different configurations, demands proper lighting to be properly seen; their spatial relations are largely geometric. The comment of lighting designer Jennifer Tipton, addressing the cast during rehearsals of *Hamletmachine*, seems illuminating here: "May I add it's easy for human beings to cheat but light goes in straight lines."

There is a kind of communication that never takes place between the director and cast. At one point Gaby Rodgers confers with Wilson about "2": "I think she's searching for her basic identity. . . ." The director says nothing. Rehearsal continues. Near the end of the scene, "2" says to the audience, "i am going to figure this character out."[30] Interviewed during rehearsals of *Hamletmachine*, Wilson says , "How an actor fills a gesture remains mysterious," adding that one actor had "built a whole subtext of what's going on ["why he's doing what he's doing"], but I didn't feel I had to understand what he was thinking."[31]

If Wilson has no interest in the actor's subtext, actors themselves are often protective of their privacy. During the August rehearsals of *Golden Windows* the director says to Jane Hoffman: "It's so curious: you're smiling at him [David Warrilow] right now" (as the actor hands her a gun). The actress replies, "Well, *I* know why I'm smiling but I'm not going to tell you."[32] Actors often choose not to reveal what it is that finally meets the needs of the event the director is staging. It is not necessarily what the director says or feels or knows that "works" for the actor, though there is a necessary interchange between them. Each has certain inexpressible "secrets" but the actor needs privacy in an absolute sense. Appropriately, it is just this bargain that allows Wilson's vision to live only when it draws life from a repository in actors that remains as mysterious and unknowable as the "characters" they inhabit.

Wilson has said of *The Golden Windows*,

> The visual book was written with no regard to the text. The text was written with no regard to the visual. And then they were put together. You can find relationships between the two, but the visual does not necessarily decorate the text. I made the gestures without thinking about what the text was saying. Do this gesture here, I told the actor, and this gesture here. The actor was given the gestures at the beginning of rehearsals

like he would be given choreography. He learned the gestures
independently of the text. He may *find* a relationship, but. . . .
The Golden Windows is a little like having a radio play and a
silent movie put together. They don't have to share the same
text.[33]

His directions in rehearsal, "More space under your chin. Head
up. Eyes closed," provide the actors with no access to the meaning of either the gestures or the verbal text. Precisely positioned
bodies and parts of bodies seem at first not to give expression to
the actors' feelings or intentions. An actor can "establish" a gesture but it is not so easy to "justify" it. In a sense, the actors
themselves do not endow any of their gestures with significance.

Jane Hoffman is one of the founding members of the Actors
Studio and the Ensemble Studio Theatre. She has performed on
and off Broadway, in film and on major network television. Her
experience, as I observe it in rehearsal of *Golden Windows*, may
illustrate the dilemma Robert Wilson poses for the professionally
trained actress. In early August I watch her execute odd haunting
gestures, beautiful in their precise quirkiness. Taking exactly one
minute and forty-five seconds, she walks three steps from left to
right, holding a revolver, as flashlight beams from the side of the
playing area cue her. Complimented by the director ("Excellent"), the actress nods skeptically, "If I can remember it. And
then I'll find things later." The actress has followed blocking
directions step by step with grace and good humor. She has "set"
the surface without finding out what, if anything, is below it. A
little later I hear her say to assistant to the director Ann-Christin
Rommen, "So much of it is *non sequitur*. I have to make up things
to put in."

During rehearsal the next day, the actress, her back turned
toward David Warrilow as he delivers his lines while artificially
amplified, asks if the actor is speaking live or if she is hearing
his prerecorded voice on tape. Warrilow laughingly replies,
"Sometimes I don't know either!" But it is a genuine problem for
actor and audience. Earlier I find myself asking Cynthia Babak
which of the simultaneous sounds of a woman crying and a
woman laughing for fifteen seconds is prerecorded. The actress
is surprised that it is not clear to the auditor that her crying
is live. As in the Akalaitis and LeCompte rehearsals, artificial
amplification and prerecorded tapes of the actors' voices are
disorienting (only the production soundman knows for sure);

such effects reflect and create the postmodern dislocation of character. In *The Golden Windows*, personality is decentered or absent; in the unpunctuated script, *i* is always lower case. Speakers, played by alternate casts, are listed either as "1," "2," "3," or as "E1," "E2," "E3," if the voice is electronically produced. The boundary between what is "inside" and what is "outside" is put in question. Speech issues from an indeterminate source, cannot be precisely located in terms of either actor or character. During rehearsal the text of *Golden Windows* almost seems to have found an alternative performance mode when the production stage manager reads the lines aloud, not differentiating individually assigned speeches by tone or pacing, while the actors perform silently, without sound tape.

At one point Hoffman raises the kind of question often posed in the Chekhov rehearsals: "Is this line [delivered] to her [Cynthia Babak]?" Wilson replies slowly and hesitantly, "Well, you can do it to her if you want." When Babak then asks how much she takes in of Hoffman, Wilson hedges, "You can see her or not see her. She can be in your mind. It can be so many things. She can be in your way. Whatever you want. What do you think?" After a few minutes of conversation, I hear Babak say, "Well, I'll experiment with several different things." When Gaby Rodgers rehearses the role of "2" a few days earlier, Wilson makes the same kind of comment to Babak: "Maybe you're Gaby's young self, or her daughter, or her lover, or her rival. Any one or all. I don't know what. You'll have to decide."

Later that day Wilson carefully rehearses the precise timing of Hoffman's blocking and then says, as he leaves the playing area, "Put the lines in wherever you like." During lighting rehearsals the words in the text function as markers of time passing, almost as spaces between lit tableaux representing the multiple different changing images we take in and imprint in any given moment of our lives.

"What is acting?" Wilson asks rhetorically during a break, and answers: "Presenting a character in time and space and textures." David Warrilow says of the director, "He postulates with his lines of force on the stage the same kinds of dynamic that other playwrights do with constructed scenes. . . . A diagram of a tennis match is closer to a Wilson piece [than is a scripted naturalistic dialogue]." Wilson's theatre presents a kind of movement that, like music, is distinguished from chaos by its being perceived as organized. He has very little interest in stasis. His own bodily demonstrations for the actor in rehearsal, like his works in performance, seem to express the fluidity of the self in space and time. To the cast, on the next to last day of rehearsal in the Lepercq Space, the director says, "You have to always be present in theatre. There's always a continuum, always one line."

Explaining his double casting of three of the four roles in *Golden Windows*, Wilson tells the company: "It's two different ways of looking at the same thing. In this work we don't know what the story is or what the subtext is or where the punctuation goes. The actor, in a sense, brings his character to the script." It may be that controlling movement and gesture while liberating individual interpretation on the part of both actor and audience is Wilson's way of participating in and rejecting what he considers the dictatorial aspects of the directorial role.[34] For Wilson, each new actor cast is a new way of looking, an unarticulated new reading of the text. In a paradoxical way, Wilson is the most actor-centered of all the directors I observe in that the individual actor's presence *is* the only character his scripts ever legitimate.

In the playscript there is a stage direction indicating that "2" laughs for one minute.[35] During rehearsal the laugh is extended to two minutes. With no further instructions from the director, each actress playing "2" treats an initially excruciatingly difficult stage direction very differently. Jane Hoffman laughs infectiously, bringing laughter to the onlookers, laughter feeding laughter, then stops on cue. Gaby Rodgers uses her laugh as a playfully seductive attempt to affect "3," who appears above her, hanging on a rope. She first laughs up at him to provoke response, then seems to laugh at him because he does not respond, then laughs provocatively again, with small pauses between laugh sequences. These individual treatments are retained in performance on alternate evenings. Clearly Wilson's kind of theatre is not a totally forbidding fortress to actors who prefer to work with the "inner motivation" he does not solicit.[36]

"You look at a face," Wilson says to me during lighting rehearsals. "Very simply it's a mask. Consider the way we think: it doesn't have a linear structure, a beginning, middle, end. It's illogical, isn't it? The whole stage is a mask for the head. . . . The stage picture is the mask for what we hear. . . . Listen to the text. It's filled with violence, tension; it changes all the time, like molecules; it can go in any direction. All this beneath the 'beautiful' visual surface." Looking out from the darkened auditorium at the lit set which onlooker after onlooker has praised with the single word, "beautiful," during the two weeks of technical rehearsals, the director says, "I don't want that to be totally 'beautiful.' I'd like a scratch somewhere. I'd like to throw a bit of mud at it, paint a red swatch across it."[37]

During a lull in a sound runthrough, while a problem in amplification is being adjusted, Kimberly Farr ("4"), tired of standing, sits down next to John Bowman ("3"), momentarily not hanging on the rope. Suddenly there on the stage is the expected romantic image always resisted in the play. The beautiful young blond-haired woman in the elegant white gown sits next to the intense, dark-haired young man in black tuxedo, on a bench under a lovely blue star-spangled sky. The rehearsal situation foregrounds what is absent in the text, and makes clear a part of the play's "meaning," which is this very erasure of the conventional love story. In Part B of *Golden Windows*, an older couple, elegantly dressed, passes a shining object on a luminous handkerchief from one (the man) to the other (the woman). What is the object? A revolver. The visual beauty of Robert Wilson's theatre is never meant to be inclusive. In context, it is at times jarringly "scratched."

Wilson has said, "I am always concerned with how the total stage picture looks at any given moment. The placement and design (shape, proportion, materials) of furniture, the color, fabric, and design of costumes, placement and content of film, paths and gestures of performers, and lighting were all major considerations, no less important than the dialog or music."[38] In the rehearsal of *Golden Windows*, especially in technical rehearsals, these elements often war for attention from the director and yet they are all utterly dependent on each other. When a bench is misplaced, or a microphone goes off, or a special is not turned on at the right moment, or a prop is missing, or an actor fails to appear in his appointed position,[39] the production is helplessly diminished. As performance approaches, brilliant lighting effects, a superbly edited and re-edited sound track, elegantly designed costumes,[40] striking stage effects (shooting stars, falling boulders, and the *coup de théâtre*, an earthquake which splits the stage in two), highly disciplined and surprisingly vital acting with its understated comic nuances are brought to readiness. Never are all these elements perfectly realized in any single rehearsal runthrough (as is characteristic of all the productions I observe), but an ideal performance has been charted, even enacted, over a series of rehearsals. Any fully realized moment in rehearsal is indeed a moment. Unlike the film director who only needs to get it right once before final cut, the theatre director in rehearsal, however meticulous, is always revealed to be engaged in "a life-force process."[41]

At times even more clearly than the prolonged *Golden Windows* rehearsal, the three-and-a-half week rehearsal of *Hamletmachine* with fifteen student actors illuminates Wilson's directorial style. Heiner Müller's six-page text calls into question the nature of "character" by calling into question the concept of role as a set of speeches designated by the same speech-tag. The actor playing Hamlet announces at one point that he was Macbeth; Ophelia's final speech begins, "This is Electra speaking."[42] Certain stage directions announce themselves as not designed to be rendered literally: "*He steps into the armor, splits with the ax the heads of Marx, Lenin, Mao. Snow. Ice Age.*"[43] The play is an open invitation to directorial reinscribing even before questions of verbal revisions are raised.[44]

My first day of observing the *Hamletmachine* rehearsals, which take place in the tiny performance space itself, is also the first day the actors attempt to speak the text accompanying blocking they have been rehearsing silently for nearly a week. Wilson's opening words to the cast on April 18, 1986, are: "Let's try to put the text on everything."[45] The actors have been taking their cues from the sounds of small wooden sticks clicked by the director to indicate the timing of different movements and tableaux.

In the rehearsal of *Hamletmachine*, as in rehearsal of *Golden Windows*, the director initially removes the interpretive grounding of actors' work on a playtext and replaces it with choreographed movements, as if he is preparing a silent film. For Wilson there are "two primary ways in which we relate to one another":

> What I try to set up in the theatre is a situation where I can hear, and where I can see. . . . And so often I can't hear. Because what I'm seeing is interfering. And I can't see because what I'm hearing is preventing me from seeing. And we hear and see as blind people and as deaf people and as hearing and seeing people all the time. This man is blinking his eyes, so for split seconds perhaps he is seeing interiorly [sic]. . . . [In] this theatre that I do, we try to set up a situation where there is simply time for interior reflection. . . . What happens for me is that theatre frequently becomes too aggressive. . . . the box,

the frame, is rigidly defined for the audio screen and the visual screen. So if we can remove the edges of the frame, we have a different way of seeing and hearing.[46]

To the student actors rehearsing *Hamletmachine*, he says, "You're on stage from beginning to end, and whether you're speaking or not speaking, moving or not moving, it's just one thing going on, always."

On the one hand, Wilson's *Hamletmachine* rehearsals are a recapitulation of our experience of a playtext in the theatre: we see, then we hear, effects to which we attribute causes.[47] On the other hand, the rehearsal experience of both *Golden Windows* and *Hamletmachine* is a kind of Möbius strip in perpetual motion: "one continuous movement [of silence and sound, activity and stillness]," "always a continuum, always one line," "just one thing going on, always." The director cautions the cast of *Hamletmachine*, "The text shouldn't erupt: it's part of the continuum."

In the first week of rehearsal Wilson explores and establishes a multi-perspectival blocking of four of the five parts of Müller's text. In each of these parts, while the actors remain in the same pattern in relation to each other, the patterns themselves rotate as if the audience were circling the playing area. For example, in part one, we watch Lisa Brosnahan walk upstage, her back toward us, as she arrives at a high stepladder substituting for a tree. Jennifer Rohn (Ophelia) faces the audience directly while three actresses—Alana Adena Teichman, Jennifer Gilley, Jyllian Gunther—sit behind a table at a diagonal to the audience, slowly smiling. Allison DeSalvo is seated in a swivel chair downstage, her face in profile. Several other actors stand with their backs to the audience. In part four, Jennifer Rohn stands with her back to the audience while the three actresses seated at a diagonal smile, unseen, at the upstage wall. The actress who will lean against a "tree" now walks downstage. The positions of all the other actors are also reversed in relation to the audience but remain in exactly the same relation to each other.

These perspectival shifts, conceived by Wilson as rehearsal begins,[48] are fascinating. The stage picture presents figures and objects from all angles—front, back, sides—but in slow motion. As each new perspective is staged, the spectator supplements the new visual field with remembered images of what was previously perceptible to the eye but is now obscured so that as the play

Fig. 8.3. Scene from Hamletmachine. *Actors: Kevin Kuhlke (in silhouette); Alana Adena Teichman, Jennifer Gilley, Jyllian Gunther (at table); Lisa Brosnahan (leaning into tree); Jennifer Rohn (standing). Photograph by Beatriz Schiller.*

Fig. 8.4. Scene from Hamletmachine *(perspectival shift). Kevin Kuhlke, Jennifer Rohn, Alana Adena Teichman, Jennifer Gilley, Jyllian Gunther, Allison DeSalvo (in swivel chair). Photograph by Beatriz Schiller.*

progresses one "sees" both what is literally visible and what is hidden. The stage picture cumulatively seems to reveal all its secrets, all its pictorial aspects, and, at the same time, continually reminds us that it hides as much as it exposes. In this respect, it is an appropriate, if not exquisite, allusion to the Shakespearean *Hamlet* behind Müller's *Hamletmachine* as well as to the nature of the theatrical event itself.

In Wilson's staging of the text, a position is a role. Sometimes these "roles" are interchangeable, as illustrated at one point in rehearsal when five male actors switch positions. Although not so obvious as to be noticed by critics in their reviews of *Hamletmachine*, the standing position of the actors is uniform: left leg straight, left foot squarely on the floor; right knee bent; right heel lifted off the floor so that it is almost perpendicular to the heel of the left foot.[49] One actor, Leif Tilden, makes a hopscotching entrance whose final hop leaves him balanced on his left leg while his right leg is crooked backward, bent upward at the knee, with the right foot high in the air. His sole function in the entire play is to "get into a position," an exaggerated reprise of that of every actor on stage.

During the third part of *Hamletmachine*, a screen on the stage blocks the audience's view of the actors who sit upstage behind it. Müller's words appear as subtitles while the cast now performs on film in their characteristic configurations, accompanied by the recorded voice of Jessye Norman singing Schubert's *Der Zwerg*. Toward the very end of part three the images of the actors become transformed into a series of squares within a larger square in the center of the screen which then becomes smaller and smaller until it is a tiny white blank. Throughout the performance two walls surrounding the stage are always covered with black curtains while a white screen conceals the third wall; the relation of black and white changes in each part of the play. The set and blocking of the final section, part five, return us to our original perspective, after which the entire stage is enclosed by white curtains and the actors must emerge from within this "box" to receive the audience's applause. Wilson is offering "a different way of seeing and hearing" actors who alternate between living presences in our midst and blips and blanks on a screen. They perform in a continuum in which verbal and visual scripts exist concurrently without becoming equivalencies.[50]

The concept of a role as a set of speeches designated by the same speech-tag is called into question by both playwright and director. In Wilson's rehearsals, as in Müller's own German production of *Hamletmachine* the preceding year, lines in the text are not necessarily distributed sequentially to a single speaker even when they occur in a single speech. As director reinscribing his own text, Müller distributed lines differently from Wilson.[51] As playwright he establishes indeterminacy of speaker in the very first speech-tag: "FAMILY SCRAPBOOK." The speech-tag at the beginning of part two reads: "OPHELIA (CHORUS/HAMLET)." In part four Wilson has the actress playing Ophelia deliver lines assigned in the text to "THE ACTOR PLAYING HAMLET" (for example, the line, "Give us this day our daily murder").[52]

Like Foreman rehearsing *Birth of the Poet* and Sellars rehearsing *Saint Antony*, Wilson alters our hearing of the verbal text not only by redistributing lines and even parts of lines in the play to various actors but by asking that the stage directions be read aloud. He further alienates the expected sounds of the play by asking that certain lines be repeated as many as seven times at precisely timed intervals. Finally, he encourages what he calls "a microphone voice" (most of the actors' voices are artificially amplified).

His directions to the actors as they read their lines aloud are fairly uniform: "Colder. Flatter. . . . Too emotional. Too expressive. . . . Simpler, colder, harder. . . . Too forced. . . . Not using a microphone voice." The timing of speeches is as precisely established as the timing of movements. Directing Thomas Tenney to turn his head away from the audience while Allison DeSalvo and the three actresses seated at the table simultaneously turn their heads toward the audience in preparation for their comically eerie smile, Wilson says to the actresses: "You pause seven counts. . . . Smile at five [counts]. . . . Dissolve the smile in three seconds. Turn the head in four seconds," and to the actor: "Pause in four, turn back in five." (The "count" is approximately equal to one second.)

A few minutes earlier the director says to Thomas Tenney, "Repeat that line seven times, with five, then six, then seven, then eight second intervals." The actor begins, "After the fall of the monument. . . ."[53] The director interrupts, "Your count's off," and asks the actor to count out loud from one to six. After the actor complies, Wilson says, "You're a little slow. Do it again," and after the second rendition comments, "Good, as long as you're consistent." The actor explains, "I'm trying to count the

number of times I say . . . [the line], *and* then count the number
of seconds in the interval, so it's hard." The director, along with
the cast, laughs, saying, "We're just beginning," and does not
interrupt again. The difficulty Tenney experiences is that of an
actor beginning a Wilson rehearsal, not merely that of a beginning actor.[54]

Actors' voices are merely one element of the aural environment
the director is creating. Other acoustical elements are rehearsed
equally carefully, not in a sound studio but in the performance
space during the time allotted for rehearsal with the actors. Like
lighting, non-human sounds are treated as components whose
contribution to the rehearsal work is very much like that of
members of the company.

Late one evening, on April 25, 1986, the cast assembles to
rehearse *Hamletmachine* with Heiner Müller present. Wilson
spends almost an hour and a half selecting and arranging prerecorded sounds. In the dimension of sound alone, the process of
rehearsal exploration continues. For two weeks taped music and
song have been heard as background to choreographed movement with and without spoken text. Now Wilson experiments
with various intermixtures of new sounds: "wolves," "dogs," "police sirens," "machine guns," "swamp sounds" (bird whistles and
frog croaks), "phone," "bell," "crows." From the point of view of
the student actors, some of whom have already requested more
workthroughs,[55] it might seem that the director could better use
their time during the relatively brief rehearsal period. But it
seems clear that Wilson can only "hear" these sounds in their
presence. As in Akalaitis' workshop production of *The Voyage of
the Beagle*, the space of the actual performance is the space of
experimentation. In the midst of the playwright, the entire cast,
the dramaturgs, assistant directors, stage manager and assistant
stage managers, sound technicians, and lighting designer Jennifer Tipton (who is present virtually throughout rehearsals), Wilson unselfconsciously directs a "sound workthrough."[56]

On the one hand, the director is the autocrat, making all the
decisions for the group attending him. On the other hand, as
one observes him, he seems a listener among listeners, his gaze
inward as well as outward. He stands with his head in his hands,
facing Heiner Müller and leaning in the playwright's direction,
his eyes closed. It seems as if for a moment Wilson creates a
sense of solitude, but that is a state very different from solitary
creating. Even now, behind his back, one actress is convulsing

the cast with her seated renditions of the tango as tango music is played. The director turns, sees the actress' performance, grins broadly. In his most withdrawn moment the cast comes alive behind his back, at once listening and performing.

As the director mixes and doesn't quite match incongruous sounds, he presents a paradigm of his work with visual and verbal scripts. He begins, for example, by asking to hear the cries of "wolves" and "babies" separately, then together. The actors respond audibly to what they hear: "It's sexy." "It's nasty." The voices of the cast are part of the hearing experience of the director selecting sounds that will interpenetrate their vocalizations and movements. As Wilson continues to experiment, "also put in the machine guns," "wolves a little louder," he begins to make adjustments of sound levels and sound mixes in relation to the different qualities and timbre of individual actors' voices speaking lines from the text. The cast is quiet, less restless, as the director's work of aural mixing makes them feel more a part of the process, though only as one component among others.

After an hour Wilson begins to give instructions for precisely timed intervals of speech and silence, movement and stillness: "In fifteen seconds fade all the tapes except the machine gun. Then in seven seconds fade the machine gun. . . . Allison, you begin to fade your sound [the actress has been making a wordless, low, wailing noise, like that of wind or animals in the far distance]. . . . Bring in the machine gun. Keep the siren going throughout. . . . Seven seconds later add [the German song]. . . . Seven seconds later add the machine guns." When the sound assistant asks for a clarification of the last instruction, the director unexpectedly responds, "Whatever I've said, keep it going or I'll forget what's in my head." Like a performer improvising in rehearsal, the director is creating his own subtextual aural script of the play. It is not surprising that the playwright is now invited to play a directorial role. Asked by Wilson if the sounds are "decorating too much," Müller pauses, then responds, "Maybe too much. You'll find out," and Wilson replies, "I'll do it and you'll tell me."

Earlier, after a runthrough on April 25, his first day of observing Wilson's rehearsals, Müller says to the director: "I like the whole structure. And you've said everything I want to say about the way to speak it. . . . Part four is the most problematic. The problem is in the text." To the actors he says, "It sounds as if you know everything and that's not true. You could *use* your

innocence." On April 26, Müller spends about three to five minutes directing one actor's delivery of the last line in part one:
"Then let me eat your heart, Ophelia, which weeps my tears"
(54). He tries to encourage in this line, and elsewhere, a less
"tragic" reading, a rise in the voice at the end of the line, though
not the characteristic contemporary American rising inflection.

On the first day the actors add the verbal text to the blocking
they have rehearsed silently for a week, Wilson says, "With the
text [added], it's too overlaid. The action too much illustrates
[the language]." He muses, "Maybe I should have *started* with
the text and then added the rest." The cast laughs appreciatively
but the director's sense of trouble is genuine. Wilson has said, "I
think we lost the edges, or mysteries, of radio when we got films.
And we lost the edges, or mysteries, of silent film when we got
talking films. Because in a radio play one can imagine the pic-
tures. And in a silent movie one can imagine the text."[57] At
various points during early rehearsals Wilson alternates between
asking the actors to read their lines aloud as they perform and
asking them to rehearse the blocking soundlessly, so that at
unpredictable intervals one hears the director say, "No text,"
and the set becomes the scene of a silent movie. Later he says,
"Text," and the language is again "overlaid."

As rehearsals continue, Wilson makes many fine adjustments
in assignment of lines, vocal delivery, hand gestures, the tilt of
a head, body posture in seated and standing positions, the pacing
of both speech and movement. It is clear that staging and text,
with one notable exception, do not "illustrate," but are in suggestive indeterminate relation to, one another. For example, Allison
DeSalvo reads aloud the following stage directions, "*Unnoticed
by the actor playing Hamlet, stagehands place a refrigerator and
three TV-sets on the stage. Humming of the refrigerator. Three TV-
channels without sound.*"[58] These lines are punctuated by the
slow simultaneous smiling of the three actresses seated at the
table. Mel Gussow suggests that, "As a chorus, [these three
women] . . . could be a substitute for the three television screens
suggested in the text, or they could represent the witches from
'Macbeth.' "[59]

The one stage direction Wilson adheres to is the "*[t]earing of
the author's photograph.*"[60] The director demonstrates several
times for the actor the slow tearing of a piece of paper in front
of a microphone. It is characteristic of Wilson that even the
ripping of paper is to be accomplished in a particular way at a

particular pace and degree of loudness. That this is the sole stage direction Wilson follows literally is striking, especially given Müller's earlier remarks in a radio interview for *Deutschlandfunk*, April 9, 1982:

> At bottom, playwriting always means to me that a picture is torn, a picture of myself too. In one play one picture is torn, from this a new picture originates. And that has to be torn again. That is actually the process.[61]

In the performance of *Hamletmachine* that I witness on May 24, 1986, three actors each tear a piece of paper. The paper the third actor tears is visibly a photograph of the playwright. It seems particularly appropriate that Robert Wilson, reauthoring the text, repeats an action that signifies "the process" itself: the director too is implicated in the rending from which a new "picture" originates.

Fig. 9.1. Kevin Kline as Hamlet. Photograph by Martha Swope.

9

Liviu Ciulei Directs *Hamlet*

"It speaks. It isn't an empty gesture. It isn't a
furniture movement."

Liviu Ciulei was born in Bucharest where he began his theatrical career as actor, director, and designer. Ciulei's visual artistry, like that of Robert Wilson, has behind it formal training as an architect: he holds not only an M.A. in theatre from the Royal Academy of Music and Drama in Bucharest but also an M.A. in architecture. Ciulei was the Artistic Director of Romania's leading repertory company, the Bulandra Theater, for almost a decade, staging works of Shakespeare, Ibsen, Büchner, Gorky, and Brecht as well as plays by Eugene O'Neill and Tennessee Williams. He has acted in and directed a number of award-winning films, including *Forest of the Hanged* which received the award for Best Direction at the Cannes Festival in 1965. Since his 1974 American debut at the Arena Stage, Ciulei has directed and taught in this country. From 1980 to 1986 he served as Artistic Director of the Guthrie Theater. He has taught directing at Columbia University and in the graduate program at New York University's Tisch School of the Arts. In addition to his work in film and theatre, Ciulei has also directed operas, including Mozart's *Cosi fan tutte* and Berg's *Wozzeck.*

Ciulei's introduction to Shakespeare occurred at the age of thirteen when his Scottish nanny gave him the Oxford edition of the playwright's works, which is still in his bookcase in Bucharest. The first Shakespearean play he read was *Hamlet.* "I don't know how much I understood at thirteen, maybe a lot. Maybe now I know less. . . ." His first public acting was in the role of Puck in *A Midsummer Night's Dream.* Later he played Jacques in a production of *As You Like It* which he directed. He designed sets for *Othello* and *Dream* at the National Theater, as well as for *Hamlet.* "I had the great advantage and disadvantage of dealing with Shakespeare in a foreign language. You are dealing with many things but not with the words. You are dealing with the 'corset' but not the poetic equivalent, ever."[1]

Describing his direction of *Hamlet*, which I observe in rehearsal during the winter of 1986, Ciulei says that it was one of his "important failures," adding that while his Public Theater production of the play was politically clear, the protagonist was not: "I . . . [failed] to explain the kernel of the play, which is Hamlet."[2]

Kevin Kline, who performs the title role, praises the director while acknowledging tensions in the rehearsals of *Hamlet*:

> Something about . . . [Liviu Ciulei's] humanity and sensitivity and ideology has always touched me. I knew that who he is as a man and as an artist would influence the production in that it would be humanized by his 'form and pressure'. . . . [Ciulei] is brilliant . . . in being able to clarify through questions and discussion what the character is saying and doing in a given scene. . . . Some of the blocking he's given me I have eventually made my own. . . . For me the best work comes when the actor has a sense of ownership, responsibility for the work. . . . In general, I like to be left alone . . . so I can interpret it directly and the director can then make what I'm doing clear or clearer. This assumes general agreement between director and actor about what the play means. . . . The rehearsal process to me is a process of exploration and discovery. If it has already been discovered and is being explained to you in rehearsal, I get enraged. . . . Liviu has definite ideas and he also works from the actor's impulse. . . . The way I work sometimes is not to edit my impulses, to let out even silly impulses. In the *doing* of it you can discover that the scene is not just about what you thought it was about but is also about this and this and this and this. . . . The rehearsal process is the means by which the actor finds out what the scene is for *oneself*.

The actor regrets that the director at times corrects rehearsal work that is "obviously wrong": "I wish he knew . . . more [often] that I know it's wrong but it's a route to explore, to see how *not* to do it, to see where it takes me, so that eventually I can create an inevitability of choice . . . because it becomes the only place where I go." Kline adds, in a revealing postscript to the preceding remarks, "I don't believe in directors. They can go home. . . . I would have done a different Hamlet with a different director, of course. All the direction in the world cannot come near the size of that role. Eventually, it will be *my* Hamlet. At least I hope it will."[3]

The following pages highlight characteristic or suggestive moments in Liviu Ciulei's rehearsals of *Hamlet* on the Newman stage at the Public Theater and later in a seventh floor studio at 890 Broadway in lower Manhattan. Rehearsals begin on January 14, 1986, with the first preview scheduled for February 18. The production remains in preview for several weeks, opening officially on March 6, 1986. The run is sold out and eventually extended. Kevin Kline, who receives generally favorable reviews, varies his acting choices in every performance from the first preview to the end of the run.[4]

On January 25, 1986, my first day of observing rehearsal in the Newman Theater, Ciulei scrupulously rehearses the blocking of Polonius's entrance in II. i, as indicated in his opening line, "Give him this money and these notes, Reynaldo." The director, first inquiring of the actor, "Can I show you?" physically demonstrates the brisk entrance of a man in a hurry as he hands money and missives for his son to a servant. Earlier he impersonated Reynaldo, sitting with tight knees and "controlled movement" of his hands, placing a hand on the table in front of him and then drawing it back. The actor watched intently, did not immediately imitate the director. When these actions are later performed, there is no attempt, as in a Robert Wilson rehearsal, to reproduce the physical demonstration centimeter by centimeter. Ciulei, however, enunciates the principle underlying his time-consuming concern with the physical details[5] of every staged moment: "the smaller, the more suggestive."

Throughout rehearsal Ciulei suggests minute physical adjustments that establish in an instant a particular characterization of the speaker or the situation in the same way that diction and tone of voice do. At times what the director himself calls "those realistic Ciulei details" seem merely pictorial or arbitrary, an interruption or interception of the actors' own explorations in rehearsal. At other times this fastidious detailing of tiny gestural moments is a sensitive barometer of an otherwise unnoticed network of continually shifting implications.

What might seem a quibble, for example, occurs on February 7, 1986, during rehearsal in the lower Broadway studio, when Priscilla Smith, playing Gertrude, moves apart from Harris Yulin's Claudius as he describes "Hamlet's transformation" to Ro-

sencrantz and Guildenstern (II.ii.5). Ciulei, calling her improvised blocking "too much of a statement," cautions the actress
not to move so quickly. The actress argues that her action is "a
worried movement" on behalf of her son, not a turning away
from her new husband. The director agrees. Together Ciulei and
Smith work out the timing and quality of the actress' blocking.

What is at stake is the precariously poised position of the
Queen. For Gertrude a movement indicative of worried concern
for Hamlet is always on the verge of becoming a move away from
Claudius. In considering so closely a nuance in blocking, Ciulei
is working not with one character but with three relationships.
By the very last scene of the play, when Gertrude drinks from
Hamlet's poisoned cup, disregarding Claudius's command, "Gertrude, do not drink" (V. ii. 292), she completes the trajectory in
which a movement of concern for the one becomes a movement
away from the other.

During a break in rehearsal of III.iv,[6] Smith tells Ciulei that
when Hamlet describes his father ("See what a grace was seated
on this brow:/ Hyperion's curls, the front of Jove himself," 56–
57), she sees the elder Hamlet's image in the face of the son. (In
the rehearsal preceding the break, Smith gazed steadily at Kline
as he delivered these lines.) The actress suggests that Hamlet
touch Gertrude's cheek before presenting the portrait of her first
husband. Ciulei replies, "No, you touch his face." The actress sees
his point and agrees. The shaping of every small suggestive detail
in this production matters: who touches whose face is an inscribing of relationship.

At times Ciulei's directorial suggestions of physical movements and gestures pointedly "illustrate" the playtext. After he
has killed Polonius Hamlet says to Gertrude, "Leave wringing of
your hands" (III.iv.35). When Smith is asked by Ciulei to wring
her hands, she responds, "Really, you want me to wring my
hands? Oh no, it isn't right." She complies after the director later
insists that the omission of this action is a "disregarding of the
text."

On another occasion, however, Ciulei openly admits that a
"directorial gesture is forced," when he asks Smith to take off
her wig in III.iv, revealing Gertrude's grey hair underneath. In
Ciulei's production Gertrude wears a brown wig, removing it
only in III.iv, before confronting Hamlet. Smith asks, "Why am
I choosing this moment, other than for your purposes, to take
my wig off?" Answering her own question, she says, "I'm doing

it deliberately to confront him as his mother, not outfacing him as queen. Otherwise I don't see the logic." Ciulei replies, "You're right, absolutely right, logically right," then adds, "My directorial gesture is forced, is forced upon the play. Your justification of it is just fine." (The Ghost, who appears without face armor or helmet, has white hair in contrast to Claudius's brown hair. Ciulei whitens Gertrude's hair and makes Claudius's relationship to her as subject to Freudian reading as Hamlet's.)

The following lines of Hamlet, ironically cut in this production, describe successful rehearsal work: "O, 'tis most sweet/ When in one line two crafts directly meet" (III.iv.210–11). Blocking is occasionally created spontaneously by actors' explorations in the presence of a watchful director.[7] More often, however, the actors perform movements and gestures suggested by Ciulei. There is always a potential tension between what the actor needs to feel and what the director needs to see. During a break in rehearsal, Smith expresses her sense of dilemma to Ciulei: "It's not my way versus your way. . . . When I work, I can't really know what I'm doing until I know what every gesture is, but it's not the blocking that concerns me: it's the intentions."[8] Shortly after this Ciulei suggests to Kline that Hamlet need only see part of Polonius's dead body in III.iv to know his identity. The actor's response is immediate: "It would play but *I* may need to be sure who I killed. . . . Don't worry. I'll find it"—over his shoulder—"but I may *need* to be sure about who I killed."

A related conflict is illustrated in the rehearsal of an earlier moment in the play. Unexpectedly finding his uncle alone and seemingly at prayer, Hamlet raises his knife as he considers avenging Claudius's murder of his father. Ciulei interrupts Hamlet's long monologue to demonstrate standing "solidly" in profile with the knife upraised as if to strike, and then after "one painful second" moving upstage to deliver the line, "And so 'a goes to heaven . . ." (III.iii.74). Then he demonstrates an alternative position, again in profile, this time with both hands holding the knife, an "intentionally melodramatic" pose. I do not overhear any directorial comment on subtext in this complicated pivotal speech. Ciulei concludes, "I think also the *speed* of the gesture is important—speed and finish." In a striking interjection, he then says to the actor who is studying where to stab Claudius: "Do not think anatomically. . . . Reality this time works against the theatre. You shouldn't for one second think anatomically. It should be just the idea [of killing], not how we do it. In the moment when we want to do it truly, in this extended soliloquy, there is a contradiction between the poetical writing and reality. This works against us, this using reality." Kline responds, "I disagree. I think Hamlet's thinking it through." The director replies, " 'Thinking it through' in poetry works against 'reality,' 'real time.' "[9] The actor continues to discuss subtext. The director once again demonstrates a stylized way of holding the dagger.

The issues here are multiple and the conflict seems overdetermined. The actor needs to explore fully and to justify every imposed physical gesture in terms of his understanding of his role, a massive undertaking. The director seems to resist within himself a tendency, as he later puts it, to "[replace] truth with reality and [destroy] the poetry,"[10] and often finds himself in conflict with actors trained in the American tradition of naturalistic theatre.

A final example related to the dagger and its uses occurs in the rehearsal of IV.ii, when Ciulei directs Hamlet to shake hands with the soldier who comes to take away the weapon with which he killed Polonius. Of this directorially inspired comic touch, Kline says, "I'll try this and even if it doesn't work I respect your point." Then as the actor replaces the knife in his belt and accidentally touches its tip, he says to it very softly, "And I respect *your* point."

It is not always so easy to wield the dagger when cutting the text. Many small cuts are made, almost on a daily basis, during rehearsal. Sometimes lines cut on one day are restored or partially restored on the next. The cuts are determined jointly by the director, assistant to the director Chris Markle, and text and voice consultant Elizabeth Smith.[11] Some excisions are made in advance of rehearsal and others occur as on-the-spot decisions in the process of rehearsing particular speeches or scenes. These two modes of removing unwanted passages parallel Hamlet's own alternation between premeditated and spontaneous elimination of unwanted characters (Polonius, Rosencrantz and Guildenstern, Claudius).

Ciulei's intention is to reduce the running time of the production, initially over four hours, to three and a half hours. The excisions are eventually so deftly made that few reviewers take issue with them,[12] but in making cuts the director comes into unavoidable conflicts with his actors. Kline at one point refers to the text as "rewritten." Ciulei's cuts include passages that are obscure or redundant, references to religion or supernatural intervention, and lines which delay the drive of the action ("A line that holds up the action is in my way").[13] Kline protests that the lines being cut "hurt the plot but help the character: by truncating it as we have, it's almost [pause] too clear, too concise. . . . It's not Hamlet." Later Ciulei speaks of "the cuts we did, bleeding," his metaphor transposing the wound from text to director.

New excisions often become potholes in the road. In the rehearsal of III.iv, the scene skids to a stop at line 83 as Hamlet asks Gertrude, "O shame, where is thy blush?" Smith does not deliver the line, "O Hamlet, speak no more" (line 89), because she is waiting for the intervening six lines. Kline says, "That's the latest cut," and the actors begin again. The actress remarks later to the director, "It's funny when you do these cuts. It's these *precipitous* changes," her body tilting forward slightly to suggest being thrown off balance.

The difficulty of neatly eliminating what is unwanted from the text is suggested in a telling moment during a break in rehearsal on February 7. On this first day in the downtown studio, it is snowing and the wind is blowing fairly heavily. A window shade near a sputtering radiator reflects the fluorescent lights on the ceiling. During the morning rehearsal I am slightly distracted by a faint shimmering outline of a human figure that seems to appear and recede on the wavering shade. Near the end of the lunch break, Ciulei turns to me, beckons me to his side, points to the window shade, and says, "The Ghost is trying to come in." This sly comment transforms the Ghost into a literal shadow on a literal shade in a storm, yet there is also a joking acknowledgment that the Ghost wants in, after all.

What Maynard Mack says of Shakespeare's play is especially true of its rehearsal: "Hamlet's world is preeminently in the interrogative mood. It reverberates with questions, anguished, meditative, alarmed. There are questions that in this play, to an extent I think unparalleled in any other, mark the phases and even the nuances of the action, helping to establish its peculiar baffled tone."[14] The interrogative mood permeates the *Hamlet* rehearsals more persistently than any other production I observe. It is the actors' way of engaging the text and at the same time one of the difficulties of the rehearsal.

For example, Priscilla Smith queries whether Gertrude agrees with Hamlet's devastating comparison of her present and former husbands ("Here is your husband, like a mildewed ear/ Blasting his wholesome brother," III.iv.65–66) and Ciulei responds by asking if we must believe Hamlet when he describes Gertrude as "hang[ing] on . . . [his father]/ As if increase of appetite had grown/ By what it fed on" (I.ii.143–45). (The actress responds, "*I believe it.*") A prolonged discussion, initiated by Richard Frank (Horatio) and continued by several actors, focuses on the meaning of the word "Nay" in Marcellus's exit line, "Nay, let's follow him," delivered after Horatio's statement, "Heaven will direct it" (I.iv.91). Harriet Harris questions whether Ophelia's seemingly submissive response to Polonius, "I do not know, my lord, what I should think" (I.iii.104), might in fact be a moment of independence, implying that she wishes to terminate her father's interrogation. Kevin Kline questions almost everything, beginning with the initial word of his first major speech in the play: "Seems" (I.ii.76): "Am I quibbling with . . . [Gertrude's] choice of terms or am I making a point about my internal state?"

Kline's questions are the most anguished, meditative, and alarmed, though often cloaked in witty or joking repartee. But the tensions between the director and the actor playing Hamlet are not merely the result of differences in temperament. In I.ii, Ciulei asks Kline to direct a certain line to the court rather than to Gertrude: "Could you not play . . . ["For they are actions that a man might play," I.ii.84] to them in this speech about playing, for *they* also play." The actor attempts the adjustment and then tells the director, "I have trouble with your interpretation. I know what you mean but I don't know if I can play it. We have to talk about it. It is bigger than anything political. . . ."

Following Ciulei's direction, at line 84 the actor turns away from Gertrude to whom the rest of the speech is addressed. He moves his head to the right, delivers the line in a changed tone to that part of the playing area where the court will be positioned when they enter the rehearsal, turns again toward Gertrude, then slowly moves his head back and forth several times without continuing his speech, as if trying to find an internal sense of the gesture. He speaks his own subtext as actor aloud to Smith: "Excuse me for awhile, I'll get back to you," as he once more gazes to the right before turning back to address the Queen: "But I have that within which passes show;/ These but the trappings and the suits of woe" (I.ii.85–86). The actor is seen, literally, in the process of trying out the directorial note and making it his own. His unscripted comic remark shows him in resistant collaboration with the director whom he so often challenges.

Fig. 9.2. Kevin Kline and Liviu Ciulei in rehearsal of Hamlet. *Photograph by George E. Joseph.*

In asking him to "play to" the court who "also play," the director engages the actor, as the court does the protagonist, in ways that alienate him and throw him back on his own resources. In a sense, throughout rehearsals, Ciulei's attempts to shape the stage life of the actor playing Hamlet recapitulate the efforts of the court at Elsinore to redefine the role of the mourning Prince of Denmark. The actor remains in baffled communion with what he largely opposes, his rehearsal work paralleling the role he plays.

Ciulei and Kline are both in rapport and in conflict with each other throughout rehearsal. This is not surprising, since Hamlet himself plays the role of director, both generally in his tendency to stage events and literally in his instructing the players in line delivery, gesture, blocking: "Speak the speech, I pray you, as I pronounced it to you, trippingly on the tongue. . . . Nor do not saw the air too much with your hand, thus. . . . Suit the action to the word, the word to the action," even forbidding comic improvisation: "And let those that play your clowns speak no more than is set down for them . . ." (III.ii.1–2, 4–5, 17–18, 38–40). Hamlet even violates "the integrity of the text" by asking the Player to add a speech in the performance of *The Murder of Gonzago*: "You could for a need study a speech of some dozen or sixteen lines which I would set down and insert in't, could you not?" (II.ii.546–48).

In II.ii, Hamlet enters reading. When Polonius asks, "What do you read, my lord?" Hamlet replies, "Words, words, words." When Polonius rephrases his question, "What is the matter, my lord?" Hamlet answers with a question, "Between who?" (191–95). In rehearsal Kline improvises and then reworks a masterfully wacky blocking. While Leonardo Cimino's Polonius delivers a long aside, Kline walks across the stage and sits reading behind a tall upholstered chair. When Cimino turns away from the audience, he is literally surprised not to see Kline; then the actor *plays* his surprise. After he spies Kline, Cimino delivers his line, "What do you read, my lord?" to a hidden figure who replies unseen from behind the chair, "Words, words, words." In rehearsing the scene a second time, Kline tears pages from his book and tosses them over the top of his chair at Polonius as he says, "Words, words, words." Ciulei demonstrates a broader, more antic reading of Hamlet's line, "Between who?" to a somewhat dubious Kline and says, "Try it." After the actor tries the new delivery, he makes a suggestion of his own: that Hamlet place one of the pages he tears from his book on Polonius's bald pate, "as if pasting a poster on a blank posterboard," as if to say, Kline adds, "Here's a transcript of everything I've said." The actor demonstrates by placing a page on the top of the director's own slightly balding head. Ciulei smiles, says nothing.[15] Kline turns to production stage manager Alan Traynor and says, "Make a note." It is an arresting image of an actor giving back the words he reads to the director, but in fact when he gives the words to the director he comically appropriates the director's role: "Make a note." Like the playwright, the director is a giver of "words" to the actor, not literally, as Hamlet with the Player, but as reinscriber of the authorial text.

When Ciulei says, "It reads well," to an actor in rehearsal, he suggests that his directorial reinscribing will be legible to the audience-as-readers. In rehearsal actors reading the script are being "read" by a surrogate for a "reading" audience, a process in which the actor is seen as making a text legible for observers, chief of whom is the director. But the director, though often using the language of reading, is still very like Pierre Menard, the Borges character who reauthors several chapters of Cervantes' *Don Quixote* without changing a word: "He multiplied draft upon draft, revised tenaciously and tore up thousands of manuscript pages. He did not let anyone examine these drafts and took care they should not survive him."[16] In a sense, this book is an attempt to reconstruct such drafts.[17]

In a provocative footnote, David Cole writes, "On some level, one can only direct a play in the teeth of the kind of thing a play is—or at least, in the teeth of the kind of reading a play invites. . . . As a playwright I have a vivid appreciation of all that a director can do for a text in the exercise of a function that is, nevertheless, a systematic undoing of it."[18] The notion of a director's function as "a systematic undoing" of a previously prepared text is already suggested in the etymology of the word *rehearse*: "to harrow again." The harrow, with its iron teeth, breaks up, pulverizes, ploughed ground. The playtext is rather "in the teeth of" what harrows it. Thus, when the director and actors in rehearsal begin "to recapitulate the writing process" of the playwright, they put in question a completed text by treating it as " 'an incomplete process' " that includes "constant change and movement rather than stability."[19]

It is fair to say that *Hamlet* as a literary text defeats all attempts to postulate with confidence any particular view of its nature:

"you would pluck out the heart of my mystery."[20] When Smith asks if her dialogue with Hamlet in I.ii "changes from [a] private to [a] public [scene]," Ciulei responds, "No. Always, in each scene, the public is included in the private, and the private is included in the public." Earlier in this rehearsal, however, he describes to the cast "a very simple situation that we must obey because it determines the play. Hamlet is in mourning; that's normal. What's not normal is that Gertrude is not in mourning. . . . Gertrude gave up the mourning and married, and wants Hamlet to join her in this marriage and this normality. . . . That's life and life has its demands on the human being." The actors playing Claudius and Hamlet seem to indicate agreement with the director's views. The actress playing Gertrude remains silent. Ciulei's emphasis on mourning as the controlling situation has much to recommend it,[21] but raises complexities when staged.

Ciulei's view of what controls a situation in certain scenes is characteristically interwoven with a discussion about the placement of a chair. In an early runthrough, Hamlet enters in I.ii, is greeted with slight bows from the court, takes the chair placed for him by the side of the Queen and moves it downstage left where he sits impassively, eyes downcast, while Claudius delivers his long opening speech. When Kline queries the directorial staging: "How important is the placement of Hamlet's chair?" Ciulei responds: "I could do it differently, if you want. . . . [but] we reduce it to close-ups if we don't use the chair. This way it's stage story-telling. The court is my curtain. When you come in, this is the beginning of an action."

The actor suggests that the placement of the chair apart from the King and Queen is an act of rebellion. The director replies: "No, it's more than rebellion. This is isolation, holding aside; it's keeping the shadow around you, not just rebellion. It speaks. It isn't an empty gesture. It isn't a furniture movement. It shows us an attitude and a position." Speaking to the actors a few minutes later, he says, with a little more than normal force, "Let me try something and then we'll discuss it." One might say, though Ciulei doesn't, that the shadow Hamlet keeps around him in this scene anticipates the Ghost, who in Ciulei's production is as solidly present as that chair and in fact actually touches Hamlet in their first scene together.[22]

Ciulei's concern with chairs is expressed at various points throughout rehearsal, culminating in a carefully arranged pattern of seated positions that is either unnoticed or treated dismissively by critics.[23] Ciulei is very precise about when and how actors sit or stand. Striking instances of unexpected seated positions include the following: Hamlet begins his first soliloquy seated in a chair in I.ii; Claudius begins his sole soliloquy seated, eventually kneels, in III.iii; Ophelia's first mad scene in IV.v occurs as she sits in mourning dress at a banquet table;[24] the opening lines of her second mad scene ("They bore him barefaced on the bier . . .") are sung while seated (IV.v.165–67); Hamlet, as mentioned, sits immediately after his entrance in I.ii, and delivers his famous speech, "What a piece of work is a man . . ." (II.i.303–16), seated; Polonius delivers his much-quoted instructions to Laertes (". . . to thine own self be true") seated, with Ophelia standing behind him nodding in mock solemnity over his head to her brother who stands at a distance facing Polonius and Ophelia (I.iii.55–81). Finally, in a disputed[25] but brilliant staging, Ophelia sits alone as she delivers her monologue near the end of the "nunnery scene" (III.i.151–62) and remains seated in a pool of light, her incipient madness ironically unnoticed by father and king as they exit on Claudius's line, "Madness in great ones must not unwatched go" (III.i.189).

One effect of Ciulei's staging of so many seated moments in the play is that the act of simply rising from a chair is potentially thunderous. For example, Kline stands up on the line, "Seems, madam? Nay, it is. I know not 'seems' " (I.ii.76), and Ciulei, watching, says, "Good, and that's a conflict already." On the other hand, the actors often see sitting as less variegated, less rich in acting possibilities, than does the director who both envisions and demonstrates a world of possible nuances in a seated posture. At one point, late in the rehearsal period, Ciulei demonstrates *en passant* six or seven different ways of "sitting in a chair."

Objecting to Ciulei's suggestion that Hamlet be seated during part of Horatio's description of the appearance of the Ghost of his father, Kline remarks that sitting would be "sedating the emotion." Ciulei demonstrates Hamlet's sitting as a way of representing "deep listening" to what Horatio is telling him and a drawing of what he hears into himself. I think I hear the director add: "Sitting protects us."

A very different implication of a seated posture emerges in rehearsal of the dialogue between Laertes and Ophelia in I.iii, just four days before the first technical rehearsal. Ciulei suddenly removes a chaise longue from the set. Replacing it with two

chairs, he calls this alteration "a sea change" and asks rhetorically, "Why should there be a chair? It was descriptive merely."
Ciulei redirects the scene, quickening its pace and suggesting
new blocking. Now Ophelia sits downstage right. Laertes moves
toward her and sits on her upstage side, forcing her to twist her
body and head toward him to listen to his words of caution
about her relationship with Hamlet. Ophelia's chair, Ciulei says,
becomes "her torture chair," though he adds that he does not
know if the audience will perceive it.[26]

Ophelia is forced into a twisted, awkward, and finally gro-
tesque position simply by her attempt to listen to Laertes's Pol-
onius-like version of reality. Held in that posture by the political
discourse that controls her family life, Ophelia finally escapes
momentarily by rising and moving upstage left where she sits
on a bench at her dressing table. Laertes follows and joins her
there, sitting again on her upstage side. Ciulei directs Laertes to
kiss Ophelia who then looks away from him. Laertes rises and
moves downstage into her view. Capturing her attention, he sits
downstage as he continues his parental lecture. On his lines, "[If]
. . . your chaste treasure open/ To his unmastered opportunity"
(I.iii.31–32), Ophelia laughs and leaps into her brother's lap, then
rises and chimes in on one of his subsequent phrases, as Ciulei
has suggested. Laertes, sitting in the chair Polonius will soon
occupy, is becoming a perfectly predictable replica of their
father.

Ciulei rehearses the first 51 lines of I.iii for almost an hour. At
the end of this session he says to the actor playing Laertes, "Don't
be afraid to do more. It's easier to reduce it later." He asks the
two actors to continue to rehearse this small section of the play
with assistant to the director Chris Markle in the adjoining studio. It is entirely characteristic of Ciulei's directorial style that
a Shakespearean "sea change" should begin with the removal of
a chaise longue. Ophelia's "torture chair" in I.iii prepares the
way for her seated monologue at the end of III.i and prefigures
her crazed outbreak at the banquet table in III.iv.

Ciulei's staging of seated postures at unexpected moments—
during soliloquies, monologues, and intense dialogues—is striking in itself and also because it is situated midway between
theatrical realism and symbolism. This doubleness is reflected
in the visual style of the production. Ciulei's *Hamlet* inhabits a
set defined by eighteen-foot gleaming bronzed columns moving
magically on stage in different configurations, often diagonal

sections, in different scenes, much like actors with abstract blocking of their own. In seeming contrast are realistic Bismarckian costumes and richly detailed furnishings: smartly tailored military uniforms,[27] diplomatic sashes, Hamlet's black frock coat with mourning band, his white linen shirt and cravat, Fortinbras's Prussian greatcoat, the banquet table with lace tablecloth, candelabra, and elaborate floral arrangements.

Kline speaks both of Ciulei's "formal, image-conscious style of directing"[28] and his being "not at all shy about telling a story physically through a kind of choreographic image: if you were deaf you could almost get the story without hearing it." Choreographing[29] a new scene which he intends, Hamlet-like, to insert in the performance of Shakespeare's play, Ciulei asks Kline to rush into the playing area with a candle, place it on the floor, take a sword and circle the candle.[30] Kline asks, "Why? Because I'm crazy?" Ciulei's inaudible answer is followed by Kline's performing a kind of odd mincing dance around the candle. Ciulei, suddenly reminiscent of Robert Wilson, demonstrates, saying, "No . . . you don't get the shadows [created by the lit candle] right. . . . It's like the shadows are dancing."

The apparent disjunction between Ciulei's story-telling impulse and his formalistic attention to striking images is not unique and takes many forms in theatre rehearsals: the seeming tension between the narrative and the pictorial, the tension between purely "aesthetic" and social-political agendas, even the tension between the tradition of American naturalistic acting and the more stylized traditions of European and Oriental theatre. Finally, the need to reconcile the materiality of theatre, its origins in the body of the actor or dancer, with its reliance on illusion or artifice remains the paradox it always was.

During technical lighting rehearsals at the Newman Theatre, as Kline delivers Hamlet's last soliloquy, he cannot tell if he is in or out of the light or exactly how he looks while facing different parts of the theatre. Ciulei asks the actor to take off his cloak and join him in the auditorium while stage manager Pat Sosnow, wearing Hamlet's cloak, stands on stage, first in left profile, then in right profile, then full face toward the audience. After a few moments of watching, Kline strides onto the stage and resumes his cloak and role. My last image of the *Hamlet* rehearsals is of the actor's giving up his role as actor in order to gain a directorial perspective on it. Having the perspective he wants, he takes back the role: a very Hamlet-like solution to a Hamlet-like dilemma.

Fig. 10.1. Peter Sellars rehearsing at the Kennedy Center. Photograph by Joan Marcus.

10

Peter Sellars Directs
Two Figures in Dense Violet Light

"The image is unshakable."

Peter Sellars, whose work with the Wooster Group I have already discussed in chapter six, began his theatrical career as a puppeteer at the age of ten. He has since directed more than 100 plays and operas, including works by Aeschylus, Shakespeare, Mozart, Chekhov, and Gertrude Stein. After graduating from Harvard, where he first studied Kabuki theatre, he was a Sheldon Traveling Fellow in Japan, China, and India. In 1983 he was named a MacArthur Fellow and in 1984 he was appointed as Director of the American National Theater at the Kennedy Center for the Performing Arts in Washington, D.C. After leaving the Kennedy Center in August of 1986, Sellars became director of the Los Angeles Festival. He continues his work in theatre, opera, and film in this country and throughout the world.

In late July and early August of 1986, I observe only a few rehearsals of Peter Sellars's last production as Director of the American National Theater at the Kennedy Center, *Two Figures in Dense Violet Light*, a collocation of three short works: Samuel Beckett's *Ohio Impromptu*; Ezra Pound's translation and adaptation of *Tsunemasa*, a Japanese Noh play; Wallace Stevens's poem "Angel Surrounded by Paysans." Sellars's departure from his post at the Kennedy Center and the discontinuance of the American National Theater are announced in *The Washington Post* on the day *Two Figures* opens in the Center's Free Theater. David Richards's respectful though muted review brings these events into alignment:

> Stripped of surface animation . . . [*Two Figures in Dense Violet Light*] qualifies primarily as a meditation. . . . Embedded in

> its murky depths, I suspect, is a troubling
> awareness of mortality. That Sellars
> should stage this piece after a beleaguered
> tenure at the center . . . is at least ironic.
> It is also rather madly and gallantly
> courageous. With "Two Figures," a swan song
> on more than one count, Sellars remains Sellars
> to the end.[1]

Performed by Richard Thomas and David Warrilow, *Two Figures* is scheduled as a two-week engagement beginning August 9 and is extended through August 30. Its last lines, those of Stevens's poem, seem to evoke the figure of the director:

>   Am I not,
> Myself, . . .
> A figure half-seen, or seen for a moment,
> . . . an apparition apparelled in
>
> Apparels of such lightest look that a turn
> Of my shoulder and quickly, too quickly,
>   I am gone?[2]

In this final production of the American National Theater, Sellars stages hints and signs of the director's roles in rehearsal along with his own leave-taking.

Rehearsal of *Two Figures in Dense Violet Light* takes place in the Kennedy Center's Free Theater, a small performance space (127 feet long and 71 feet wide) with 20-foot high windows facing west. For this production, the theatre, with its 300-person maximum capacity, is divided into three approximately equal performance spaces, separated by floor-to-ceiling green curtains. The audience for *Two Figures* will be limited to 100 persons, with additional room for four or five others who may sit on the floor.[3]

On July 31, 1986, his first day of rehearsal with the full cast, the director talks about light as natural phenomenon: "When the show is set at twilight, we get the dense violet light. If twilight hits right on, it is unbearably moving to feel the light fade; [it is] a primal feeling to *feel* the light fade. . . . This light is changing every minute. The figures will change shape and take on the qualities of three-dimensional shadows. The image is unshakable."

Production stage manager John Beven has a detailed schedule

of exactly when sunset occurs each night during the rehearsal and the run. Unlike Robert Wilson, with whom he is compared in his staging of this production, Sellars relies almost entirely on natural light in both the rehearsal and the performance of *Two Figures in Dense Violet Light*.[4]

At one point in the failing light of rehearsal I am startled to see my own shadow fall diagonally across the page of my notebook as I write. When I look up toward the actors, I see a longer shadow on the floor diagonally to my right where the director sometimes sits. In other rehearsals I have invisibly shadowed the director. In the "real" light of Sellars's rehearsals my shadow shows, as does the artificiality of the attempt to exclude one's own imprint from one's observations.

The attempted synchronization with natural changes in light is in its own way as difficult to achieve as Wilson's carefully plotted artificial lighting of discrete objects and persons. Sellars tells the cast that because of the changing light "every night will be dramatically different." David Warrilow remarks at one point, "It's very tricky. We need to know how we look at a certain moment in a certain quality of light which is changing nightly." To this actor, accustomed from his work with Robert Wilson to the precise coordination of movement and lighting changes, Sellars replies simply, "The basic criterion is . . . feeling. . . . The play begins each night when you feel ready."

Sellars's reliance on natural light in his staging of *Ohio Impromptu* is a conscious rejection of Beckett's opening stage directions: "*Light on table midstage. Rest of stage in darkness.*"[5] The director remarks to the cast that what Beckett intends is a "positive impact in a negative field, but we're doing the reverse: in this [natural, fading] light there is this dark concentration. . . ." "One senses a rhythm of nature. The speed of a natural process is the time scale that governs what we do."

The following pages focus on Sellars's rehearsals of Samuel Beckett's *Ohio Impromptu*, the longest and perhaps most familiar of the three works which compose *Two Figures in Dense Violet Light*. For Beckett, the successful realization of his plays depends to a great extent on a director's observing his meticulously detailed stage directions and implicit rhythms. Although Warrilow has just returned from Paris where he as Reader and Jean-Louis Barrault as Listener rehearsed *Ohio Impromptu* with Beckett in attendance,[6] one of Sellars's first remarks to the cast tells the story of his rehearsal: "I've never stopped in my life to think,

'What will the author think?' I feel that what I'm doing is the only authentic production."

Although he makes no changes at all in the text of the play, the director violates almost all of the playwright's directions for set, lighting, costumes, and physical placement of the actors in relation to each other. Beckett's opening stage directions continue:

> Plain white deal table say 8 . . . [feet] × 4 . . . [feet]. Two plain armless white deal chairs. L seated at table facing front towards end of long side audience right. Bowed head propped on right hand. Face hidden. Left hand on table. Long black coat. Long white hair. R seated at table in profile centre of short side audience right. Bowed head propped on right hand. Left hand on table. Book on table before him open at last pages. Long black coat. Long white hair. Black wide-brimmed hat at centre of table.
> Fade up.
> Ten seconds.
> R turns page.
> Pause.

In Sellars's staging of the play there is no light on the table, which is square and brown rather than rectangular and white. Brown stools replace white deal chairs. (The sets for the Beckett play, the Noh play, and the Stevens poem are identical: a square brown table and two brown stools.) The long black coats are replaced by Indian silk robes. (David Warrilow remains in a saffron silk robe throughout; Richard Thomas wears a saffron robe for the Beckett play, dons a scarlet robe for the Noh play, and appears in a white robe while delivering the lines of the Stevens poem.) There are no white wigs to produce Beckett's desired "long white hair" and there is no black wide-brimmed hat at the center of the table. The only prop that remains is the book which R reads.

In addition, Sellars alters the positions of the actors. L (Listener, played by Richard Thomas), seated at the square table, is facing diagonally upstage right (not facing the audience, as the playwright stipulates). R (Reader, played by David Warrilow), seated at the side of the table to L's left, is also facing diagonally upstage right. Thus, while Beckett indicates that the actors sit near the same end of a rectangular table, one facing the audience and the other in profile, Sellars positions his actors so that both

Fig. 10.2. Richard Thomas and David Warrilow in Ohio Impromptu. *Photograph by Joan Marcus.*

face in the same direction, one diagonally behind the other, each with left hand and arm resting on the table top, heads slightly bent. It is a meticulously arranged restaging in which the two figures are suggestively united by the similarity of their postures (their bent heads and left arms and hands positioned alike) and placement (both on the diagonal). They seem alternately and then simultaneously a figure and his shadow as well as two distinct figures working in tandem though nearly stationary, one mobilized in words, the other in the sound of one hand knocking on a small wooden table.

Sellars's use of natural light—his initial departure from Beckett's stage directions—seems to be rooted in his own experience of Noh theatre:

> The real mystery is Noh. . . . It's that experience I don't think
> Beckett has had . . . that theatre happens with life and is part
> of it, that life doesn't stop when theatre happens.

On the first day of rehearsal he tells the actors of "one of the four
greatest experiences of my life" which takes place on an island
just opposite Hiroshima where there is one of the oldest Noh
stages in Japan. For several days each year five Noh plays are
performed every day on the island. The performances begin at
9:30 a.m. and last until dusk. The audience sits on grandstands,
the stage is on stilts in the bay. The natural light recreates the
changing water patterns on the actors' gold-embroidered costumes. As the plays continue, the tide recedes so that between
the audience and the stage there is no longer water but sand and
pebbles. Sand crabs and deer wander through, and beyond the
stage people are seen boating. During the last play the night
overtakes everything and the tide comes in. "It's overwhelming."
As the cast sits listening, the late afternoon August light, continually changing, streams through the windows facing the terrace.
The director, telling his tale as he begins to rehearse the telling
of a tale in which "little is left to tell," seems to evoke the figure
in Stevens's poem:

> Yet I am the necessary angel of earth,
> Since, in my sight, you see the earth again.[8]

Warrilow says of his role as Reader in *Ohio Impromptu* what
is true of his role as actor in rehearsal: "The story can never be
changed but we must keep reading it to gather new meanings in
it." He tells me privately that in rehearsal and performance he
feels it is important actually to read the text whenever he has
sufficient light to do so. The book as prop and the book as playtext
are the only elements Sellars preserves without alteration in
Ohio Impromptu. Giving notes to Warrilow, the director refers
to "that experience of reading about the book you're reading." In
the play Warrilow reads aloud a story in which a man reads
aloud a sad tale nightly and then disappears without a word.
With one possible exception, nothing is said in the play but what
is read from the book; when the book is closed, there is silence.
In the silence there is a brief mysterious mutuality of gazing
which brings the play to an end.

Ohio Impromptu dramatizes the interrupted voicing of a text.

An unnamed Reader reads aloud from an open book to an unnamed Listener who at intervals interrupts the Reader by knocking with his left hand on the table at which they both sit. In the
narrated scene of reading there is no interruption of the tale.
Only in the enacted scene of reading and listening is the Reader
interrupted by the Listener. In other words, *Ohio Impromptu* is a
text of interrupted reading that narrates scenes of uninterrupted
reading. The start-stop process is by now a familiar sign of the
rehearsal process. The Reader is the figure of the actor just as
the Listener is the figure of the director.[9] (Initially, in fact, Sellars
himself "takes the role" of Listener since he rehearses with David
Warrilow alone for several evenings before Richard Thomas arrives.) Beckett's play is partly a reflection of the process of its
own realization in rehearsal.

At one point Sellars says to Warrilow, "You're reading to him
[the Listener] but at the same time he's in control." The actor
responds, "Oh, yes." The Listener's knocks control at what point
the Reader must stop and start again. The knocks require the
Reader to pause and repeat earlier lines; they also signal approval or acknowledgment of the repeated reading. The following excerpt from the play illustrates these functions:

> Then turn and his slow steps retrace.
> [*Pause.*]
> In his dreams—
> [*Knock.*]
> Then turn and his slow steps retrace.
> [*Pause. Knock.*]
> In his dreams he has been warned against this change. Seen
> the dear face and heard the unspoken words, Stay where we
> were so long alone together, my shade will comfort you.[10]

The first knock requests a repetition of the preceding line; the
second knock permits the Reader to continue. The longest period
of uninterrupted voicing in the play is the Reader's narration of
nightly scenes of uninterrupted reading. The interrupted reading
of a text about uninterrupted reading also encodes rehearsal's
relation to performance.

Sellars suggests to Warrilow that there is a connection between the line, "They grew to be as one," and the subsequent
announcement that there was "no need" for the Reader to present
himself again to the Listener.[11] No longer performing their roles

as Reader and Listener, actor and director, the two figures can meet finally in an unblinking mutual gaze.

Exploring the physical act of knocking is the form that exploration of character assumes in the second day of rehearsal. For example, Richard Thomas does not want his arm to return after each knock on the table to a "pre-knock position." Warrilow agrees that each knock must be an independent action, a starting over from the beginning. Thomas is apprehensive about knocking with his fingernail[12] because he doesn't want to sound "nervous." The director talks about an "interruption knock" and a "repetition knock." Thomas speaks of a "delaying knock" and Sellars refers to knocks that say "continue."

Sellars's intimate style of directing allows him to conduct a conversation that melds considerations of physical technique with analyses of the intricate possibilities in so seemingly constrained a dialogue between Listener and Reader. In this quiet moment of rehearsal work director and actors break down the binary distinction between precise Robert Wilson-like attention to the physical positioning of every finger and the psychologized probing of "inner life" that includes awareness of motivations, goals and objectives. In rehearsal, talking about the timing, volume, and "quality" of a soft knock on a wooden table and talking about a human relationship are two modes of talking about the same thing. Sellars moves without transition, suggesting that none is necessary, from the analysis of knocking as a finely nuanced and technically complex language to straightforward, precise directions on the pace and angle of Thomas's turning of his shoulder and head to face Warrilow at the end of *Ohio Impromptu*.

Sellars interrupts Warrilow almost immediately in the first workthrough to ask the actor to pause longer before repeating his opening line:

> R: [*Reading.*] Little is left to tell. In a last—
> [*L knocks with left hand on table.*]
> Little is left to tell.
> [*Pause. Knock.*][13]

Appropriately, the first directorial interruption of rehearsal of *Ohio Impromptu* occurs in response to one of the play's own disruptions of the reading aloud of a text. The timing of pauses, so crucial to the playing of the piece, is not prescribed by the author. I overhear the director tell the actors that he wants the pauses to be "more acute." To Warrilow, he says, "[In the pauses] it's not just catching your breath. It's desire. Or need for acknowledgment."[14] As Thomas notes, the knocks which seem to request repetition are strangely delayed. The speaker is allowed to read new material before he is requested to repeat previous material. In his directing of the pauses after the knocks, Sellars forces the audience to "hear" silences differently.

As he is about to begin the first runthrough, Warrilow says to the director: "I'm not going to be lively. I'm not doing it for you." Sellars responds, "Good. Do it for yourself," and retires to listen in darkness to the actors.

In performance *Ohio Impromptu* is presented twice. The audience is first placed within a dark curtained-off area while the unseen actors perform the Beckett play in an adjoining "theatre." Then, led by ushers into that identically shaped rectangular space, the audience hears and sees the same play performed again.[15] After the second performance of *Ohio Impromptu*, the audience moves to a third adjoining "theatre" where the Noh play and Stevens poem are performed. The two experiences of the Beckett play—listening to a reading followed by hearing and seeing the play on its feet—parallel the usual sequence in rehearsal of a readthrough followed by a runthrough. In fact, in Sellars's extraordinary first day of rehearsal with the full cast, the readthrough is followed, after the dinner break, by a full runthrough of *Two Figures in Dense Violet Light*.

At first Sellars entertains the notion of a largely unseated audience, free to move about in the curtained-off "hearing space." During the initial runthrough, performed without artificial amplification, I see Sellars himself represent the spectator by peeping at the performers through flaps in the curtains. The directorial gaze now becomes overtly voyeuristic, more like that of the film audience watching a framed picture in a dark room. When the director decides that the audience will all be seated, "clamped in like a coffin," his language seems to suggest that the suppression of spectatorial desire in the theatre is a kind of death.

The last rehearsal I observe occurs on a particularly dark night. As Warrilow begins the second performance of *Ohio Impromptu*, there is an almost magical feeling of being bound together in a room by a voice. Suddenly a storm breaks: lightning flickers through the theatre. There is the roar of thunder and the lightning flickers again. The Noh conditions Sellars spoke of on the first day of rehearsal prevail, for the rehearsal performance "happens with life and is part of it . . . life doesn't stop when theatre happens."[16] As *Ohio Impromptu* continues, the thunder rolls are almost continuous but quiet. The flashes of lightning come every few seconds. Against this rhythm the two actors perform in seemingly natural counterpoint. In a sense, theatre is appropriating nature's ever more dramatic effects, yet

> over that art,
> Which . . . adds to Nature, is an art
> That Nature makes.[17]

The thunder rises precipitously in volume and the wind rises as well. The actors are intermittently illuminated as if by a giant flashlight whenever the lightning strikes. And yet the marvel of the storm is matched by the marvel of the actors' discipline. Warrilow's voice and Thomas's knocks continue, their rhythms joined with those of the tempest. It is a brilliant and undoubtedly a unique rehearsal performance. Afterwards, on the terrace of the Kennedy Center, one of the actors asks, "Shall we have notes?" Sellars, in a Prospero-like renunciation of his role, responds by asking, "Do you expect notes on *that* performance? You need notes from God *and* me?"

Fig. 11.1. Lee Breuer, with Elena, the Bunraku puppet, and the Bunraku puppetmaster, Tamamatsu, rehearsing The Warrior Ant. Photograph by T. Charles Erickson.

11

Lee Breuer Directs *The Warrior Ant*

"You move from one to another, bringing them to life."

Like JoAnne Akalaitis, writer-director Lee Breuer is a founding member of the theatre collective, Mabou Mines. He has directed plays since 1970, beginning with Beckett's *Play* and including his adaptations of Shakespeare and Wedekind as well as his own works. With his long-time collaborator, composer and musician Bob Telson, Breuer has conceived and directed *The Gospel at Colonus*, an adaptation of Sophocles' *Oedipus at Colonus*, and parts of a music theatre piece, *The Warrior Ant*. While rehearsing *The Warrior Ant* in New Haven, he served as Co-Chairman of the Directing Department at the Yale School of Drama, where he also taught.

Breuer's tendency, like that of Elizabeth LeCompte, is to rehearse major works over long periods of time. *Lear*, his gender-reversed adaptation of Shakespeare's play, starring Ruth Maleczech,[1] was in rehearsal for several years before its appearance in New York in 1990. *The Warrior Ant* has been in development since 1984. A 45-minute concert version was presented at the Dance Theatre Workshop in Manhattan in June of 1985. The Prologue and Epilogue were performed a year later at Lincoln Center's Alice Tully Hall. In early January of 1987, Bob Telson's band, Little Village, performed the latest versions of the music at Sounds of Brazil in Manhattan. Part IV, "The Ant in Hell," was first presented in Manhattan at Performance Space 122 on February 6, 1987, as a work-in-progress. Sections of *The Warrior Ant* were performed in New Haven in the fall of 1987 and the fall of 1988, as well as at both the Spoleto Festival in Charleston, South Carolina, and the American Musical Theater Festival in Philadelphia in the summer of 1988. A three-hour version inaugurated the Brooklyn Academy of Music's Next Wave Festival in the fall of 1988 after its world première at Yale University. When produced in its entirety, the 12-part mock epic will be performed over three evenings.

The rehearsals of *Warrior Ant* that I observe occur in mid-October of 1987 and in late September and early October of 1988, in preparation for work-in-progress performances at the Yale School of Drama's 100-seat Experimental Theatre on October 25, 1987, and eight performances at the larger 670-seat University Theatre in the fall of 1988. The following account records traces of a rehearsal journey that continually returns to its earliest impulses in collaborative improvisation.

On October 12, 1987, the first day of the New Haven rehearsals of Part IV of *The Warrior Ant*, the floor is not yet marked with tape to indicate the exact dimensions of the playing area. In a nearly bare and at first barely lit or heated studio, once the initiation room of one of Yale's secret societies, Lee Breuer, using tapes of an unfinished musical score, still writing and revising the script, relying largely on non-professional student actors, mobilizes his directorial imagination. He has the fewest possible ingredients for what will become, he tells me a year later, a half-million dollar production. The rehearsal space is, in Wallace Stevens's words, "a room/ In which . . . /The world imagined is the ultimate good."[2]

Despite its history of previous work-in-progress performances, Breuer tells the cast: "This is like a draft. . . . Basically I don't want to have too many ideas set, so we're starting out and doing everything together." On the third floor of the Gypsy, a building next door to the Yale University Theatre, Breuer has brought together four American puppeteers, two Master Bunraku puppeteers from Japan, several translators, a set designer, student actors, collaborator-composer Bob Telson, producing director Liza Lorwin, production liaison Ryan Gilliam, administrative associate Kara Vallow, and his own young son, Joseph.

The author-director explains the "Ant in Hell" section of *Warrior Ant* to the Bunraku puppeteers, pausing while each sentence is translated into Japanese: "This is Part IV. What has already happened is that the warrior ant has had his first series of battles, and the results of his battles are very confusing. He doesn't know whether he's won or lost or what he's fighting for." Part IV begins with an allusion to the opening line of Dante's *Inferno*: "Midway in its life the Warrior Ant found itself in a dark hole."[3] Breuer comments:

The ant is in a dark hole and will be conducted down to hell [by a worm named Maeterlinck]. . . . The 'dark hole' is a metaphorical statement of a state of confusion in the soul. At the same time we are using the literal metaphor [sic] of the dark hole as stage setting.

Set designer Alison Yerxa, sitting next to me, sketches one image after another as the author-director continues to discuss the imagery in the text:

When the ant looks up, he feels as if he's been drawn up, sucked up. And when he looks down, he feels as if he's being sucked down. The idea that we want to establish is that the ant stays there day and night, day and night, by his hole. At noon, when the sun gets very hot, the ant crawls into its hole because it's afraid of the sun. . . . At night the ant is afraid of the dark hole beneath. So it never knows whether to go up or down. It looks up and thinks an anteater is going to eat it from above; it looks down and thinks a spider is going to eat it from below. Nothing protected it and nothing helped it get away. Then everything changes. The earth opens up as if in an earthquake. The ground rises up like a great wave and keeps turning and twisting as if the ground is water. The ground is like a whirlpool which sucks the ant down into hell. . . . This is what we just heard on the [music] tape before the drum roll. It's about four minutes.

After Telson's music is played on tape, the director says, "So the first thing we want to do is to get an idea about how to stage this."

When the set designer is asked if she would like to share any visual ideas with the puppeteers, she responds: "I don't know. I just did some sketches while you were talking." She removes several sheets from her sketch pad and shows them to the director and the Bunraku masters. As Breuer describes the ghost-like appearance of a five-and-a-half-foot worm puppet on whose writhing back the Bunraku warrior ant puppet will ride, Japanese master Yoshida Tamamatsu suddenly stands up, holding the set designer's sketch in one hand, and moves with great energy toward the playing area. But the puppeteer's attempt at physical enactment is defeated: there is as yet no context for action and he returns to his seat.

Later that same day three American puppeteers practice manipulating the accordion-like worm puppet while Telson plays the synthesizer, the director watches, and the set designer continues to sketch. Tamamatsu's skilled hands deftly lift up his Bunraku puppet and place it astride the sinuously rotating worm. The action, nearly indescribable, is the first moment of collaborative improvisation in the rehearsal. Breuer, beaming, says to the set designer, "That is one beautiful move. Gorgeous. . . . It's gonna work." He leaps slightly in the air and gives a little kick while the rehearsal exploration of worm movements continues, watched closely by Tamamatsu, now seated in a chair. Breuer then gives a note in a more sober tone to be translated for the Bunraku master: "But these are just beginning ideas. Tamamatsu should understand that it's not just *one* idea about riding [the worm] but that it changes as the riding continues." Whatever prior discussions may have suggested about the setting and staging, the set designer and director are clearly discovering visual images in rehearsal as they watch the puppet-actors.

The first day of Breuer's 1987 Yale rehearsals is an elementary introduction to the way discrete elements in a theatrical production gain their full effect from their admixture. Three American puppeteers and the set designer rehearse the manipulation of the worm puppet,[4] while across the room four student actors sit reading the playtext aloud to the author-director who, as he listens, makes cuts and revisions in the script. The actors then read the revised text aloud to the puppeteers while the director stops and restarts the reading at various points in order to describe set and action. Telson is asked to play the synthesizer against the background of taped music. Finally, when the score is added to the sounds of the actors' voices reading, and the worm's mouth and body move in concert with the spoken dialogue, a distinctly new effect begins to emerge.

The shaping of text, sound, gesture, and movement occurs in different locations of the same room in the fall of 1987 and in different cities in the fall of 1988 as the production of *Warrior Ant* grows to become an international community of 100 artists, eventually including a Brazilian samba band, a Trinidadian steel band, an 18-foot-high steel and wire female ant puppet, an aerialist, a Moroccan dancer playing the santir, belly dancers manipulating Chinese glove puppets, breakdancers, gospel singers, an Arab band, eighteenth-century costumed narrators, Bob Telson's funk band, along with American and Japanese Bunraku puppeteers.

The Warrior Ant is a gigantic non-realistic representation, a mythic saga, of life, death, afterlife. It is ironic, chaotic, subtle and cornball; meditative and exuberant by turns; raucous, parodic, recklessly postmodern in its appropriation of heterogeneous styles and cultural traditions; at once low-brow and exalted, seemingly out-of-control and precisely executed, tongue-in-cheek and reverential, epic in scope and deeply personal: an ambitious, high-camp, outrageous yet earnest endeavor. That all the varied elements in this cross-cultural "performance art"[5] could be mediated by a single directorial vision might seem, on the face of it, impossible. And yet, on another occasion, Breuer has said of his role as director, "It's my job to see."[6] Difficult though it is to document such a claim, I regard the rehearsals of Breuer's *Warrior Ant* as a pervasively improvisatory collaboration seen into life by its author-director.

In both the 1987 and the 1988 Yale rehearsals of *Warrior Ant*, there is no director's table. Breuer never has a fixed seat or place to stand. His physical motility finds a parallel in his flurry of seemingly contradictory, even at times unplayable, suggestions for line readings. To actor Tom McGowan, Breuer gives the following notes in rapid succession: "Fellini cum Middle East. . . . Like a silent Yiddish movie [the actor looks dumbfounded; an actress repeats, "*silent* Yiddish film?"] . . . perhaps Viennese. . . . [interrupting] *Simpler*. Just *straight*. . . . In other words, a deadpan voice."[7] Like Akalaitis, Breuer is not interested in immediately achieving a particular tone but in establishing a range of possibilities and dislodging the actor from preconceptions or personal mannerisms invoked too early in the rehearsal process.[8]

Exploring what he calls different "takes" on each speech in his script, the director discovers what (and whose) voice will be best, as he listens for the balance between musical and vocal expression. On the day before the workshop performance, I overhear Bob Telson give general directions to the newly arrived Arab band whose music will accompany a long monologue of the termite who fathered the warrior ant. After listening to a tape of Dennis Scott's delivery of the speech, the musicians make suggestions about which instruments should be more dominant in different parts of the score. Telson listens and discusses various options with the musicians, as he had with Breuer earlier in rehearsal, and as Breuer had with the actors. The relationship among musicians working with a basic score and improvising within general prescribed limits is clearly one model for the *Warrior Ant* rehearsals.[9]

In the 1987 Yale rehearsals, Breuer often stands in a kind of liminal space somewhere between the audience section and the playing area. When he wants to introduce or reinforce a particular dance movement or puppet position, his own body involuntarily enacts it. As he watches rehearsal he is frequently in motion, not imitating but somehow carrying the rhythms of the performers in his body. After a runthrough of one section of Part IV, he says to the student chorus of belly dancing puppeteers: "I learned something very important. The best gesture the little [Chinese glove] puppets can do is clapping because it keeps them joyful and animated. Keep them clapping."[10] In the fall, 1988, rehearsal at the University Theatre, Breuer dances as he directs the performers on stage. His own body becomes the ever-changing book of the play.

There is a striking lack of closure in Breuer's rehearsal. The runthrough, often invoked as a means of preparing for and setting the conditions of performance, is used in the *Warrior Ant* rehearsal as an occasion for seeing possibilities for change. At times the first full runthrough of Breuer's works-in-progress may even coincide with the first public performance.[11] After a runthrough of one small section of Part IV, the director responds characteristically, "It's good to see it all together. I have a couple of ideas for variations." In the fall of 1988, five hours before the opening performance at the University Theatre, Breuer is still introducing new ideas and new staging.

In the rehearsals I observe on the third floor of the Gypsy, the puppet is cherished. Here is the magic of rehearsal in one of its most haunting forms. The secrets and techniques of puppetry are discussed and exposed in this small room. There is an undecipherable intimacy between the human figures and the nearly life-size wood-and-cloth Bunraku dolls. In the rehearsal studio, but not in performance, one sees the eyes of the puppets open and close. The puppets are animated by a life not their own and yet not simply that of their handlers. They are not alive and yet they appear so:[12] the actors lend their voices and the beautiful Bunraku dolls seem to speak.

For a full appreciation of the work of the Bunraku masters, some knowledge of the Japanese puppet theatre may be helpful. Combining puppetry, storytelling, and shamisen music,[13] Bunraku originated in the sixteenth century and has changed very little since the mid-eighteenth, when puppeteer Yoshida Bunzaburo developed a three-man system of doll manipulation. Barbara Adachi's description of the puppet theatre suggests its collaborative nature:

> Bunraku might be described as the "art of threes": the spellbinding coordination of the three puppeteers manipulating one doll, the unity achieved by the three independent elements—puppet, narrator, and musician—and the intersecting lines of communication established between puppeteer and narrator, narrator and musician, musician and puppet, as well as between and among the trios of puppeteers. *This interlocking and continual shifting of artistic triangles formed by words, music, and movement* continues to fascinate . . . (italics added).[14]

In her repeated viewings of Bunraku at the Osaka Theatre in Japan, Adachi reports a sense of alternating experiences very like my own in watching rehearsal:

> Forgetting the intricacies of the complicated situation that has excited the characters on stage, one intermittently returns to the matter at hand. How are the dolls moved? . . . It is this combination of continuous movement and sound that draws one back into the drama, ready to ignore again the physical complexities involved in its creation.[15]

The physical complexities of operating the puppets are considerable. Bunraku puppets are delicate four-foot-high dolls, each of which is manipulated by three puppeteers. The chief handler animates the head and right arm, the second handler manipulates the left arm, the third operates the legs. All puppeteers perform in full view of the audience. In Bunraku theatre an onstage reader speaks both the dialogue and the narration. A Bunraku puppeteer may spend ten years operating the legs of the puppet and another ten years handling the left arm before animating the head and right arm.

Yoshida Tamamatsu, a master puppeteer with the Osaka Kukuritsu Bunraku Theatre, the national puppet theatre of Japan, explains the effect of this training: "I've had ten years with the legs, ten with the left arm, and [more than] ten as chief puppeteer. All the years of training blend together when three puppeteers begin to move a single doll at dress rehearsal. . . . If the legs aren't right, that puppet dies no matter what the head puppeteer does. . . . All three puppeteers must focus on the back of the doll's head. . . . For the doll to be alive, all three must *be* together—

must share intuition and must feel that they are inseparable. One plus one plus one equals more than three in Bunraku, but three minus one equals zero."[16] The splendid puppetry of the Bunraku masters, at the center of the rehearsals I observe, provides a model of the intricate, precarious, at times miraculous work of collaborative creation.

On October 5, 1988, a female Bunraku puppet drinks coffee from a miniature china cup with matching saucer. Tamamatsu operates the right hand which takes the dainty cup from the saucer held in the left hand operated by Barbara Pollitt, one of the first Americans to puppeteer with the Bunraku master. The left hand of the puppet continues to hold the saucer; the right hand takes the china cup, raises it to her lips, and returns it to the saucer in the left hand. A perfectly united action, seemingly natural and effortless, is created by the right hand of the chief puppeteer and the right hand of the left-arm manipulator whose fingers in this case actually hold the saucer beneath the puppet's fingers while the cup passes to the waiting fingers of the Bunraku master.

Now the puppet begins to dance. Invisibly Tamamatsu's left hand grasps the headgrip attached to the neck of the doll. His middle and ring fingers operate the main wooden toggle, the *choi*, that controls the up-and-down or nodding movements of the head. His thumb manipulates the small toggles attached to heavy silk threads that animate the puppet's eyes, mouth, and brows.

Tamamatsu's unseen right hand animates the puppet's right arm and hand movements by operating a toggle connected to silk cords running the length of the hand and arm. Barbara Pollitt's unseen right hand operates the left-arm toggle by means of the *sashigane*, a wooden armature attached to the puppet's left arm. The puppeteer's index finger and middle finger control loops of twine which, pulled or loosed, move the toggle within the armature. Leg operator Kanju Kiritake crouches as he manipulates the hem of the female puppet's kimono to suggest movement, bending his arm and clenching his fist to suggest a knee line.[17] (Female dolls usually do not have legs.) As the puppet dances the cha-cha-cha with more and more élan, the rhythm is transmitted kinetically to the other two puppeteers by the chief handler whose own graceful swaying body and dancing feet are visible beneath the Bunraku doll. Watching Tamamatsu in rehearsal I think of Goethe's description of piano playing as the soul passing into the fingers.[18] The hands of three puppeteers seem to be orchestrated by a single consciousness; the technical intricacies of each millisecond of coordinated movement produce the uncanny effect of a puppet spontaneously dancing.

What role does the chief puppeteer play in a rehearsal where the puppet is the star? On October 4, 1988, narrator Frederick Neumann reads the script aloud on microphone while the director and, slightly behind him, Tamamatsu sit listening. As interpreter Yoko Totani translates the English words into Japanese, the puppetmaster stands up and begins to move his empty right hand. At times his hand rehearses what the audience will never see: the special fingering used to produce certain effects with the puppet.[19] But more often Tamamatsu himself performs the puppet's actions—for example, puts his own hand over his own heart.

This is not an insignificant distinction. The first kind of movement is that of the choreographing hand of the chief puppeteer; the second is something between a director's physical marking of an emotional moment and a performer's enactment of it.[20] The master puppeteer enacts with his body what his hands alone will later create: "I become the puppet. I measure out the playing area and the space in the music—seeing where I should stop and make *mie* [freeze-frame poses], finding out the form."[21] In the *Warrior Ant* rehearsals Tamamatsu is partly director and partly performer. He rehearses in the role of the puppetmaster and he rehearses in the role of the puppet. Onstage in performance he animates a figure that replaces his own.

At times in the 1988 Yale rehearsals Tamamatsu exuberantly partners the director, with Breuer's full encouragement, in conceiving the stage actions to be explored. On October 1, 1988, for example, Breuer begins rehearsal of the final scene by describing the narrative action (the warrior ant concludes its life by climbing a redwood tree and mating with a death moth). He then poses the problem of the moth puppet's initial position on stage: "She should be in a strange position. I don't know. I wanted to discuss this with Tamamatsu. . . . If not upside down, perhaps curled up." (He curls his own body in front of Tamamatsu as the interpreter translates his words.) Several minutes later the puppeteer interrupts Breuer's continuing presentation of the scene to suggest exactly how the puppet could be wrapped up in a ball and then slowly unfolded. Director and puppeteer trade ideas excitedly, slowed down only by the need to have their dialogue translated.

The director notes that Tamamatsu's idea works well with the lines in the English text but that the lighting will have to be adjusted. A multitude of technical details must be considered before Tamamatsu's idea is deemed stageworthy, but he has essentially formulated the staging of the first appearance of the death moth.

When the scene is rehearsed, Tamamatsu takes the female Bunraku puppet in his arms and revolves slowly as white gauze wrapped around her body slowly unwinds and is slowly re-wrapped onto a bamboo pole held high in the air. In this striking moment I see Tamamatsu's eyes clearly as they focus on the puppet-actor. I feel a shock of recognition. His gaze is steady, impassive, ineffably poignant. It is a gaze I have seen before but not on the stage itself. It is the gaze of the director: performed, public, visible, as it never is except in rehearsal. The directorial gaze that I observe in rehearsal is, like Tamamatsu's, not that of longing or desire, but of absorption in and detachment from the other, as if the viewer is inside and outside what is viewed. Not easily categorizable, it is what I have called the "maternal gaze" in its ideal aspect. Neither purely voyeuristic nor purely posses-sive, it is a taking in and letting go.

The chief puppeteer inhabits two kinds of space simultane-ously: the space of representation and the space where stage images are received and reconstructed by the spectator.[22] His paradirectorial role is shared by other performers in Breuer's rehearsals, as it might be in any theatre piece with music and dance. Elena, a Middle Eastern dancer and choreographer, di-rects and performs with her ensemble of belly dancers. Lead vocalist Denise Delapenha directs the movements of a troupe of Brazilian musicians, Empire Loisaida Escola de Samba, whom Breuer has encouraged to dance as they accompany her on the drums. Pat Hall-Smith rehearses her troupe of adult dancers in New York while Estelle Eichenberger rehearses a youthful chorus of local public school students in New Haven whom she will join in performance. Bob Telson rehearses his own band, Little Village, and the Trinidadian steel band, Moods Pan Groove, in New York and somehow manages to direct both bands simultaneously on stage in New Haven as he accompanies them on the synthesizer.

This abundance of paradirectorial figures,[23] as much as the trio of puppeteers handling each puppet, reflects the collaborative nature of Breuer's rehearsal work. Singers, dancers, musicians, narrators, puppeteers, puppet-actors meet in a rehearsal space where the cross-cultural[24] multilayered texture of *The Warrior Ant* is continually exposed. What may look in performance like the work of an impresario,[25] a booking-agent extraordinaire, has as its invisible subtext the fragile intricacies and resistance to closure of collaborative improvisation.

In the fall of 1988 Elena dances with the warrior ant and worm puppets. Improvising movements as the director watches, she stamps one foot lightly and, bowing her head, throws her long black hair forward. Tamamatsu immediately recreates these actions so that the warrior ant puppet's black ponytail is flung out in rhythmic greeting to the belly dancer. She twirls, the puppet twirls; she flicks her hair, so does he; she shakes her head, he shakes his. Breuer asks that Elena introduce additional movements, then interjects a few minutes later, "It can be an embrace but the [puppet's] arms should always dance."

Tamamatsu suggests blocking, asking Elena to move behind the ant puppet and give him a slight push. (Breuer later changes this so that the worm puppet pushes the ant puppet toward Elena.) As she and Tamamatsu dance together without the puppet, Elena continues to initiate and explore new choreography. Members of the cast quietly suggest alternate possibilities to the director but he resists: "Let's let them work it out for awhile." After the dance is rehearsed with a trio of puppeteers, Breuer suggests certain hand movements to Elena. The dancer asks, "Lee, should I exaggerate my gestures?" and the director replies, "Yes. [pause] I don't know. I really don't know yet."

Later that evening Elena dances with the worm puppet while Ruth Maleczech reads aloud its long monologue. Breuer demonstrates a two-step wiggle to be performed by the worm; the movements of the director's feet and torso are recreated by three pairs of hands. Breuer synchronizes the complex manipulation of the puppet by its trio of handlers (Patrick Kerr, Eren Ozker, and John Ludwig), Elena's electric movements, and Maleczech's wonderfully raspy vocal rhythms with the taped score by Bob Telson. He concentrates first on variations in line delivery ("Ruth, the key to the rap is making it evil. . . . Just hit the stresses"), then on changing the worm puppet's blocking, then on introducing new choreography for the belly dancer. Illustrative of the continually shifting "artistic triangles formed by words, music, and movement" is Breuer's continual revision of his script. He restores a phrase, "down there" (cut earlier in rehearsal), in order to accommodate choreography created by the puppeteers, after conferring with Ruth Maleczech about the effect of the restored words on her newly adjusted speech rhythms. At the end of the evening rehearsal the director says simply, "It's basically getting clear now."

On occasion rehearsal exploration is confined to the director's own body. For example, on September 30, 1988, after gracefully demonstrating certain movements of the arms and body of the warrior ant puppet in the presence of the puppeteers, Breuer immediately rejects it, "I don't think so." In rehearsal Breuer usually physicalizes his directorial comments. When he suggests where in the playing area a particular dancer or puppet is to be, he often moves there and makes an appropriate expressive gesture associated with that figure's role or presence. Walking out the blocking, demonstrating a movement or dance step, is the director's way of exploring the staging he envisions even as he indicates to the performer what is to be explored.

Breuer's demonstrations of blocking "for the puppet" are problematic. The actual movements required to animate the Bunraku doll do not in the least resemble the gestures of the director who is always illustrating the result, not the intricately coordinated process, of collaboration among three puppeteers. Breuer's physical demonstrations in the puppetry rehearsal are signs, gestures indicating an idea rather than actions to be imitated. Alternately, they are punctuation marks, establishing for the non-English-speaking Bunraku puppeteers certain parts of the sung or spoken text as separate playable units. At one point in rehearsal, Breuer demonstrates three or four exaggerated poses of shock "for the warrior ant puppet." When the director presents *mie*, he provides an expressive marker. The discovery of the form and means of enactment is left entirely to the Bunraku puppeteer.

In Breuer's *Warrior Ant* the "character" of the puppet-actor seems to be splintered into many different forms of stage presence: narrators Ruth Maleczech, Leslie Mohn, Isabell Monk, and Frederick Neumann present the speaking voice; lead vocalists Sam Butler, Jr., Denise Delapenha, and Jevetta Steele perform the singing voice; a multitude of bands and dancers enact the musical rhythms and kinetic energy; Bunraku and American puppeteers animate the gestural life. But "splintered" does not do justice to the sense of overlapping renderings of "character" in rehearsal. At one point Denise Delapenha, dancing with the Bunraku warrior ant puppet as she sings in a very high voice, says suddenly to her small partner, "That sounds like *your* voice." Earlier I watch the moth puppet rehearse a scene narrated by Leslie Mohn. An actress seated on a bench talks into a hand-held microphone while six feet away two men in kimonos and a woman in a black robe handle a female Bunraku doll dressed in white. I see the actress in full view reading from the script, but I hear the puppet say the lines: "each one / struggles to become the other; / once the other, back itself again . . . an exchange of souls."[26]

I watch Tamamatsu and Elena again rehearse their dance without the puppet. Tamamatsu practices on his own the belly dancer's remarkable semi-revolving thigh and hip movement, then dances with Elena once more. When he animates the puppet, the puppeteer's bodily and facial expressiveness, even the warmth of his dancing style, are suddenly reconfigured in the Bunraku doll.[27] And I wonder, as I watch, who is dancing when the puppet dances?

The Warrior Ant opens with a festival celebrating the conception and birth of its protagonist. Breuer's description in the program suggests the tone:

> Once a year, ants fly: this night is a night of great passion on which ants are conceived. All the earth must prepare itself. From the noon to the moonlight hour to the flight of the virgin queen, the rains and the breezes, the smell of the flowers, the taste of all the earth's juices, the rhythms of insects calling, the flashes of twilight falling, the embraces of shadows, and the very air of the earth prepares itself for the love of ants.
>
> And the love of ants is a thing of mid-air, and there is a certain message here, or at least a certain metaphor, for the queens live and multiply, and the drones live and die.[28]

On October 6, 1988, four days before the first performance of *Warrior Ant* at the Yale University Theatre, actress Isabell Monk and Moroccan musician Hassan Hakmoun rehearse their roles in the opening section of the mock-epic. Monk narrates the celebration of the conception of the warrior ant. Hakmoun sings and dances as he plays the santir, a three-stringed lute-like instrument. As they perform, the stage will be filled with several bands and troupes of dancers, lead vocalists and a youthful chorus, puppeteers and puppets, other narrators, and a giant female ant. In the small studio the director rehearses two performers.

Breuer begins by describing what the stage will look like: "Everyone [is] in a Carnival tableau . . . frozen. When the music starts, they will move. [to Monk] Now what you're doing in telling the story is . . . more [of] . . . a conjuration. . . . I'd like you to move, to incorporate moving rhythmically slowly, unless you feel uncomfortable. If you feel uncomfortable, don't do it. But I'd like you to move slowly among all these frozen figures and bring them to life." A few minutes later the actress comments, "I hear you saying what the stage looks like but until I get much more familiar with this I may not be able to move around as much as you like."

Monk begins to read aloud lines from Breuer's newly revised script, first in an unaccented voice and then in a voice which carries the accents of South African speech. Hakmoun, sitting two feet away, spontaneously begins to sing in a mixture of Arabic and South African dialect as he strums the santir. The director, seated nearby, listens, head slightly bent, eyes on the floor, as he nods rhythmically. The actress begins to move in her chair, rocking slightly, right hand moving over her head. Suddenly she says in a normal voice, "I don't understand that [line]," and continues to read the script aloud as previously accented.

Monk suggests that in the next section of the narrative Hakmoun first begin to play and that she follow his lead. Breuer says to the musician, "One idea, Hassan, is that we use three different songs or three different tempos. We're looking for ways that excitement increases. *I don't know how, because I don't know what music you're going to play*, but the third one should have a lot of [percussive sound] . . . on the santir" (emphasis added). He then says, "I love this song. That will be the first one," and the actress agrees.

The santir player's mode of participating in the improvisatory collaboration is to perform, not to discuss or analyze. He plays another song, this time in a lower register, and Breuer asks the actress to begin reading the third section of her narration:

> In the heart of the night of the
>   flight of the virgin queens begins [sic]
>   the beatings. . . .
>
>   (. . . Rubbings

> And scrapings and the claxings
> > they are the oowheegings and the
> > tintinkings), such as they are
>
> They are the percussions . . .
> > They are the languages the gods speak
>
> They are God's
> > Body languages. . . .[29]

As Monk reads aloud, Breuer says, "Hassan, sing," and as the santir player sings in a language unknown to the director and actress, Breuer says to Monk: "Just ride with it."

Coordinating the rhythms and timing of her narration with music and song she is hearing for the first time, the actress is finding her way simultaneously through Breuer's script and Hakmoun's song, two texts spontaneously placed in juxtaposition. But this is not all. "Tell me, Hassan," the director asks at the conclusion of the song, "is the third piece easy to dance to?" Without answering, the santir player attaches a shoulder strap to his instrument, stands up and begins to move slowly and tentatively in response to his own playing. As he listens to himself, his dance steps become more patterned and exciting. The actress remains seated, reading aloud. The director, head bent, first watches the musician's feet dancing, then closes his eyes, listens, nods rhythmically. Afterwards he says, "That's beautiful, man. Just beautiful. . . . That's going to be a solo."[30] And then, spontaneously reversing his earlier note to Monk, Breuer says to Hakmoun: "It's like you're in a street . . . full of Trinidadian Carnival dancers—forty to fifty people on stage, like statues. The only person moving is you. So music and dancing is to bring them to life. . . . You move from one to another, bringing them to life." To the actress the director says in a striking phrase: "Let the demonstration of bodily language be Hassan."

After watching the Moroccan musician improvise a dance as he plays the santir, the director transfers to the dancer's body the role he earlier assigned to the actress' voice reading his words ("the story is . . . a conjuration") as she moved. Despite the fact that Hakmoun is improvising, the director seems to see the dancer's "bodily language" as a reinscribing of the spoken text.

The director briefly describes his sense of what is musically appropriate to the second section of the opening narration:

"Softer than the first one. . . . Also sing in a different way, maybe with the mouth closed to make people feel like coming in . . . more inside." There is no literal shift from outside to inside in the narrative nor does Hakmoun take the director's suggestion about technique literally. With mouth wide open he sings a beautiful soft low song. As the actress begins to read aloud, the director says to her, "Softer, maybe in a whisper." She slows down and softens her delivery but does not whisper.

All three songs are now rehearsed with the spoken text as the director listens and suggests further adjustments in pace and volume. As rehearsal continues, the originally improvised alternation and overlapping of spoken text and song is replaced by a formal establishing of cuing devices to control when Hakmoun sings and when Monk speaks. During the last runthrough of this opening section, Hakmoun performs the second song softly on the santir, with lips closed; only the actress' voice is heard. The director raises three fingers to cue the final song without interrupting the rehearsal. Hakmoun dances, plays, sings. The director stands outside the playing area, listening, his feet moving rhythmically in place. His gaze seems to rest on the floor between the two performers. Then he cues a fade, and says, "Great." The stage manager announces the timing: seven minutes, thirty-five seconds. The staging will be refined—Monk's blocking, for example, will be altered several times before opening night—but the essential form of three pages of *Warrior Ant* has been created for two performers.

After a short break the director rehearses with Frederick Neumann, who delivers a long lecture on ants before Monk and Hakmoun enter. The actor begins with a quiet, low-key reading, interrupts himself, begins again. As the reading continues and becomes more expressive, the director begins to discuss verbal changes in the script, soliciting the actor's opinion of revised phrasing and variation in accented speech. Characteristically Breuer encourages experimentation with different acting styles and attitudes ("Camp it up, Fred, camp it up"; "Take it pretty deadpan").

Like Fornes, Breuer revises the script in the presence of the actors. In this rehearsal he composes several questions to be delivered by actors planted in the audience. He dictates, and revises, phrases that the actor and stage manager write, erase, rewrite in their scripts. Authorial and directorial roles interrupt and supplant each other. On the one hand, Breuer fastidiously

Fig. 11.2. The eighteen-foot-high ant puppet, Tamamatsu, the Bunraku puppet, and Barbara Pollitt in rehearsal of The Warrior Ant. *Photograph by T. Charles Erickson.*

corrects the actor's inadvertent alterations in phrasing as the new lines are repeated (e.g., "this" rather than "the"; "explain" rather than "briefly describe"); on the other hand, he includes a phrase suggested by the actor. After the actor finishes reading the lecture aloud, he asks, "Is it too long?" and Breuer replies, "That's the way it should be played. The rest is politics, logistics, economics."[31] Members of the company enter from behind the closed door of the rehearsal studio and compliment the actor on his delivery of the speech.

The Warrior Ant is a theatre piece that presents in its opening Carnival section the birthing of the puppet-actor and at its close a scene of sexual union[32] that presumably culminates in a new birth. As I watch the very last moments of rehearsal a few hours before the play opens in New Haven, what dominates the stage is an eighteen-foot-high ant puppet dancing in the air above the other dancing figures on the stage and the director dancing in the aisles of the darkened theatre. The giant female figure who dances as she gives birth to the Bunraku warrior ant puppet is the emblem I've been searching for without knowing it. Rehearsal is a dance of creation, of continually recirculating energy, of comings together and cross-fertilization, through which new life is born. It seems to me that the creation of life in the theatre can find no better emblem than this dancing puppet, the figure of pure dramatic presence.[33] From one point of view, rehearsal is a process by which a construction (the dramatic text) results in another construction (the theatrical event). And still one wants to ask: who is dancing when the puppet dances?

Epilogue

The last rehearsal I record is a kind of return home, an observation of and gradual absorption into the process of rehearsing
Sophocles' *Antigone* on the campus of Albertus Magnus, the college where I teach, just before I embark on an extended sabbatical to write this book. No less than in the earlier documentation
of award-winning theatre professionals, I encounter the truth of
W.B. Worthen's remark: "To describe how the theatre subjects
texts and performers to its process is a daunting challenge. . . ."[1]
My purpose in ending with this project is simple. It is an occasion
for discovering to what extent the rehearsal work of a company
of untrained, inexperienced actors and a student director may
elucidate that of professional theatre artists. The names that
occur in the following pages will be known to very few. The
dilemmas, frustrations, disasters, triumphs, and above all trust
in the process itself are surprisingly familiar.

Rehearsals of *Antigone*, directed by Martin Marchitto, a senior
at the college, take place from March 9 through May 5, 1988, in
various locations, indoors and out, on the campus of Albertus
Magnus College in New Haven, Connecticut. A single performance is scheduled for the afternoon of May 6, on the steps of
the library, Rosary Hall, the college's oldest building. In what
will prove to be a significant omission, there is no rain date.
Although I initially attend rehearsals, and even one pre-produc-
tion meeting, as a faculty observer, I eventually become dramaturg and thus a member of the company. In a spatial representation of this change in function I am asked midway through
rehearsals to abandon my usual position diagonally behind the
director in order to sit by his side. In the *Antigone* rehearsal, my

gaze approximates the director's own more directly than in any other.

On the evening of March 9, 1988, after the first readthrough of the play by the cast seated in a circle in a sectioned-off area of the upstairs dining hall, Marchitto's first words are: "The whole rehearsal process is trying new things. *Now* is the time to try it all. That's the only way we're going to grow and make those choices so that we come to full production." Speaking of the script, he then adds a caveat that will come back to haunt the production: "We need to get rid of this crutch." A month later he tells Kathy Shave, playing the guard who informs Creon of the unauthorized burial of Antigone's brother, Polyneices: "We're seeing your character want to grow but holding onto your script is stunting your growth." Although Marchitto seems to be alluding to a more conventional notion of "character" than do most of the directors I have observed, his final "your" is just indeterminate enough to suggest that it is the actor's growth he is encouraging, not that of the "character."

For this student director, as much as for Wilson or Breuer, "the body is his book."[2] Not only is his own body continually responding to the staging of the text but Marchitto's comments to the actors reflect an emphasis on corporeality. After he reads aloud certain lines in a playtext from which he never deviates,[3] Marchitto tells the actress playing the messenger:

> Push through. Use your body. Work through the storytelling with your body. That will help you. In a lot of ways acting has nothing to do with the script. . . .

To Mary Lee Vitale, who delivers the messenger's 50-line monologue narrating the death of Haemon to Eurydice, played by Ellin Regis, the director says: "Visualize the graphic details. [Go] . . . to the tomb. *Make* it a true account. Like that accident on Rt. 95 last night. These are the gaps you need to fill in as an actress so that *you're making the account happen*" (emphasis added). Later he will say to the cast, "You have to experience this play now in the rehearsal moment. You can't just use memory. You have to create."

What is created in any particular rehearsal is never precisely reproduced. Speaking to Mary Vitale, whose electric rendering of the messenger's speech midway through the rehearsal period is never quite recaptured, the director remarks, "You did something beautiful last week but it has to be fresh tonight. You can't try to recreate it. . . . You can recreate subtext perhaps but you can't try to recreate that exact performance."

At one point in rehearsal Marchitto tries to accelerate and sharpen a certain exit line and exit. The director says exactly what he wants and then demonstrates verbally and physically, speaking the line himself as he exits from the playing area. The demonstration could not be clearer. When the actor playing Creon attempts the line and the exit, both the delivery and the action are slower and less crisp than the demonstration. The director does not repeat the note to the actor. Later he remarks privately, "I could do it because *I* could see it," a wonderfully paradoxical statement. The entire company could see the "it" of the director's demonstration. What "it" could the director "see" that the actor could not?

Successful directing is not rooted in clear demonstration, however irresistible and necessary that may be. Nor is the intelligibility of the director's comments the *sine qua non* I had supposed when I began this project. The actor's self-negotiations, passing through the arc of the directorial vision, are fundamental to the rehearsal work of every director, from the most collaborative to the most seemingly autocratic. What the director "sees" into reality on the stage is invariably dependent on the physical skills, imaginative elasticity, and rhythms of receptivity of particular actors.

Sometimes this mutual dependency of actor and director is mutually nourishing. For example, I watch Marchitto block the dialogue between Creon and his son, Haemon. As Haemon moves one step diagonally upstage left, Creon simultaneously moves two steps diagonally upstage right. Later Marchitto tells me, "I try to establish boundaries and let the actors work within them. I had blocked this moment generally and told Creon, 'You're always one step ahead of Haemon.' I told Haemon to take one step and I told Creon where I wanted him to start and end up when Haemon moved but *Creon himself found the pace and rhythm of the movement by which he crossed Haemon's upstage move*" (emphasis added). I respond, "It's a collaboration"; the director replies, "Yes, and a miracle."

During a workthrough on the stage of the campus theatre, the cast is able for the first time to rehearse moving up and down actual stairs in preparation for performance on the stone steps leading to the library. In this new space Marchitto gives a new blocking direction to the actor playing Creon after he falters in delivering a long monologue. He asks the actor simply to descend one step each time he says the word, "this," repeated three times in a line and a half of verse:

> This destroys the state;
> this drives men from their home; this wicked
> teacher . . . (ll. 297–98)

What may seem a literal-minded blocking succeeds in eliciting a more effective incantatory voicing of the speech. It is an elementary but illuminating example of how a director may evoke certain verbal effects through the simplest of physical means: how slight an adjustment of bodily position or movement can alter pace, tone, and pattern of stresses in the speaking voice.

Because of Marchitto's trust and openness, I am given an unusual glimpse of the director conceptualizing the staging during rehearsal. As he watches the final scene of the play, Marchitto muses in a low voice: "Perhaps Creon could take Haemon's hand here. . . . There will be blood on Haemon's face and hands. . . . Perhaps Creon could get blood on his hand. . . ." I listen quietly to "this dialogue of one,"[5] marveling at the director's need to speak his thoughts as they occur, then surrender to my own need to verify my assumption. I ask if he is in fact reconceiving the staging as he observes rehearsal, and he responds, "Well, it's really happening now. I knew I wanted blood on Haemon's body. . . . [But Creon's bloody hand] just came to me now *as I was watching*" (emphasis added).

Four days later, as he watches the first rehearsal on the steps of the library (the college's oldest building and hence its original "house"), the director says to the actor playing Creon: "Maybe when your bloodied hand touches the steps, and gets blood on the steps, it's as if you have bloodied the house."[6]

On other occasions Marchitto introduces preconceived blocking during the actors' early rehearsal explorations. On April 6, for example, he tells Chris Russo, playing Haemon, to take two steps diagonally toward center stage, moving down one level of stairs as he does so: "You're making a choice. In this scene [with Creon] you act on your choice. *We're seeing those decisions made*" (emphasis added). If the blocking represents making choices and acting on those choices, the actor is being asked to "choose" the director's choreography—two diagonal steps downward toward center—on behalf of his "character," somewhat as the director claims to have chosen those moves on behalf of the spectator. The choreography is a representation of the process of decision-making. A diagonal movement toward downstage center is generally considered one of the strongest crosses an actor can make. But this one will not have its fully intended force until the actor has made the directorially imposed blocking his own.

A problem I first noticed in Elinor Renfield's rehearsals of Chekhov's *Cherry Orchard* emerges in the rehearsal of *Antigone*. The cast experiences difficulty with the director's insistence on a presentational staging in which actors are asked to face the audience when they speak, rather than each other.[7] The students in the cast, not unlike many professionally trained American actors, continually try to position themselves naturalistically and are continually reminded by the director to "face out" toward the audience. Finally Chris Russo asks, "What should I look at? Just straight forward?" as he gestures toward the empty space beyond the back of the director. There is no answer to this question as posed. The director merely replies, "I know it's hard." So the actor playing Haemon has to find the object of his own gaze. His eyes search the farthest corners of what would be the audience section of the performance space, the movements of his head perhaps compensating for a bodily position facing Creon which the director has checked. In this moment the perennial question of "where to look" seems connected to the presence of the directorial gaze in rehearsal, as if the actor must be found looking not at what looks steadily at him but always somewhere else, anywhere else, so that he may be seen to *be* looking elsewhere.[8]

At one point Marchitto asks Jennifer Tarbe, playing Antigone, to give fuller expression to her own "thrusting emotions" by facing out diagonally. A few minutes later he leaps to his feet, and asks the actress, "rather than being so tight," to "talk to these positions," as he stands first to the far right and then to the left of what would be the last row of the audience section. He tells me privately that the actress is beginning to affect him and that he wants her "to turn to reach . . . more of the audience." The director is using two distinct techniques to motivate the same blocking. First he justifies facing out diagonally in terms of the actor's need to find a bodily position appropriate to the emotional force of Antigone's speech. Then he justifies the movement in terms of the audience's need to be addressed and included in that speech. This eclecticism is characteristic of most directors I have observed. But the two approaches are also two versions of the same necessity: to make manifest an otherwise invisible imagined life in the presence of an imagined audience, represented in rehearsal by the director's continual presence.

Early in the rehearsal period the director revises his blocking of the scene between Haemon and Creon by having Haemon face the audience not directly but on a slight diagonal, stage right. He confirms privately that this new blocking occurs to him during rehearsal as Chris Russo begins to move in this direction spontaneously. The actor, freed from the necessity of watching himself, but secure in the sense that he is nonetheless being watched and watched over, makes a tentative exploratory or merely random movement. Even were the actor fully conscious of this alteration in the prescribed blocking and even were he looking at himself in a mirror, he would not see *this* movement but only an image distorted by the fact of self-scrutiny. He would see a different self, a self-observing figure, a figure literally altered by its attempt to take itself in.[9]

Like Peter Sellars rehearsing *Two Figures in Dense Violet Light*, Marchitto intends to use artificial amplification and natural light in his production of *Antigone*. How fascinating it is to watch the evening outdoor rehearsals on the steps of Rosary Hall. Shadows fall on the steps and on the actors, lit only obliquely by a lamp hanging from the ceiling of the library portico.[10] Some faces are in full light, others totally unlit, a few half lit. As the cast rehearses on May 4, I notice all about me other ongoing signs of preparation for performance. Assistant to the director Priscilla Clark sits on the grass behind the director's chair painting half-masks[11] on the faces of chorus members Diane Edwards, Julia Funck, Tara Kane, and Debbie Sanguineti. Set and costume designer Melanie Rood sits on a grassy slope to the side of the playing area, completing final alterations on one of the costumes she has made and creating coverings for the library windows. Just beyond her, prop mistresses Morganna Payne and Laura Kiritsy are laboriously constructing the scrolls which the chorus members will hold. As I look behind me I glimpse the college president, Julia McNamara, leaning against a tree, unobtrusively watching the rehearsal in the deepening twilight.[12]

Two days later a relentless downpour on the day of the scheduled performance drives the production indoors, where, on a quickly improvised stage, a raised blue-carpeted platform, approximately eight feet by twelve feet, in the all-purpose room of the college's Campus Center, *Antigone* is performed without artificial amplification in cold stark white light to a standing-room-only audience.

As the play begins, the actor playing Creon falters, throwing off the actresses playing Antigone and Ismene by giving Mary McKelvy (Ismene) the wrong line as cue. The energy level on stage plummets visibly. The audience shifts uneasily. The legs of the director, who is standing beside me with his back pressed against the rear wall of the auditorium, bend backward and forward as if he is pedaling a bicycle. In rehearsal the director would stop and restart the actors, restoring the rhythm of the scene. In performance the actor must "save himself," a phrase Marchitto repeats frequently in the last weeks of rehearsal.

But this is not possible. Throughout rehearsals the actor playing Creon resists learning his lines, especially those at the end of the play when he must openly mourn the loss of son and wife; he is unable to imagine a context in which mourning is the only possible response.[13] The actor's dilemma in rehearsal is Creon's dilemma in the play. The only actor still "on book" during the first runthrough, he carries the script with him as he rehearses. At one point, while the director gives notes on the final scene to the whole company, the actor playing Creon balances his script on his upturned face as he lies on the stage, listening. It is an appropriate image of his situation: his script hides his face, he is hiding behind his script. In theatre terms, he won't come "off book," for he has not ingested the text. It is both too much with him and not enough his.

In performance Creon remains uncertain of his lines, and does not "save himself." But the company as a whole achieves at times a startling intensity. Vivian Frazier's Teiresias maintains a newly achieved uncanny presence; Haemon is meticulous in his attention to the nuances and details of his blocking. But it is Antigone herself who, like Creon, but with a totally different impact, almost breaks under the strain of her stage role. In her final speech the actress can barely hold back sobs as she begins her exit on the line, "Look what I suffer" (l. 942). Her face is ravaged as she leaves the stage to spontaneous applause. Overtaken by emotions that had never appeared in this form during rehearsal, the actress still does not lose a syllable of her scripted speech: in the text her own feelings find a voice. Finally we hear the self-mourning that the actor playing Creon has been unable to perform.[14]

It is not only student actors who are subject to this involuntary welling up of emotion in performance.[15] Antony Sher describes an early performance of a Royal Shakespeare Company production of *Richard III* in which he played the title role:

> The Nightmare scene is unfelt and technical. Different funny voices coming out. I had hoped it might release in performance, but not yet. Afterwards, in the Ratcliffe scene ("O Ratcliffe, I fear, I fear!"), my failing voice cracks badly, giving me a terrible fright. Fear that it won't last and the relief that we're coming to the end produces a flood of real tears. I stop it instantly . . . [when I say] "play the eavesdropper" [seven lines later]. Real emotion is so useful to act with—wish I had more access to it.[16]

. . .

My account of rehearsal is a narrative in which the story is a process. Now, at the close of the story, I finally apprehend the essential aloneness of the director. José Quintero has written that after opening night a director feels

> left out, useless, alone because there is nothing more to do. . . .
> The play belongs to the actors and the audiences and you feel
> that they are both saying, "Get out of the way."[17]

I watch Martin Marchitto exit into the pelting rain that has taken away his outdoor performance space and removed his production to an indoor playing area in which the company had never rehearsed until barely an hour before the performance. His retreating back soon becomes as invisible to me as his literal presence was to the audience. I feel the difficulty of his act of relinquishing, just as I feel my own, for this is the end of my journey into the hidden world of rehearsal.

Notes

Chapter 1

1. The phrase is Michael Goldman's describing an actor playing the role of Othello, in *Acting and Action in Shakespearean Tragedy* (Princeton: Princeton University Press, 1985), 148.

2. George Bernard Shaw, *The Art of Rehearsal*, quoted in Toby Cole and Helen Krich Chinoy, eds., *Actors on Acting* (New York: Crown Publishers, 1962), 197.

3. Molière, *L'Impromptu de Versailles*, in *One-Act Comedies*, trans. Albert Bermel (Cleveland: World, 1964), 107.

4. The desire to watch rehearsal, violating the theatrical taboo against observers, may, of course, be viewed as voyeuristic, but perhaps no more so than sociological or anthropological observation.

5. My observation of Joseph Chaikin's rehearsals of *Trespassing* is recounted in Susan Letzler Cole, *The Absent One: Mourning Ritual, Tragedy, and the Performance of Ambivalence* (University Park: The Pennsylvania State University Press, 1985), 101–114.

6. Norris Houghton's invaluable account of various directors' rehearsals in Moscow is the only precedent I know: *Moscow Rehearsals, An Account of Methods of Production in the Soviet Theatre* (New York: Harcourt, Brace and Company, 1936).

7. The one apparent exception is Liviu Ciulei, a Romanian. Ciulei, however, has been directing in this country since 1974 and is the former Artistic Director of the prominent Guthrie Theater in Minneapolis.

8. *The American Heritage Dictionary*, 1097.

9. Part of this information is taken from the OED; it has been supplemented and verified through correspondence with Charles R. Planck, an independent farmer in Purcellville, Virginia (April 1, 1989).

10. Cf. director Mike Nichols: "Kurt Russell and Cher called me 'Dad' while we were shooting *Silkwood*. . . . I think the role of director satisfies me partly because I am creating a father that I miss," quoted in an interview conducted by Barbara Gelb, "Mike Nichols: The Special Risks and Rewards of the

Director's Art" (*New York Times Magazine*, May 27, 1984), 41. Cf. also John Huston directing his father, Walter Huston, in the film, *The Treasure of the Sierra Madre:* "On the set, the director is always the father, and in directing him, I became my father's father" (CBS Evening News, March 24, 1986).

11. Director and psychotherapist Stephen Aaron sees "the maturation of a character as being akin to the birth of the ego," and, in the context of "this psychoanalytic perspective of ego development," notes "yet another way in which the actor experiences the director: as 'mother' to both the actor and the character." *Stage Fright: Its Role in Acting* (Chicago: University of Chicago Press, 1986), 47.

   Simon Callow writes of director Robert Walker rehearsing *Measure for Measure* at the Lincoln Rep: "What was . . . indispensable was Rob's capacity to create *the amniotic fluid* in which creativity can flourish" (italics added). Later he describes the director's role, affixing the male pronoun to the same maternal image: "The director's job in all this is parental. In the early stages of rehearsal, he must flood you with *amniotic fluid*, then, as the performance begins to take shape, he has to guide, nurture, offer himself as buffer, sometimes disciplining, but always respecting, your individuality. It's as difficult a job as parenthood, and one as little appreciated by the beneficiary" (italics added). *Being An Actor* (New York: St. Martin's Press, 1984), 32, 147.

12. Mike Nichols says of the process of directing, "It is in some ways like being an ideal parent." Gelb, *ibid.*

13. Cf. Peter Hall's distressed recognition: "Peter Stevens said my most common stance in rehearsals had been that of a teacher. I said I was aware of it and did not at all think that that was what a director should be. . . . I think more and more that rehearsals should be divided quite clearly between the learning of technique, and the creative process of the actor. We shouldn't confuse the two, and that is what we always do. We part teach, part impose, part encourage from the inner life of the actor. I would like to sort all that out. There's teaching technique, and there's trying to provoke imagination, but separate them, separate them." *Peter Hall's Diaries: The Story of a Dramatic Battle*, ed. John Goodwin (London: Hamish Hamilton, 1983), 81, 421.

14. Marvin Carlson, speaking of Goethe, says, "His role now became much more that of the modern director, the *invisible* artistic guiding presence that shapes and controls the production from first reading to public performance" (italics added). *Goethe and the Weimar Theatre* (Ithaca: Cornell University Press, 1978), 305.

15. Cf. actress Linda Hunt, "I can never hold my work outside myself. You can never really *see* or objectify it" (emphasis added). Interview conducted by Susan Zielinski, "Actress Linda Hunt On Campus: A Transforming Experience," *Radcliffe News* (Winter, 1989), 13.

   John David Cullum, during rehearsal of Irene Fornes's *Abingdon Square*, tells me that when he attempts to be his own director, "it is impossible [as an actor] to be your own third eye" (private conversation, September 18, 1987). Fornes, describing her directing of *Uncle Vanya*, says: "You just have your eye. You just have to get it in focus" (private conversation, November 20, 1987).

Director Nigel Jackson adds an interesting perspective on the third eye: "There are two 'me's' at rehearsal, one observing the other. One is immersed in the play as a sort of innocent John Doe who has never seen the action before and responds or does not respond. The other 'me' watches that John Doe, figures out why things work for him or do not. It's a weird kind of schizophrenia, but always interesting." Quoted by Robert Benedetti, *The Director At Work* (Englewood Cliffs: Prentice-Hall, Inc., 1985), 165.

16. Cf. Laura Mulvey, "Visual Pleasure and Narrative Cinema," *Screen*, 16, no. 3 (Autumn, 1975), 6–18, especially her discussion of woman as the object of the voyeuristic male gaze. The view in this well-known essay is somewhat modified by Mulvey's later article, "Changes: Thoughts on Myth, Narrative and Historical Experience," *History Workshop*, 23 (Spring, 1987), 3–19.

17. Cf., e.g., Anna Freud's discussion of the ego as observer in *The Ego and the Mechanisms of Defense, The Writings of Anna Freud*, vol. II, rev. ed. (New York: International University Press, Inc., 1966). See especially 6–8.

18. The metaphor is my own, but Peter Hall notes in his diaries that director Trevor Nunn says "he doesn't know where he's going and undertakes *a voyage of discovery* with the cast (italics added). Hall adds: "I go on voyages of discovery too. . . . We both often find things we didn't know were there and which we certainly weren't looking for" (Hall, *Diaries*, 15).

   A more concrete version of this metaphor is frequent reference to rehearsal as a mountain-climbing expedition, with the director as its leader. Antony Sher, rehearsing David Edgar's *Maydays* in March of 1984, writes in his diary: "In these last few, hectically busy weeks it felt like climbing a mountain." *Year of the King: An Actor's Diary and Sketchbook* (London: The Hogarth Press, 1985), 131. Albert Finney, rehearsing the role of Hamlet, uses the same metaphor of a difficult ascent, complete with references to pack animals, medical supplies, and oxygen: "Where were we going anyway? At this point he looked up and did a huge double take. We're Not Going Up There!" (Reported by Hall, *Diaries*, 191). Harris Yulin, playing Claudius, says to me during a break in rehearsal of *Hamlet*: "This play [in rehearsal] is like climbing Mt. Everest—in winter—with no gear." Later that same day Yulin and director Liviu Ciulei discuss the rehearsal experience of exploring the play. To the actor's comment, "It's a big mountain," the director replies with careful emphasis, "It's a *huge* mountain" (February 1, 1986).

   Playwright-director John Patrick Shanley, describing the experience of directing his own play, *Italian American Reconciliation*, which opened at the Manhattan Theater Club in the fall of 1988, offers a more detailed version of the metaphor of a mountain-climbing expedition: "[A good director is] a person who understands process. So that you do not, on the third day, want the third act emotionally there. It's like trying to find the way up a mountain, and there are six paths, and some of them get really close to the top, but then you have to go back down again to find the one that leads all the way to the top. After that, you know the path." Interview conducted by Sonia Taitz, "The Education of a Playwright Turned Director," *New York Times* (October 13, 1988), H5, H36.

19. Cf. Gordon Craig's account of the autocratic ship captain: "The captain of the vessel is *the king*, and *a despotic ruler* into the bargain. . . . Until discipline is understood in a theatre to be willing and reliant obedience to the manager

or captain no supreme achievement can be accomplished" (italics added). See Edward Gordon Craig, *On the Art of the Theatre* (New York: Theatre Arts Books, 1956), 171–72.

20. "The actor must go, and in his place comes the inanimate figure—the Über-marionette we may call him, until he has won for himself a better name." *Ibid.*, 81. It is interesting to note that Peter Sellars was a puppeteer before he became a director.

21. "[Peter] Shaffer describes the process we are going through with *Amadeus* as carving out a play with actors." Hall, *Diaries*, 466.

  Both Robert Wilson and Liviu Ciulei were trained as architects before they become theatre directors. Robert Wilson's primary and characteristic method of communication of his initial and continuing images of his theatre pieces is to draw sketches. Irene Fornes was initially a painter.

22. Robert Benedetti describes the director: "During this [exploratory] phase of rehearsal, you are the midwife at the birth of the score." (He defines the score as "the underlying sequence of objectives which stirs the actor to physical action.") Benedetti, *Director At Work*, 135, 166.

23. The actor Jeremy Irons has said of director Mike Nichols, "He's like the best of lovers: he makes you feel he's only for you." Gelb, "Mike Nichols," 41.

  Irene Fornes remarks, during a break in rehearsal of her play, *Abingdon Square*: "When I work with an actor and the work goes well, I feel a love that is as intimate as with a lover. But I am not aware of it at the time. I don't notice it while it's happening. But in the middle of the run if an actor leaves, I feel a sense of betrayal as if a lover has left. And yet there is never a question that it may lead to a more personal relationship. And yet it is a strong love."

24. Liviu Ciulei described the rehearsal process in this way to Kevin Kline: "It's a marriage between an actor and a director." (Kevin Kline, private communication, February 9, 1986). Peter Hall, in writing of his relationship with actor Paul Scofield after the first day's rehearsal of Ben Jonson's *Volpone*, uses a similar metaphor: "I get very much the feeling it's our second honeymoon." Hall, *Diaries*, 284.

25. See especially chapter 9 on Liviu Ciulei's *Hamlet*.

26. "We [Peter Brook and Peter Hall] both feel that in a sense the concept of the director is moving away from the *autocratic interpreter*, the *conductor* who presents his view of the work, to someone who is much more like the *trainer of a football team*. The director trains and develops the group, but the group of course has to do the play, or play the match" (italics added). Hall, *Diaries*, 101–102. At least three different metaphors overlap here.

27. Actor Antony Sher describes director Bill Alexander during rehearsals of Shakespeare's *Richard III:* "We've all got different solutions to the problems in these scenes and no one can agree. Bill, the most democratic of directors, sits silently, looking miserable. . . . Bill should decide this one [whether there should be outbreaks of physical violence in the court], but he continues to sit obstinately on the fence, so it's left unresolved." Earlier, the director says to the actor: "You must allow everyone their [sic] own rehearsal process." Sher, *Year of the King*, 211, 186.

28. Stephen Aaron's dual profession as psychotherapist and director is suggestive. A more extensive definition is that of actor and director William Roerick: "A director is a psychoanalyst, father, mother, brother, sister, mistress, lover, friend. Author's surrogate, actor's conscience, and ideal audience." (Private communication, July 3, 1985).

29. "To be read to is thus to have wholly at your disposal another on whom you wholly depend. . . . Conversely, to read *to* another is to be wholly at the disposal of one whose intake you wholly control." David Cole, *Acting as Reading* (Ann Arbor: University of Michigan Press, 1992). Cole is discussing the reader-listener as well as the actor-audience relationship, but his description seems highly illuminating as applied to the relationship of the director and the actor, especially the actor still "on book." Cf. also Robert Brustein: "There comes a time . . . when the director must reimagine himself as a spectator, and try to experience the production the way an audience will. At the same time, he must maintain a critical distance in order to push the production forward to its final realization." Quoted by Benedetti, *Director At Work*, 164.

30. The director in rehearsal re-authors the playtext, even if not a word is changed. The directorial role is at times very like the astonishing project of Jorge Luis Borges' Pierre Menard: "His admirable intention was to produce a few pages which would coincide—word for word and line for line—with those of Miguel de Cervantes," and its more astonishing result: "Cervantes' text and Menard's are verbally identical, but the second is almost infinitely richer. (More ambiguous, his detractors will say, but ambiguity is richness.)" Jorge Luis Borges, "Pierre Menard, Author of the *Quixote*," in *Labyrinths: Selected Stories and Other Writings*, eds. Donald A. Yates and James E. Irby (New York: New Directions, 1964), 39, 42.

31. The play is born from a broken text. Rehearsal is the breaking of the book of the play, the harrowing again of ground already ploughed and planted. Cf. Edmond Jabès: "It was necessary for Moses to break the book in order for the book to become human. . . . The book is always born from a broken book. And the word, too, is born from a broken word." Paul Auster, "Book of the Dead: An Interview with Edmond Jabès," in *The Sin of the Book: Edmond Jabès*, ed. Eric Gould (Lincoln: University of Nebraska Press, 1985), 23.

   The metaphor of the gardener is elaborated in actor Brian Cox's description of director Deborah Warner: "She works like a gardener: prepares the bed, plants the seed, waters it and watches it grow." Quoted by Joan Dupont in "Life and Death Are the Actors on Her Stage," *New York Times*, April 23, 1989, H36.

32. Dr. Daniel Stern, an experimental psychiatrist whose films of infants in interaction with their mothers have profoundly affected the director Robert Wilson, has said: "Mothers and children play all sorts of exaggerated verbal-visual games." "*It's like a sort of dance that precedes speech, with specific action and reaction going on all the time. In some ways, it's remarkably like what Bob [Robert Wilson] is doing in the theater—the way he works with people. In fact, when I see what he's doing, sometimes I wonder why I'm doing what I'm doing*" (italics added). Quoted by Calvin Tomkins, "Time to Think," in *The Theater of Images*, rev. ed., The Contemporary Arts Center

and The Byrd Hoffman Foundation (New York: Harper and Row, 1984), 67–68.

Kenneth Kaye, in *The Mental and Social Life of Babies*, notes that "The maintenance of mutual gaze during face-to-face interaction is a universal goal among mothers, but in its intensity it is a source of variation from one dyad to another. Several investigators have noticed that mutual gaze is also a variable distinguishing disordered infants from normals. . . . Infant gaze aversion may be an early sign of autism before other symptoms appear." (Chicago: The University of Chicago Press, 1982), 258. Is the mutual gaze of mother and infant—"the pre-oedipal pair, inhabitants of the original nurturing environment"—the gaze theatre needs to mask (literally, in classical Greek theatre) in order to *be* theatre? (Quotation above is from Edward Snow , "Theorizing the Male Gaze: Some Problems," *Representations*, no. 25 [Winter, 1989], 37).

33. E. Ann Kaplan, "Is the Gaze Male?" *Powers of Desire: The Politics of Sexuality*, eds. Ann Snitow, Christine Stansell, and Sharon Thompson (New York: Monthly Review Press, 1983), Headnote, 309; 318.

The deconstruction of the subject-object polarity of the gaze is a striking, and, to my knowledge, unexplored aspect of theatre. The first radical act I saw in the theatre was the initial moments of the Living Theatre's performance of *Mysteries and Other Pieces* when a single actor entered and planted himself at the extreme downstage-center point of the apron, silently staring at the audience. It was uncomfortable, seemed a violation of some unarticulated taboo. We in the audience were there to observe, to place ourselves in the subject position, not the object position, unless we identified with the latter on stage. Above all, we did not attend theatre to experience mutual gazing though we might be spectators to its onstage enactment. The pleasure of seeing the other and being seen by the other is suggested by the physical structure of most theatres, but the originary pleasure of mutual gazing, with its prototype of mother and child, has been ironically appropriated as the phallocentric pleasure of the voyeuristic gaze.

34. A full exploration of this speculation is beyond the limits of the present undertaking. The passage from Proust is translated and quoted in Cecile Nebel, *The Dark Side of Creativity* (Troy, New York: Whitston, 1988), 136. The original ("Le travail nous rend un peu mères,") can be found in *Cahiers Marcel Proust*, vol. 8 ["Le Carnet de 1908"], ed. Philip Kolb (Paris: Gallimard, 1976), 69.

35. Snow, "Theorizing," 31. The "negative capability" to which Snow refers is Keats's phrase: "I mean *Negative Capability*, that is when man is capable of being in uncertainties, Mysteries, doubts, without any irritable reaching after fact & reason." (Letter to George and Thomas Keats, December 21, 27 (?), 1817). Cf. also Goethe's provocative statement, "Alles faktische schon Theorie ist" (everything factual is already theory), quoted by J. Hillis Miller, in his 1986 presidential address, "The Triumph of Theory, the Resistance to Reading, and the Question of the Material Base," *PMLA*, vol. 102, no. 3 (May, 1987), 281.

36. From Freud's "Instincts and Their Vicissitudes" (1915), quoted by Janet Malcolm in *The New Yorker*, April 20, 1987, 95.

37. Interview conducted by Benedict Nightingale, "A British Grande Dame Comes Into Her Own," *New York Times*, January 20, 1985, H14.

38. Nikolai M. Gorchakov, *Stanislavski Directs*, trans. Miriam Goldina (New York: Grosset and Dunlap, 1962), 250.

39. "The new tyrant is the auteur-director." Mimi Kramer, review of Steven Berkoff's production of Shakespeare's *Coriolanus* at the Public Theater, *The New Yorker*, December 12, 1988, 140.

40. Michael Goldman, *The Actor's Freedom: Toward a Theory of Drama* (New York: The Viking Press, 1975), 101.

41. Joseph Papp, watching Liviu Ciulei's rehearsals of *Hamlet* at the Public Theater on February 2, 1986, remarks, "The director is a living writer: he has a say."

42. The Wooster Group's readthrough is a notable exception.

43. *The Tempest:* I.i.14; I.1.24–27, italics added. All citations of Shakespeare are taken from *The Complete Signet Classic Shakespeare*, ed. Sylvan Barnet (New York: Harcourt Brace Jovanovich, 1963).

Chapter 2

1. "Cross Left," *The Village Voice*, July 30, 1985, 88. Chekhov's characters' names are spelled as in the theatre program for Renfield's production of *The Cherry Orchard*.

2. Quoted by Gaby Rodgers, "An 'Orchard' Close to Home," *The East Hampton Star*, July 4, 1985.

3. Mark Zeller (Pishchik) is a theatre educator and director. Joanna Merlin is, like Karen Ludwig (Charlotta), an acting teacher: she is also a casting director. William Roerick, a veteran actor for fifty years, having performed with Ethel Barrymore and Katherine Cornell, has also directed.

4. Paul Hecht played Charles, Allie's former husband, in the CBS series, "Kate and Allie." William Roerick performs the role of Henry Chamberlain in "Guiding Light" in the morning and rehearses *Cherry Orchard* in the afternoon and evening.

5. This is not generally true of the directors I observed. Irene Fornes's approach to Chekhov's stage directions in *Uncle Vanya* is at times innovative; Peter Sellars consciously violates all of the playwright's stage directions in Samuel Beckett's *Ohio Impromptu*.

6. In theatre rehearsal, "notes" are writing and talking: what the director writes and says, what the actor hears and writes.

7. *The Cherry Orchard*, a newly revised version in English by Jean-Claude van Itallie (New York: Dramatists Play Service, Inc., 1979), 25. Unless otherwise noted, all citations to *The Cherry Orchard* are to the van Itallie translation used in the Renfield production.

8. *Selected Poems* (Ithaca: Cornell University Press, 1968), 140. I am not speaking, of course, of a literal walk, i.e., blocking, discussed later in more detail. My mistake was to take the director's words to the actor too literally, as if they were fixed ideas. David Selbourne, in his account of his observation of

Peter Brook's rehearsals of *A Midsummer Night's Dream*, reveals, I think, a similar misunderstanding of the directorial strategy when he writes: " 'The whole play,' [Peter Brook] . . . said to . . . Hippolyta, 'is about sex.' " "It is not," Selbourne adds. *The Making of* A Midsummer Night's Dream (London: Methuen, 1982), 83.

9. Benedetti, *Director At Work*, 146. Benedetti continues, "Your aim [as director] is to create the conditions in which the actors can generate the blocking impulses which you then extend, edit, and refine. . . ." This approach to blocking is not literally practiced by the directors I observed, with the exception of Elizabeth LeCompte and Lee Breuer, although in every rehearsal the directors responded to and incorporated, in varying degrees, blocking generated by the actors' impulses.

10. In a later rehearsal, when the cucumber Charlotta eats during her act two opening monologue was missing, a banana I had brought for lunch was conscripted, and, to my dismay, entirely consumed.

11. Charles Segal, *Interpreting Greek Tragedy: Myth, Poetry, Text* (Ithaca: Cornell University Press, 1986), 78.

12. In one sense, the actor is the site of this interlocking, but on behalf of the role, not of the play as a whole. The playwright as well might be conceived of as such a site (this is certainly Charles Segal's point), but only fully insofar as the playwright acts as director, which he may well have in the classical Greek theatre.

13. See David Cole, *Acting As Reading, passim.*

14. The subtext, for the actor, is like an unspoken interior monologue, an unwritten text buried beneath the written text, which inscribes the character's unstated desires, thoughts, feelings.

15. van Itallie, 26.

16. Beginning to rehearse act four, Renfield says, "Rather than staging, I'm just shaping impulses here."

17. Interview conducted by Mindy Aloff, "Home on the Road," *Village Voice*, April 18, 1989, Special Dance Supplement, 5.

18. "No, dear friend. Please stay. We'll find a way [together]. . . . Don't leave. I beg you" (van Itallie, 28). The word "together" has been added to the van Itallie translation.

19. Spoken under the words of the interviewer, Michael Billington, in the documentary, "Dame Peggy," produced and directed by Derek Bailey, a Landseer production, 1987. At one point, she contrasts theatre and film acting by saying, "[In the cinema] you *are* entirely in the hands of the director."

20. This is my own term, introduced to express a connection I feel between blocking as it is conventionally understood and the establishing of an oral-aural trajectory in space and time as speech moves across the stage from speaker to auditor.

21. The translation of the stage direction is that of Ann Dunnigan in *Chekhov: The Major Plays* (New York: New American Library, 1964), 348. The silence is first broken by Firs's subdued mutterings in act two; Firs alone is on

stage, possibly muttering, at the end of the play when the distant sound is heard once more.

22. "[The Greek] *theatron*, 'theatre,' is a space for beholding, derived from the verb *theaomai*, to behold with wonder." (Segal, *Interpreting Greek Tragedy*, 75).

23. van Itallie, 34.

24. Mark Zeller defines *beat* for me as "any section of a play where an objective is lost or won [i.e., completed]" or as "any time anyone wants something from someone else." Elinor Renfield defines heat as "a unit of time—like a musical beat. To get from one beat to the next beat is called a transition." At one point in rehearsal Renfield refers to "just an eighth of a beat." Robert Wilson's usual substitute for the beat is the "count," e.g., "You pause seven counts." The Robert Wilson count is approximately equal to one second, the agreed-upon duration of the beat in Emily Mann's rehearsal of *Execution of Justice*.

25. I do not mean to imply that Anya and Trofimov are lovers, only that there is an underground affinity between them.

26. Each character in this first unit of action has at least one prop: Yasha a cigar; Charlotta a shoulder gun and, briefly, a cucumber; Yepikhodov a guitar and, briefly, a revolver. Important props in the next unit of action are Ranevskaya's coin-filled purse and a telegram, Gayev's ever-present candies and ever-forgotten overcoat carried in by Firs.

27. van Itallie, 25.

28. In rehearsal of *The Cherry Orchard* Elinor Renfield rarely gives line readings, demonstrations of a particular inflection or intonation in the delivery of a line as if to be imitated precisely by the actor, although she may occasionally suggest certain verbal emphases. In the afternoon rehearsal, for example, she indicates to Trofimov that he might "hit one word hard in Ranevskaya's ear"—the word *philosophizing*—during his monologue in act two (van Itallie, 32).

29. In addition, the cast seems to take on characteristics of the characters they play. The actor playing Firs frequently speaks of "the old days," even uses this phrase. He tells me, during a break in rehearsal, "What is called ensemble acting now, we used to call 'acting.' " Small specific echoes of the play in rehearsal: the actor who plays the money-borrowing Pishchik borrows small sums of money continually for a week; the actor playing the accident-prone Yepikhodov has a tendency towards small physical maladjustments to the demands of his role; the actor who plays the stationmaster hands out the train schedule for the Long Island Railroad trip to the East Hampton playhouse.

30. David Magarshack, *Chekhov The Dramatist* (New York: Hill and Wang, 1960), 169–72.

31. Chekhov writes: "Let the things that happen onstage be just as complex and yet just as simple as they are in life. For instance, people are having a meal at table, just having a meal, but at the same time their happiness is being created or their lives are being smashed up." Quoted by Robert Brustein in his Foreword to *Chekhov: The Major Plays*, x.

32. van Itallie, 10.

33. By "private moment" I do not mean the kind of acting exercise described by Shelley Winters: "That year, 1954, I began to attend [sessions at the Actors Studio] regularly and tried to work on something called a 'private moment,' which is very difficult for me to do. . . . It is something you do in front of the class that you would only do in the privacy of your home, alone, such as acting out a fantasy, conducting an orchestra . . . pretending you're greatly accomplished . . . since no one is watching or listening to you— except the entire class." *Shelley II: The Middle of My Century* (New York: Simon and Schuster, 1989), 15.

34. A vivid example of this is a problem first noticed near the end of rehearsal. The John Drew Theater has no "legs" (fairly wide pieces of cloth, usually hung in pairs to stage left and right, creating wing space). The set designer wishes to place a white lace surround at right angles to the edge of the stage and beyond the set. Upstage behind the surround there will be a white muslin bounce drop (lights bounce off it so as to suggest a sky). The white lace surround is intended to create the feeling of a cherry orchard in blossom surrounding the action set inside the house. But when the actors exit, they will be seen through the lace surround after they leave the stage. In certain scenes this lingering sense of the characters in some other space is exactly what is wanted. But more often what is wanted is a definitive exit, especially in comedic moments. The set designer, lighting designer, stage manager, and director in a joint meeting decide to resolve the problem through lighting adjustments in technical rehearsals at the theatre. The cast is alerted to the advantages and potential disadvantages of the lace surround awaiting them in East Hampton. (The production is darker than I had anticipated, despite the white lace of the surround.).

35. van Itallie, 55.

36. In early rehearsals of this moment in act four, Varya explored different acting choices, e.g., tears; head lowered on hand; no response at all to her mother's questioning look; shaking her head "no." There was no coat-folding.

37. Constantin Stanislavski, *An Actor Prepares*, trans. Elizabeth Reynolds Hapgood (New York: Routledge/Theatre Arts Books, 1989), 312. Cf. also Robert Benedetti: "A living thing cannot happen exactly the same way twice" (*Director at Work*, 135).

38. Tortsov, the director, describes the physical movements Kostya performed while playing the role of Othello. Kostya confesses, "Now that you tell me about what happened, I seem to remember my actions." "But without me you could not have understood the ways in which your feelings found expression?" the director asks. "No, I admit I couldn't," Kostya replies (Stanislavski, *An Actor Prepares*, 12–13).

39. Cf. Benedetti on blocking: "The danger is that the physical actions will become habitual, rather than the score ["the underlying sequence of objectives which stirs the actor to physical action"] which generates them . . ." (*Director At Work*, 166).

40. Cf. Kevin Kline, "Rehearsals are, for me, a way to find out every possible way *not* to play the part" (private communication, February 9, 1986).

41. J. Laplanche and J.-B. Pontalis, *The Language of Psycho-Analysis*, trans. Donald Nicholson-Smith (New York: W. W. Norton & Co., 1973), 488–89.

42. Renfield does allow alternate translations for some of the lines in the play, in lieu of the Jean Claude van Itallie translation used in rehearsal. Only once is a line altered because of the physical appearance of the actor (Ranevskaya's reference to Trofimov's thinning hair).

43. Jan Kott, "Theater—The Eternal Art of the Particular Moment," *New York Times*, September 2, 1984, H5.

Chapter 3

1. Unless otherwise noted, all citations to *Uncle Vanya* are taken from *Plays by Anton Tchekoff*, trans. Marian Fell (New York: Charles Scribner's, 1916).

2. Rehearsing a scene in act two, in which Chekhov's stage directions merely indicate that Yelena withdraws her hand as Vanya bends down toward it, Fornes has Austin Pendleton (Vanya) approach Alma Cuervo (Yelena) with outstretched arms and grab her; they struggle for several minutes until she tears herself away; Vanya falls and grabs Yelena's legs as he lies on the floor. Later Fornes tells the actress to fight harder. When the scene is repeated, Vanya and Yelena tangle physically with such vigor that the actress accidentally falls down. Fornes jokingly cautions Cuervo to "watch out" since Pendleton is a Method actor and the actress replies, laughing, "I am, too."

3. Charles Marowitz argues that "the act of interpretation is every bit as creative as authorship." Directors (such as Liviu Ciulei) may "rejig . . . , restructure . . . , and occasionally complement . . . the original play with new material." Fornes's astonishing achievement is to give a sense of newness without violating what Marowitz calls "the formal limits of the work as originally written." *Prospero's Staff* (Bloomington: Indiana University Press, 1986), 33, 36, 37.

4. Gordon Rogoff describes her production of *Uncle Vanya* as "languourous" and refers to "Fornes' infatuation with drift and pause" (*Village Voice*, December 22, 1987, 132, 133). Mel Gussow also accuses Fornes of having "made the play languorous" and counsels her to "speed . . . up the tempo" in "a production that mistakenly communicates boredom by being boring" (*New York Times*, December 15, 1987, C21). Mimi Kramer, however, admires "the gentle, becalmed pacing. . . . What makes most productions of 'Uncle Vanya' so boring is the murky miasma of actors' personalities that you have to grope through in order to get to the play. The acting in the C.S.C. 'Vanya' is not trying to . . . impress us with how realistic it is." (*New Yorker*, January 4, 1988, 59). (Mimi Kramer is one of the rare critics to note in the course of her review significant differences between two performances of the production she is discussing: in this case, one before and the other after the appearance of a negative review in *The New York Times*.).

5. Cf. director Charles Marowitz, "Is it not possible to use theatre to reflect states of mind more accurately . . . ?" (137).

6. Chekhov's characters' names are spelled in the program as rendered by Marian Fell in her translation of the play. Thus, Vanya appears as Voitski.

7. Fell, 45.

8. With somewhat different effect, Robert Wilson deconstructs Heiner Müller's *Hamletmachine*, assigning sequential lines in a single speech to different actors.

9. With her characteristic scrupulousness about language, Fornes adds: "I said, 'taking away' . . . [to the actress] but I meant 'taking over.' " I think, however, that she meant both taking away and taking over.

10. Cf. Stanislavski on the difficulty of sitting on stage in *An Actor Prepares*, 33–37. The actor Kostya describes the attempt to sit quietly on the stage: "My legs, arms, head, and torso, although they did what I directed, added something superfluous of their own. You move your arm or leg quite simply, and suddenly you are all twisted, and look as though you were posing for a picture. Strange! . . . It was infinitely easier for me to sit affectedly than simply. I could not think what I ought to do." The Director comments later: ". . .the external immobility of a person sitting on the stage does not imply passiveness. You may sit without a motion and at the same time be in full action. Nor is that all. Frequently physical immobility is the direct result of inner intensity, and it is these inner activities that are far more important artistically. The essence of art is not in its external forms but in its spiritual content" (34, 37).

11. Fell, 23.

12. All references to *Abingdon Square* are to the version published in *American Theatre*, February, 1988 (vol. 4, no. 11), 1–10 (separately numbered insert). An earlier rehearsal version of this scripted stage direction read: "as if in a deep emotional trance."

13. The next day, rehearsing another two-person scene with different actors, Fornes characterizes Marion's cousin, Mary, whose role it is to remain silent in a scene composed entirely of Juster's long monologue, as "a generous ear." This kind of comment mediates between literary analysis of her playtext and directorial suggestion to the actress.

14. What Juster reads is a description of the fertilization of flowers in language that is at once highly technical and erotic. The excerpt was originally much longer, but when the speech needed to be shortened Fornes ended up excising what had originally drawn her to the passage, a description of someone walking in a garden saying farewell to the plants.

15. As in the Renfield rehearsal, the characteristic Chekhovian extended family with its retainers seems to find a representation in the company assembled for rehearsal. In the *Vanya* rehearsals, there are again particular echoes: an actor whose stories seem to go nowhere plays a long-winded character; two gossipy actors play gossipy characters; the actor playing the most repressive character in the play requires that I leave the rehearsal whenever he is there. More generally, however, people who don't necessarily know, understand, or even like each other, who criticize each other's actions implicitly or explicitly with sudden intensity or sly humor, who may never really enter into each other's lives, come together in a space where whatever is going to go on between and among them is going to go on.

16. *The Collected Poems of Wallace Stevens* (New York: Alfred A. Knopf, 1969), 524. All citations of Stevens are to this edition.

17. In rehearsal of the scene in act three in which Astroff embraces and kisses Yelena just as Vanya enters the room with a bouquet of roses, Yelena pulls away from the doctor and delivers the line, "This is awful!" (rehearsal version; also Dunnigan's translation, 211) to Astroff and herself, without appearing to notice Vanya. In the performance I attended on December 19, 1987, Yelena sees Vanya watching, as she seems about to kiss Astroff for the second time, and says, "This is awful!" (The stage directions in the text indicate that Yelena sees Vanya, leaves Astroff's embrace, goes to the window, and then says, "This is awful!").

18. Fell, 45.

19. Fell, 17.

20. Interestingly, shortly after this, the actor offers his own version of this precept in what I call a "private moment" in rehearsal. He begins to discuss what he has worked out in understanding Astroff's seeming betrayal of Vanya, then stops himself: "Better to keep that a secret."

21. Fell, 34.

22. Fell, 35–36.

23. The actors playing Telegin and Sonia arrive, as pre-arranged, one and two hours, respectively, after Vanya and Astroff begin work on the scene.

24. Cf. Charles Marowitz's anecdotes:

    > An actor refused to wear the costume provided by the designer of the production, insisting it was 'wrong' for his character. "But it's exactly like the drawing we showed you on the first day of rehearsal, and then you thought it was marvelous."
    > "That man died three and a half weeks ago," the actor replied.
    > "Why," said the director to the intransigent actor, "why can't you play this role the way you did on the first reading?"
    > "For the same reason the chicken cannot get back into the egg," answered the actor. (*Prospero's Staff*, 174–76).

25. *Abingdon Square*, 8.

26. In the performance of *Abingdon Square* that I saw on November 18, 1987, the rigidity Fornes had encouraged was somewhat modified but still present.

27. Quoted by Benedetti, *Director At Work*, 129.

28. The script of *Abingdon Square* is not only in revision but without a final version of the last scene during the rehearsals I watch. The actors' reactions to this vary, but nervousness prevails. On the eighth day of rehearsal I overhear an actress ask, "Irene, when will we have [copies of the final revisions of] the last scenes?" The following day one actor says, "I'm having trouble not knowing the end of the play," and a second actor responds, "That makes us like the characters." It is Fornes's usual practice to begin rehearsals of her own plays with an incomplete or unfinished script. She tells me, "There are things that only happen in rehearsal and could not happen if the script were complete. *But* there are things that don't happen because you don't have time to sit down quietly and write. You have to make quick decisions in rehearsal. But it's *exciting* to work in this way." (Private communication, December 7, 1985).

29. In rehearsals of *The Cherry Orchard*, as already indicated, Elinor Renfield's body and face at times respond in tandem with the actor's. Renfield's body grows tense during scenes of anger; her face softens during delicate scenes. I glimpse the staccato beat of her head during a scene of emotional frenzy. When her head is still, her hands involuntarily take up the rhythm of a scene. Here is a detailed description of Irene Fornes as she sits watching Astroff rehearse his transformed scene of drunkenness in act two.

The director's hands *jump* as Astroff stamps the floor twice while Telegin plays the guitar. She crosses her left knee over her right knee and places her hands in her lap, the right hand clenching a clenched left hand. The fingers of her right hand make short, jerky movements in response to the beats in the scene. Her hands unclench. The left hand with fingers out-stretched remains in her lap while the fingers of the right hand play momentarily on the left hand, seemingly counting out beats of silence (pause) as well as vocally expressive units in the scene. Otherwise, her entire body is still, her gaze steadily on the actors. Sonia enters, Astroff exits followed by Telegin. Fornes's left hand moves to her head for a moment. Her left elbow juts out to the side, her left hand on her hip. Her right hand is semi-clenched, the fingers still moving. I sense her waiting to be utterly stilled. (This description covers a period of about four minutes of rehearsal time.) Earlier, during a break, Fornes tells me, "I experience it. . . . I experience what [the actors] . . . say, feel. I care. . . . I and the stage manager see this production over and over, and I always want to be interested. That's the thing."

At one point in the rehearsal of scene 23 in *Abingdon Square*, as she watches and listens to Juster deliver his monologue, Fornes herself seems almost as if in a state of waking trance. She sits with her hands folded over her right knee, her script on top of her crossed hands. Then her hands fall to her sides, clenching the seat of her aluminum chair. Now she is nearly motionless. Her mouth is slightly open; her eyes are half-closed but focused on the actor delivering the monologue; her lips move almost imperceptibly. At the end of the scene she says quietly in a low voice, "That's very beautiful." This is one of the few times I hear her utter that frequently over-used term of praise in rehearsal.

30. Some of these in-rehearsal revisions may seem minute but all are treated with equal importance by the playwright. Revisions which are made during my observation of rehearsal include occasional addition of a few lines, frequent elimination of words, and changing of some contractions to their full grammatical form. A few examples follow.

Fornes changes Michael's line in the scene in which he is playing chess with his father from "No, I'm not good enough to win" to "No." In rehearsal of scene 25, Fornes dictates a line she is adding to Juster's long monologue: "Then she said, 'This is a love letter.'" The actors and stage manager write down the new line. In consultation with the actor playing Juster, she changes the word "uniform" to "clothes" in his long monologue in scene 20, to avoid the unwanted implications of a *military* uniform. (All these revisions appear in the text of *Abingdon Square* as published in *American Theatre*.) Finally, after listening to actor John David Cullum reading aloud Michael's line, "I'm going to school outside of the city," Fornes stops him, saying "That line doesn't sound right." When the actor responds, "I'm just fooling around," Fornes clarifies, "No, I mean the line itself doesn't sound right."

In consultation with the actor, Fornes tentatively changes the line so that it reads: "I'm going to *a* school. . . ." (This line does not appear, in either version, in the text published in *American Theatre*.).

31. Ross Wetzsteon, however, quotes Fornes as saying, "I had all this creative energy I had to use. I never really loved painting," in his fine article, "Irene Fornes: The Elements of Style," *Village Voice*, April 29, 1986, 42.

32. The visual composition of scenes in the rehearsals of *Uncle Vanya* is made particularly difficult by the fact that the performance stage is a foot wider than the rehearsal studio. Fornes is never literally able to see scenes in rehearsal from the vantage point of the audience at The Classic Stage Company theatre: "I try in some way to project my eye from the side." At times during rehearsal Fornes will sit far downstage in the playing area itself in an attempt to ascertain whether an actor will in fact be visible to the audience in the theatre. Cf. Elinor Renfield's comment, delivered fairly good-humoredly during rehearsals of *The Cherry Orchard*, "I'll be able to see this when I'm twelve rows back!" Her director's chair is approximately four inches from the downstage edge of the playing area. The *Vanya* and *Cherry Orchard* rehearsals are exacerbated versions of the situation of every director who must rehearse somewhere other than in the performance space itself.

33. Cf. Ross Wetzsteon: "Fornes's trademark as a director . . . is a gestural and intonational formality, . . . that rejects the cumulative effect of naturalistic detail in favor of the spontaneous impact of revelatory image, that rejects emoting, behavioral verisimilitude, and demonstration of meaning in favor of crystallization, painterly blocking, and layers of irony" ("Irene Fornes," 43).

34. When I first ask if the the scene as she directs it is like a painting in her own mind, Fornes answers affirmatively. She later clarifies that she does not literally have a particular work of art in mind but that her stage image of the penitent has some resemblance to certain Mexican paintings.

    A famous example of the complexities of tracing an artist's images to their supposed sources is the controversy surrounding Keats's indeterminate depiction of a particular or a generic or an imagined artifact in the visual composition of the scenes in his "Ode on a Grecian Urn."

35. Fornes's rehearsal script version. Fell's translation is: "This is agony!" (I, p. 27). Fornes considers Vanya to be the penitent in this scene. As my description suggests, in rehearsal I see two penitents trying to rise "from the flames below."

36. Chekhov has not specifically indicated an exit and re-entrance for the purpose of bringing tea to the professor, although it is theoretically possible for the nurse to leave and return during the tea-drinking scene in act one.

37. Later Fornes adds, "I prefer to tell the actors about my shortcomings and let *them* try to cover up for . . . [the shortcomings] rather than to try to cover up my shortcomings from the actors." The child does appear in one scene. The stage directions for scene 19 indicate a prominent position for the objective correlative, if not the child himself: "*Center stage, there is a playpen with a teddy bear sitting in it. Marion enters from left. She carries Thomas, eight months old. She takes the teddy bear*" (*Abingdon Square*, p. 6). Of this

scene, in rehearsal, Fornes says that if Thomas is played by a real child as she would like him to be, the child's presence in Marion's arms will be a tremendously potent image.

38. I understand Fornes's silence on the question of where the child is when it is not in the play in the same way that I might imagine Shakespeare's response to the question of where Lady Macbeth's children are.

What complicates this situation, of course, is the fact that Fornes is both playwright and director, as Shakespeare himself might conceivably have been. For a recent view of the question of Lady Macbeth's missing children, and the position of the child in tragic drama, see Bennett Simon, *Tragic Drama and the Family: Psychoanalytic Studies from Aeschylus to Beckett* (New Haven: Yale University Press , 1988), 140–75 and *passim*. Although he takes quite seriously the question of the Macbeths' missing offspring, Simon remarks that the poet offers no "explicit answer or resolution" (148).

39. As Ross Wetzsteon notes, Fornes does not focus on causes or consequences of pivotal moments in a relationship so much as on the pivots themselves, and this is reflected in the kinds of scenes she likes to construct and direct: "I don't like scenes to build up or peter out. In fact, I don't even like to present the entire scene—most of my scenes actually start in the middle, almost at the climax. That way, both the writing and the acting go from one critical moment to the next." (Quoted by Wetzsteon, "Irene Fornes," 43).

40. Fornes's style is clearly difficult to define in a single phrase. Wetzsteon refers both to "the subliminal hyper-realism of her staging" and the "compassionate realism" of her plays (*ibid.*, 43–45).

41. Quoted by Wetzsteon, *ibid.*, 43.

42. Fornes stresses that Juster's offer of money to Marion is not an act of kindness but "more in the nature of a kind of honor, like not fighting an unarmed man."

43. Near the end of *Abingdon Square*, Juster in murderous rage fires his gun twice in Marion's presence without harming her; Chekhov's Vanya twice attempts unsuccessfully to shoot the Professor at the end of act three. In each play the first shot is offstage, the other performed onstage. In both *Uncle Vanya* and *Abingdon Square* a young woman marries a much older man with whom she has no passionate connection. I am struck by these parallels in the two plays that Fornes is rehearsing within a period of approximately three months. (Fornes herself, however, is not.).

Chapter 4

1. The text of *Still Life*, like that of Mann's first play, *Annulla, An Autobiography*, is drawn from tape recordings of the persons on whom the principal characters were based.

2. Emily Mann, correspondence, July 11, 1985. This may not be true merely of America. British actor Simon Callow writes, "For a long time, my mother couldn't work out what rehearsals were for. 'Once you've learned the lines and the director has told you where to stand, what do you do?' " (Callow, *Being an Actor*, 134).

3. Quoted in *New York Times*, October 22, 1985, A18.

4. *Execution of Justice*, 51, 41 (Playwright's Note). All citations to *Execution of Justice* are from the revised script as published in *New Plays USA, 3*, eds. James Leverett and M. Elizabeth Osborn (New York: Theatre Communications Group, 1986).

5. Quoted by Leslie Bennetts, "When Reality Takes to the Stage," *New York Times*, March 9, 1986, H4.

6. Once I overhear Mann, in response to an actor's request, introduce the possibility that she might add a transitional phrase, such as "I don't know." I am not sure if the transitional phrase was ever added or, if added, whether it was drawn from other transcript material.

   At the end of the second week of rehearsal, Mann announces to the cast that she needs to look again at her "own writing" because the testimony of one witness, Carol Ruth Silver, now seems funny rather than horrific. A week later I hear Marcia Jean Kurtz, the actress playing Silver, ask the assistant stage manager for "a clean copy" of this scene because "there have been so many rewrites that I'm a little confused." Presumably these "rewrites" continue to make use of words actually spoken.

7. Cf. Richard Foreman: "Rhythmic organization is 98 per cent of directing." Foreman emphasizes "uncovering and fixing in place the *rhythms* that will allow the idiosyncratic quality of each performer to serve properly the text." (Quoted in Benedetti, *Director At Work*, 167).

8. The first quotation occurs on page 33 of the rehearsal script. The second quotation is taken from a photocopy of script changes, dated February 5, 1986, handed out by the stage managers to the company.

9. *The American Heritage Dictionary of the English Language*, 1471.

10. At the end of the last day of rehearsal in the studio after the technical equipment is moved to the theatre, the director says, "This play is fantastic without video, without anything on it. I watched it today and felt we could invite people to see it in this room." But, she then adds, "It's really a mind-blow with the lights and the video."

11. *Execution of Justice*, 70.

12. Quoted by Bennetts, "When Reality Takes to the Stage," H4.

13. I am alluding to Lacan's usage of *se voir se voir*, as translated by Ellie Ragland-Sullivan: to see oneself being seen. The reflexive verb form, *se voir*, can, depending on context, be translated as "to be seen" or "to see oneself." Lacan's comments on the gaze develop the implications of line 35 in Paul Valéry's poem, "La Jeune Parque": "Je me voyais me voir."

14. Ellie Ragland-Sullivan, *Jacques Lacan and the Philosophy of Psychoanalysis* (Chicago: University of Illinois Press, 1986), 94. Stefan Brecht, performing in Robert Wilson's *A Letter for Queen Victoria* (1974–1975), gives a startling portrait of the directorial gaze during rehearsal. He first writes of Wilson, "Once the choreography was settled, he sat and sat, silently, while we went through the piece over and over, and his notes to us at the end of each rehearsal were few." Then, as if reversing the relationship between performer and silent gazing figure, Brecht writes in a remarkable footnote: "He [Wilson] will sit there, hands wringing, except they are not moving (so they are clasped), straight-sitting, head up, bird nose upsweeping, dead eyes

(red-rimmed blue behind dark glasses) unerringly fixed on what somebody is doing, an idiot's knot of concentration in the sinoidal spot behind his eye-bridge-bone above . . . *the unseeing eye's gaze/stare* [italics added], a dead center from which spins off, but only because he is a genius, . . . food for directorial, directed, shaping thought: ideas on how to do it otherwise, save the situation superlatively, make something of it: but it still is that *Idiot's* immersion in the present idiotic fact that's feeding the imaginary brain, a debility, an almost getting buried . . . , an almost coming to a stop, or even . . . the dead halt, through which a believed-in momentum carries him off into a further great arch or loop of flight." Stefan Brecht, *The Original Theatre of the City of New York: From the Mid–60s to the Mid–70s. Book I. The Theatre of Visions: Robert Wilson* (Frankfurt am Main: Suhrkamp, 1978), 276, 276n. To Brecht's comment might be added one of Gerard Manley Hopkins's 1871 journal entries: "What you look hard at seems to look hard at you." *Gerard Manley Hopkins, Journals and Papers*, eds. Humphrey House and Graham Storey (London: Oxford University Press, 1959), 204.

15. Ragland-Sullivan, *Jacques Lacan*, 94.

16. Northrop Frye, *Fearful Symmetry: A Study of William Blake* (Boston: Beacon Press, 1962), 16–17.

17. Teresa de Lauretis' notion of the constructed self (to be constructed is to be), especially the construction of gender identity, is related to my view, though my focus is, of course, on construction of "self" by actors in rehearsal. Hélène Cixous' view is somewhat different from my own: " 'Seeing herself see herself,' [is] the motto of all phallocentric speculation/specularization." Hélène Cixous and Catherine Clément, *The Newly Born Woman*, trans. Betsy Wing (Minneapolis: University of Minnesota Press, 1987), 94. As I have indicated, I believe that the originary pleasure of mutual gazing, which finds its prototype in mother and child, has been defensively, and ironically, appropriated as the phallocentric pleasure of the controlling/voyeuristic gaze.

18. "Poetry," longer version, 1.24, in *The Complete Poems of Marianne Moore* (New York: Macmillan Publishing Co., Inc., and Penguin Books, 1982), 267.

19. Teresa de Lauretis defines that "elsewhere" as "spaces in the margins of hegemonic discourses, social spaces carved in the interstices of institutions and in the chinks and cracks of the power-knowledge apparati." *Technologies of Gender: Essays on Theory, Film, and Fiction* (Bloomington: Indiana University Press, 1987), 25. I appropriate her term without all of her implications.

20. After the runthrough Mann puts this ability in question when she asks Gerry Bamman, playing the prosecuting attorney, "Did you decide to nail that witness earlier than before . . . [or] was that just me? [referring to the fact that she had been taking notes while watching rehearsal]." First the actor is not certain whether he altered the scene, then admits that he inverted two lines. Although it turns out that Mann is accurate in her perception of the alteration in the actor's playing of the scene, still she expresses her awareness of the difficulty of "taking it all in," especially for the note-taking director.

21. Earlier this day, before the runthrough, John Spencer greeted me warmly,

saying, "Glad to see you again. You're becoming one of us." I am later told that he was upset by the large number of invited guests present as audience during the runthrough. I too must have been an initially unnerving presence for the actors. A stranger in the house has to become perceived as a friend of the house. In every rehearsal I observe, actors tactfully seek me out, graciously introduce themselves, establish contact in some way—despite, or to counteract, the strain placed upon them by the presence of an outsider.

22. The derivation of "inspire" is from the Latin *inspirare*, to breathe into.

23. Andrzej Wajda's production of *Hamlet*, presented by the Stary Theatre of Cracow at SUNY-Purchase in July, 1989, is designed to create for the audience the perspective of looking over the shoulder of the actor as he observes the backs of his fellow players. Cf. Alisa Solomon's review: "Wajda seats us beneath the theater's flies; we spy on the action like Polonius behind the arras, like everyone in *Hamlet*. . . . The production opens with fanfare and pageantry as Claudius, Gertrude, and all the rest of Elsinore's court assemble on the big stage; we see their lushly costumed backs from a distance. . . . But our attention is riveted on Hamlet, who emerges from behind the dressing screen so close to us, yanks black suede boots up to his knees, and waits for the cue to enter." She adds, "The feeling of privilege is exciting: from our concealed position, we see the most private affairs of an actor's preparation." *Village Voice*, July 18, 1989, 91. Of course, "the most private affairs of an actor's preparation" is what no one, including the director, ever really sees, however privileged or concealed one's position.

24. Quoted by Michael Kuchwara, " 'Justice' Result of 'Volcanic Reaction,' " *Asbury Park Press*, March 2, 1986, G6. The title of Kuchwara's article refers to Mann's description of her early research on the streets of San Francisco: "When I mention the names of Moscone, Milk, or White, I got a volcanic reaction."

25. *Execution*, 112.

Chapter 5

1. Don Shewey, "A Revue for the Nuclear Era Moves from Stage to Film," *New York Times*, November 9, 1986, H15.

2. By characterizing this production as a "workshop," I do not mean that it represented evolving experimental work, only that it was prepared under something like staged-reading conditions.

3. One of these, Yolande Bavan, defines herself as an actress who sings rather than as a singer who acts, though she sings professionally with a jazz vocal trio (Personal communication).

4. Quoted by M. Elizabeth Osborn, "Directors At Work," *American Theatre* (September 1985), vol. 2, no. 5, 30.

5. *The Voyage of the Beagle*, JoAnne Akalaitis and Jon Gibson, unpublished script, 16. All following citations are to the draft of the script used in rehearsal.

6. Unfortunately, I was not invited to the auditions for any of the rehearsals I observed.

7. Rehearsal script, 25. Three days before the performance, however, Akalaitis cuts the jokes altogether.

8. *Ibid.*, 47.

9. *Ibid.*, 33.

10. *Ibid.*, 11.

11. John Donne, Meditation XVII.

12. Rehearsal script, 37.

13. These mothers are in evidence during final rehearsal. After repeated shouts from the green room below the auditorium, one mother moves rapidly in that direction. She emerges a few minutes later, holding a small plant sprayer which she has confiscated from the boys. She explains her action quite audibly to the adults in the darkened auditorium: "I won't have it."

14. Rehearsal script, 18.

15. *Ibid.*, 49–50.

16. Quoted by M. Elizabeth Osborn, "Directors At Work," 30.

17. *Ibid.*

18. Rehearsal script, 51.

19. Although Akalaitis is well aware of the manipulative aspects of the director's role in rehearsal, this example of her directorial strategy seems more an illustration of extreme efficiency under pressure of time than of manipulativeness.

20. Rehearsal script, stage direction, 19.

21. For a fuller account, see Susan L. Cole, *The Absent One: Mourning Ritual, Tragedy, and the Performance of Ambivalence*, 101–114. The discussion summarized here occurs on pp. 106–107.

22. Rehearsal script, stage direction, 14.

23. *Ibid.*, 50, 38.

24. Rehearsal script, 26.

25. Those inclined to date the origins of directing only from the mid- or late nineteenth century might reflect on the variety of directorial tasks assumed by Peter Quince in *A Midsummer Night's Dream*. Quince gives notes (on the lion's roar, I.ii.75–77); settles casting disputes (all of them initiated by Bottom, who is subdued by directorial tact, 84–86); rules on costume choices ("why, what you will," 90); schedules rehearsals (99–100); inserts material (16–21); solves lighting problems (46–47); devises non-naturalistic stagings ("Some man or other must present Wall," 66); blocks scenes (71–74, 80); interprets action (89–91); and prompts entrances and lines (97–98, 99–100).

26. Cf. Charles Darwin, *On the Origin of Species* (New York: Atheneum, 1967), 101.

Chapter 6

1. James Leverett, "In Search of Dafoe," *Interview*, vol. xviii, no. 6 (June 1988), 38.

2. *Ibid.*

3. I also attend the first readthrough of the production of *Antigone* discussed in the Epilogue but as dramaturg rather than merely as observer.

4. See David Cole on rehearsal "at the table," *Acting as Reading*. My observation of the Wooster Group, completed before I read *Acting as Reading*, receives confirmation from this eloquent book.

5. I later learned that when actor Ron Vawter lay dangerously ill in a coma in the fall of 1986, Elizabeth LeCompte along with Kate Valk and Peyton Smith "sat beside his [hospital] bed and read aloud for hours at a time from the plays in which he had appeared, hoping to make some kind of connection through the words to which he'd devoted his life." After four days he suddenly awakened from his coma. (Ross Wetzsteon, "Saint Ron, New York's Best Unknown Actor," *Village Voice*, October 17, 1989, 41).

6. Low-keyed delivery of lines during the first readthrough is fairly common. Vanessa Redgrave, described by director Charles Sturridge, is a notable exception: "The English [actors] usually stumble cautiously along, tentatively putting a toe in the water [during the first rehearsal reading of a play]. . . . Vanessa throws the character around the room and gets into every conceivable corner of the part, not all of them logical. It's very noisy and adventurous and terrifying to watch, but it does fill you with ideas. It gives you 17 directions to go and 27 *not* to go in." (Quoted by Benedict Nightingale, "An Actress in Love With Risk," *New York Times*, September 17, 1989, H14).

7. In (. . . *Just the High Points* . . .), the Wooster Group appropriated parts of the text of Arthur Miller's *The Crucible*. After legal pressure by the playwright, the Wooster Group was forced to abandon his text but replaced it with "a mischievous version in double talk" (Leverett, "In Search of Dafoe," 38).

8. Ingmar Bergman, *The Magician*, in *Four Screenplays of Ingmar Bergman*, trans. Lars Malmstrom and David Kushner (Simon and Schuster: New York, 1969), 344. All citations of *The Magician* are from this edition.

9. Marvin Carlson, *Goethe and the Weimar Theatre*, 305.

10. *Frank Dell's The Temptation of Saint Antony*, 35, 40, 48, 36, 10, 41, 65 (rehearsal script, January, 1989).

11. Norman Frisch tells me, in June of 1986, that the first piece in the trilogy, *Route 1 & 9*, "theoretically finished in 1981 is still being revised" as is Part Two, (. . . *Just the High Points* . . .). In September of 1989 dramaturg Marianne Weems declares Part Three finished. I begin writing this chapter with the January, 1989 version of the script in hand.

12. David Savran refers to Flaubert's *The Temptation of Saint Antony* as "a distant pretext" for LeCompte's *Temptation* in his article, "Adaptation as Clairvoyance: The Wooster Group's *Saint Anthony* [sic]," *Theater*, vol. 18, no. 1 (Fall/Winter 1986), 40. In the revised form of the piece, the "pretext" is not so distant.

13. This is the title of the Cummins book as cited in the script and theatre program. The edition of Cummins I saw in rehearsal was entitled *The Road to Immortality, Being a Description of the After-Life Purporting to be*

Communicated by the late F.W.H. Myers Through Geraldine Cummins (Pilgrims Books Services: Norwich, England, 1932).

14. The Ursula Easton videotape never appears in any of the public versions of the theatre piece. Nonetheless, the work-in-progress performances in the fall of 1987 and in the fall of 1988 as well as the final version in the fall of 1989 are dedicated to Ursula Easton, who seems to haunt the production along with other "ghosts."

    During the extended development of this theatre piece, dramaturg Norman Frisch is succeeded by Marianne Weems; Michael Kirby drops out; actress Nancy Reilly—replaced by Mary Hestand—appears only on videotape as does Willem Dafoe who is away making a series of movies during the latter stages of rehearsal and performance.

15. Stephen Holden, "Wooster Group on Love, Lust and Lenny Bruce in 'St. Antony,' " *New York Times*, April 3, 1987, C3.

16. Elinor Fuchs, "End of the Road?" *Village Voice*, October 25, 1988, 104.

17. Savran, "Adaptation as Clairvoyance," 41. Cf. the last stanza of William Butler Yeats's "Byzantium."

18. Quoted by Savran, "Adaptation as Clairvoyance," 38.

    Cf. LeCompte discussing *Temptation* in an interview conducted by Elinor Fuchs in April, 1988: "The process here is the work." In this interview LeCompte also discusses her role as "conceiver": "Because of the position I am in in my work I am not seen as an artistic entity. . . . Because I am first of all part of a collective, a certain kind of collective. As a result, I am not viewed as the conceiver—though I am the conceiver of all the work. I never write on the [theatre] program, 'Conceived By.' I don't write it for many reasons. Besides, I'm not sure how important conceiving is. Nurturing or whatever it is that comes after that is equally important." Quoted in Fuchs, "Quilting, Passion Plays, and the Female Body: Reflections on New Women's Work in the American Theatre" (Paper delivered at the Sixteenth Amherst Colloquium on German Literature, "From Word to Image: The New Theatre in Germany and the United States," April 1988), 17.

19. Interview with Peyton Smith, September 25, 1989, at The Performing Garage.

20. Richard Foreman, *Reverberation Machines: The Later Plays and Essays* (Barrytown: Station Hill Press, Inc., 1985), 204.

21. *Frank Dell's The Temptation of Saint Antony*, 42, 58. All references to the play are taken from the January, 1989 version of the script.

22. Quoted by Savran, "Adaptation as Clairvoyance," 40. I have altered his spelling of *Antony*.

23. Whatever one may think of LeCompte's sense of the "object-ness of the written word and its inherent lifelessness" in general, the text must become a script before it has life in the theatre. Dramaturg Marianne Weems, who with Elizabeth LeCompte prepared the final form of the written playscript, notes that "[literary] texts are evidence of what the piece uses as points of departure" and further cautions that there can be "no exact relationship [even] between [the final version of the] script and performance." (Interview, September 28, 1989).

24. *Frank Dell's The Temptation of Saint Antony*, 15, 37, 10, 33, 44, 37, 32, 63, 25, 40.

25. Quoted by Ellen Pall, "Jon Amiel Tracks Life in the Dreamy Lane," *New York Times*, September 10, 1989, H28.

26. Interview with Norman Frisch, June 24, 1986, at The Performing Garage.

27. Gustave Flaubert, *The Temptation of Saint Antony*, trans. Kitty Mrosovsky (New York: Penguin Classics, 1983), 68. Unless otherwise noted, all citations of Flaubert's *Temptation* are from this edition.

28. These quotations are taken from LeCompte's notes to the actors in rehearsal on November 2, 1985, May 28 and May 29, 1986, respectively.

29. The viewing I observed occurred on May 28, 1986. The company had seen Bergman's film in its entirety before the first readthrough of the screenplay.

30. The Wooster Group has had legal troubles of its own. *Route 1 & 9*, with its use of blackface, was considered racist by certain New York critics and funding organizations. Arthur Miller threatened a lawsuit when the Group used excerpts from his play in (. . . *Just the High Points* . . .) (originally titled *L.S.D.*). Even friendly critics have described parts of the company's work as obscene.

31. "The process of making improbable narratives from fragments that don't cohere, that often repel each other, is the work; and that is the narrative the work tells." Fuchs, "Quilting," 17.

32. "Poking" is LeCompte's version; the actors suggest "feeling" and then "tapping." What Albert is smoking is left indeterminate at this point.

33. *The Magician*, 307; the earlier actions are described on p. 299.

34. These actions do not appear in performance; Cubby, played by Willem Dafoe, appears only on videotape.

35. The "hint-wait-fulfillment" pattern occurs in the 1989 version of the piece: a gun appears and Frank fakes a suicide; the gun is waved wildly and fired; later Frank waves the gun wildly and fires again; Onna cries, "They've killed my husband! They killed him! They've killed my husband!" (41, 46–47, 59–60). Mental-process-revealed-in-quick-decision is illustrated when Frank collapses in a faint during the onstage performances of the fake Del Fuegos and Onna quickly cues Phyllis to begin the "Dunkirk" number to cover (56–57).

36. I owe this term to a comment of actress Peyton Smith, quoted later.

37. Quoted by Stephen Holden, C3.

38. Mrosovsky's translation, 85.

39. A more exact parallel in their directorial remarks, unwitnessed by each other, is illustrated by Sellars's note in the November, 1985 rehearsal of the Devil Dance, "And don't come out of character so much. I don't think that's necessary."

40. Cf. Jacques Lacan, "The gaze I encounter is, not a seen gaze, but a gaze imagined by me in the field of the Other." *The Four Fundamental Concepts of Psycho-analysis*, ed. Jacques-Alain Miller, trans. Alan Sheridan (New York: Norton, 1978), 84. Kimberly J. Devlin comments on Lacan: "The

subject is always aware of the gaze, is always watching the gaze—reflexively, not intentionally or consciously—but the gaze is not necessarily watching the subject." Devlin later notes: "Women play paradoxical roles in . . . male fantasies: physically degraded or semiotically devalued, they are yet *perspectively powerful*, their gaze functioning frequently as the arbiter of male value itself" (italics added). " 'See ourselves as others see us': Joyce's Look at the Eye of the Other," *PMLA*, vol. 104, no. 5 (October 1989), 884, 891.

41. "The gaze in its more gratifying form functions in Joyce's works as the final signifier of significance, as that which fulfills the self's desire to be acknowledged and recognized, to be a somebody rather than a nobody." Devlin, " 'See ourselves,' " 891.

   During a break in rehearsal on May 30, 1986, LeCompte tells me that the "Channel J" videotape she made in Washington the previous fall will be played on the monitors during performance "as if the cast is watching itself."

42. On "this privilege of the gaze," see Lacan, 83–85.

43. Interview with filmmaker Ken Kobland during a break in rehearsal, November 15, 1985.

44. "*Saint Antony* is the most extreme experiment in intertextuality ever mounted by the Wooster Group." Fuchs, "Quilting," 11.

45. A month later, in response to Kate Valk's question, "What [script] has the right of way right now?" LeCompte replies without hesitation, "the Bergman." But the plot as "mask for the piece" seems to shift somewhat by the final version of *Temptation*. The program for the fall, 1989 performances presents two columns of explanatory matter: the column on the left, headed "A Hotel Room in Washington, D.C.," states tersely the events of seven episodes in which Frank (Vawter) receives phone calls from Cubby (Dafoe, who only appears on videotape), talks with Sue, rehearses Phyllis (Smith) and Onna (Valk) in their dances, after which the troupe performs a magic show. At the end the King of Sweden (an allusion to the ending of *The Magician*) requests that the company perform at his palace. In the right-hand column, under the heading, "Sunset in the Desert," appear summaries of the action of Flaubert's *The Temptation of Saint Antony*. The Flaubert scenario ends with the relevation of the face of Christ.

46. Savran, "Adaptation as Clairvoyance," 39. I find Savran's simile of the performance platform as resembling the page of a giant book particularly apt.

47. David Savran interprets the ever-present bed downstage center as "both the carriage that transports the itinerant company and a miniature stage." *Ibid.*

48. The multiple endings of the 1989 version of *Temptation* seem endless. Onna receives a phone call:

> ONNA. Brrrrinnnng. Brrrrrinnnnng. Hello? Yes? What! Tonight?
> . . . . Frank! Frank! It's the King of Sweden. He wants us tonight at
> the palace. He didn't forget us! (script, 64)

Before and after this allusion to Bergman (the reference to the King of Sweden) is the appearance of the face of Christ. On videotape, Cubby, played by Dafoe, points to the cover of an Italian magazine which features a photograph of the face of the actor in his role as Jesus in Scorsese's film, *The Last Temptation of Christ.* Vogler-Antony-Frank-the fake Dr. Del Fuego-Vawter exits, followed by Dafoe's recorded voice, his image no longer visible on the monitor, poignantly calling out in the dark to an absent actor and an empty stage: "Frank . . . Frank, speak to me. Something's wrong. Frank. Something's wrong. . . . Frank, something's wrong" (script, 65). And when we think all exits are accounted for, Sue enters, running, stage right, with a bag of groceries and says, "Frank?" (*ibid.*). The lights black out, and only now does the final exit occur. Two video monitors playing Kobland's film, a meditation on *Saint Antony* and the Wooster Group rehearsing *Temptation*, finally fade and flick out. LeCompte's *Frank Dell's The Temptation of Saint Antony* has become, as Elinor Fuchs notes, a *mise en abyme* (Personal communication, October 5, 1989).

49. Mrosovsky, Introduction, 17–18. Flaubert finished the first version of *Saint Antony* in 1849; a shortened second version was finished by 1856–57; he completed the last version in 1872. LeCompte comments earlier that she intends to include an allusion to "the pig referred to in the original version of *Saint Antony.*"

50. Bergman screenplay, 379.

51. The striking parallel between "the sun [that] flashes down" in the Bergman screenplay and the dawning sun at the end of Flaubert's *Saint Antony* is noted but not reproduced by the Wooster Group. (Bergman, 379; Flaubert, 232).

52. The quoted words are LeCompte's. Cf. playwright Suzan-Lori Parks, commenting on the rehearsals of her play, *Imperceptible Mutabilities in the Third Kingdom:* "It's lit[erary]-crit[icism] live!" (Quoted by Alisa Solomon, "To Be Young, Gifted, and African-American," *Village Voice,* September 19, 1989, 102).

53. See chapter two, p. 32, and chapter three, p. 49.

54. In this community a large number of pigs were thought to be infected with African swine fever. Earlier LeCompte remarks, "In medieval times the pig represents lust. I'm interested in bringing together all these things—the pig referred to in the original version of *Saint Antony* and AIDS . . ." (May 30, 1985).

55. Flaubert, *Saint Antony,* 61. These lines appear in the Wooster Group's publicity for the world première of the work-in-progress version of the as yet untitled *Frank Dell's The Temptation of Saint Antony* in 1986–87 but not in the January, 1989 script or in the fall performances of 1989. The staging described in this rehearsal does not appear in performance.

56. Flaubert, 90–95.

57. E.g., the line, "I feed on bitter things," and the phrase, "the exhortations of friends" (Flaubert, 91, 95). The argument paraphrased by Dafoe and Vawter occurs on p. 95.

58. The lines from Flaubert occur on pp. 90–91. The lines of Vawter, which were to be varied in performance, are my reconstruction; the lines of Dafoe, which were more or less set, are taken from assistant to the director James

Johnson's notebook transcription, June 23, 1986. None of these lines appear in the January, 1989 script.

59. One of Hilarion's speeches is altered as follows: "You got yourself in trouble in Miami, impersonating the Del Fuegos. You know, they're suing you for right of publicity." That the Del Fuegos are, in part, alter egos of the Wooster Group is indicated by the phrase, "right of publicity," a technical term added by LeCompte that describes the nature of the legal suit that threatened the production of the second part of *The Road to Immortality.* (These lines do not appear in the January, 1989 script.).

60. In the January, 1989 script there are several long passages taken verbatim from section seven of *Saint Antony* (226–27, 229), though none from the dialogue between Antony and Hilarion in section three.

61. Nothing in *Temptation* is univocal. Responding to an actor's query whether Vergérus, a character in *The Magician*, is the devil, LeCompte says, "*Everybody* is the devil. *Everything* is a temptation."

62. After working long and carefully with the lines in the collectively improvised script of the Antony-Hilarion debate, LeCompte, in rehearsing the next scene, says to Michael Stumm: "Just read it. Don't play the lines. Play the part. Do you know what I mean? . . . I don't want it flat. . . . Just say it quickly and fast and natural." Later she adds: "Just say it and don't think about what it means . . . [referring to Carole Lombard and Barbara Stanwyck in films of the 1930s]. They're not thinking about or illustrating what they're saying. But it's not flat. You're thinking about what you have to do next. . . . Don't embellish."

63. The subtext of *The Magician* is the situation of a theatre troupe on the lam. The passage in Flaubert is Hilarion's speech: "The exhortations of friends, the pleasure of causing popular outrage, the vow once made, a certain vertigo, a thousand circumstances come to their help" (95).

64. In performance, voices traverse rather than inhabit characters. (For this point I am indebted to David Cole.).

65. Sher, 9.

66. Interview with Norman Frisch, June 24, 1986.

67. The "Critic" in the piece. Peyton Smith remarks after the perspective is reversed: "It [LeCompte's restaging] makes . . . [the Devil Dance] a real performance in the context of the play." In general, critical response to LeCompte's work has not noted her concern for clarity. Ross Wetzsteon, for example, refers to the Wooster Group as "maddening in its self-reflexive, almost solipsistic indifference to the canons of communication" ("Saint Ron," 48).

68. An allusion to the exposed staging of Vogler's levitation scene in *The Magician*, 354–55. The stage direction in the script of *Temptation* reads: "*Dummy on bed is raised up by FRANK's magician-like gestures, and by SUE, EVA, and JACQUES with strings from underneath the stage*" (55).

69. Savran, "Adaptation as Clairvoyance," 41.

70. "Maybe appearance is the only reality. . . . Form is perhaps the error of your senses and substance an image of your mind. . . . But in one sense are you

sure of seeing . . . are you sure of even seeing? Are you sure of even being alive?" These lines, spoken by Ron Vawter, are taken from the January, 1989 script, 5, 7. The first sentence is actually Kate Valk's repeated line on the "Channel J" videotape, spoken aloud by Vawter in the opening episode of *Temptation*. The lines of Flaubert, translated by Mrosovsky, occur at the end of section six of *Saint Antony*, 212.

In a notable omission, the *Temptation* script does not reproduce the Devil's next line, "Perhaps there is nothing!" but picks up almost verbatim the following one: "Worship me, therefore! and curse the ghost you call God!" (*ibid.*). The line in the *Temptation* script is: "Worship me and curse the ghost that you call God" (7).

Chapter 7

1. Explaining what he calls "the ontological part of [my] . . . Ontological-Hysteric Theatre," Foreman tells me an anecdote that, he says, those who dislike his theatre work would use to show why they dislike it. At dinner, at the age of nine, Foreman told his mother that the light bulb above the table was just as interesting to him as the people at table. "I'm interested in the qualities of things. That for me holds more meaning than momentary configurations of human beings. . . ." (Interview during a break in rehearsal, November 1, 1985).

2. Descriptive copy, February 26, 1985, Performing Artservices, Inc., New York. (Foreman confirmed that he wrote his own descriptive copy.).

3. "The Theater of Richard Foreman: An Interview with the Director of *The Birth of the Poet* Conducted by Roger W. Oliver, "*On the Next Wave*, vol. 3, no. 3 (November 1985), 17. Cage-Cunningham events may be seen as analogous to Foreman's "unique collaboration."

4. Michael Feingold, "An Ungrammar of Ornament," *Village Voice*, December 17, 1985, 117, 120.

5. Erika Munk, "Cross Left," *Village Voice*, December 17, 1985, 120, 117. A more characteristic criticism of Foreman's direction is not gender-specific. Edith Oliver's review of Václav Havel's *Largo Desolato* at the Public Theater, "under the tyrannical direction of Richard Foreman," refers to "that fine actor Josef Sommer" and "other blameless actors, . . . reduced to puppets" (*The New Yorker*, April 7, 1986). Gordon Rogoff, reviewing Foreman's "Miss Universal Happiness" at The Performing Garage, writes, "The most political statement, perhaps, is that the actors have not been beaten entirely into submission by the boss," having remarked earlier of Foreman, "No slouch he when it comes to saying who's boss" ("Insensate Overload," *Village Voice*, June 4, 1985, 85). Of the Wooster Group members acting in the production, including LeCompte, Rogoff comments, "The company is more than brave, it's positively heroic."

6. Quoted by David Savran, *In Their Own Words: Contemporary American Playwrights* (New York: Theatre Communications Group, 1988), 48.

7. Michael Feingold, "Presidents of Mind," *Village Voice*, January 19, 1988, 99.

8. Quoted by Savran, *In Their Own Words*, 50.

9. "Internal Gestures" [a review of Foreman's "The Cure"], *Village Voice*, June

3, 1986, 81. Michael Feingold, reviewing Foreman's "Symphony of Rats," notes that "no interpretation of a Foreman work is ever wholly valid, and the most dignified thing a critic can do is indicate for his readers the general preoccupations and imagery of the piece at hand, and then bow out gracefully" (*ibid.*).

10. Kate Davy describes Foreman's 1974 rehearsal work: "The rehearsal time for *PAIN(T)* and *Vertical Mobility* was entirely devoted to placing the performers on stage, because for Foreman 'placement is nine-tenths of the staging.' " "Foreman's *PAIN(T)* and *Vertical Mobility*," *The Drama Review: Rehearsal Procedures Issue* (T62), vol. 18, no. 2 (June 1974), 28.

11. Foreman is scrupulous about not altering Kathy Acker's text without her confirmation. In his own work, his voice uttering the word "cue" became part of the performance. Cf. Davy, "At one rehearsal [of *Vertical Mobility*], Foreman told them, 'For the change [in position] I'll put in a *boing*.' Until he got around to recording the sound, he shouted, 'cue!' Eventually, his shouting became part of the piece, and the '*boing*' was never added. Several times during the performance, Foreman shouted 'cue' from his booth behind the bleachers" (Davy, "Foreman's *PAIN(T)*," 36).

12. It is interesting, in light of his expressed interest in the word, that Foreman had originally wanted Kathy Acker's handwritten Arabic in the playtext visibly reproduced for the audience as part of the scenic design but David Salle "was against it." (Personal communication, November 1, 1985. Apparently, certain kinds of discussions did occur between the set designer and the director.).

13. Kathy Acker, *The Birth of the Poet: An Opera*, rehearsal version of the script (New York: Performing Artservices, Inc., 1981), 35. All references to the play are taken from this version of the script.

14. Cf. the following observation in Kate Davy's account of the 1974 rehearsals of *PAIN(T)* and *Vertical Mobility:* "Often what seemed to be an instruction to a performer—'Register how the word relates to the wait (pause)'—was actually Foreman in the process of thinking out loud or talking to himself. His staging process is closer to that of an artist working in private—painting, writing, or sculpting—that that of a theatre director" (Davy, "Foreman's *PAIN(T)*," 32). As may be evident by now, in some sense all the theatre directors I observe are at one point or another working "in private" in public.

15. Foreman characteristically refers to "the men" and "the women" as he directs groups of actors in rehearsal. These blocking groups tend to reflect the playtext's view of human experience as defined by gender.

16. The line from this speech most quoted in reviews of the play is, "Take out your cock and piss over me" (II.3, p. 21). Cynthia's speech, like the whole middle section of *The Birth of the Poet*, is taken, with many small verbal revisions, from Kathy Acker's previously published novel, *Great Expectations* (New York: Grove Press, Inc., 1982), which itself appropriates passages from the texts of earlier writers.

17. Quoted by Arthur Bartow in *The Director's Voice: Twenty-One Interviews* (New York: Theatre Communications Group, 1988), 134.

18. In a more conventional use of this categorizing language, Foreman at one point comments, "I think I was wrong in what I said, Frank [Dahill]," immediately giving a new direction for the physical position of the actor.

19. Acker, *Birth of the Poet*, p. 15.

20. *Ibid.*, II. 2, p. 17.

21. "Ontological-Hysteric Manifesto II" (July, 1974), in *Richard Foreman: Plays and Manifestos*, ed. Kate Davy (New York: New York University Press, 1976), 143.

22. *Ibid.*, 143.

23. "Ontological-Hysteric Manifesto III" (June, 1975), *ibid.*, 188, 192–93. The quote beginning, "Despite what people say," is Foreman's comment to me during a break in the rehearsal of *Birth of the Poet* (October 18, 1985).

24. I overhear the actress mention this fact to Foreman but when I ask him later which line this might be, he does not know.

25. Referring to "line after line of ferocious smutty longing," Munk observes, "It was during this act that people booed, and berated the performers, and walked out in droves. There was nothing sensual about the staging—quite the opposite. The words did it. Hatred spewing from the man, self-contemptuous yearning from the woman. Got to me, too. . . . Still I had to face the truth: I wasn't offended, I was *upset*. I hadn't heard a woman's voice saying these things. So much the better." "Cross Left," *Village Voice*, December 17, 1985, 120.

26. "Think of the late Picasso as the grandfather of so much that's happening in art today, with his way of attacking the canvas, letting the drips be there, of doing something fast so that the evidence of contradiction and war between levels (mastery, impulse, desire, materiality) clearly registers on the canvas—much as it registers on Acker's page." Richard Foreman, "The Art of Kathy Acker," *On the Next Wave*, vol. 3, no. 3 (November 1985), 24.

27. II. 3, p. 22. The phrase, "at her dressing-table," which occurs on p. 114 of Acker's novel, *Great Expectations* and in the script, is omitted here.

28. The next lines are, "a twelve-year-old syphilitic named Janey should wrap her cunt around that prick I hate that prick I hate those fingers I hate black hair I want his teeth to rip themselves out in total agony" (II. 3, pp. 22–23). These lines are taken almost verbatim from *Great Expectations*, 114. (In the novel the word "teenager" follows "syphilitic.")

29. III. 2, p. 27. Most of the lines in act three are written in Arabic and English in the text.

30. In a strange way the effect of these disassociated verbal cues for the actor is reminiscent of what veteran actor William Roerick (Firs, in Elinor Renfield's production of *The Cherry Orchard*) recalls in "the old days." Actors were not given complete scripts but only "sides" which contained their own lines with a word or brief phrase as cues. The "sides" Roerick remembers did not even include the name of the character delivering the cue line. If, for example, your cue was "yes," and there were several "yeses," you needed to count the number of "yeses" to be certain you were making an appropriate entrance. In Roerick's early experience of theatre in New York, blocking

was established at the very beginning of rehearsals: "I knew what my cue was from the direction [stage right or left] the line came from." (Private communication, June 29, 1985). Cf. Foreman, "Blocking is for me not the truth of what is going on between two actors."

31. Foreman says that he tries to make "a reverberation box out of scenic elements . . . so that this phrase can reverberate the most, then the next [phrase]," and so on. (Interview, November 1, 1985). See also Bartow, *The Director's Voice*, 134. Foreman's second book of plays, along with his essays, published in 1985 by Station Hill Press is entitled *Reverberation Machines*.

32. Unnumbered page preceding p. 55.

33. Acker, p. 55.

34. *Reverberation Machines*, 204.
    The following day, while the sound tape is being adjusted, Foreman works for about five minutes directing a single sound to be made by the entire cast at intervals, accompanied by what he calls a "small Middle Eastern gesture" (the movement of one hand to the head), with the intention that it be repeated throughout III. i. When the taped music is restored and the actors begin to rehearse the scene in the playing area as previously blocked, Foreman instantly rejects the repeated sound-with-gesture and does not refer to it again.

35. ". . . women are goddam sluts. They're goddam sluts because the only thing they've got going for them are their cunts" (II. 4, p. 28). In Acker's novel, the line reads: "Goddam sluts: if only the cunts were unattached" (*Great Expectations*, 121). The speaker in both texts is a male who characterizes himself as "a macho pig" (*ibid.*).

36. Foreman remarks, in an interview during a break in rehearsal on November 1, 1985, "I believe that in anything human beings do, [or] manufacture, there is an inevitable drift toward coherence."

37. In II. 4, Maecenas says, "Writing is not about egotism" (29). Certainly in Foreman's rehearsals acting cannot be about egotism in the usual sense.

38. Prologue to act three, unnumbered page.

39. Foreman presents an abbreviated version of this account in an interview conducted by David Savran the following fall. See Savran, *In Their Own Words*, 38.

40. Kate Davy, *Richard Foreman: Plays and Manifestos*, Introduction, ix.

41. Cf. David Savran who describes the style of Foreman's own plays as revealing "a desire to explore, through performance, the workings of consciousness itself" (*In Their Own Words*, 36).

Chapter 8

1. David Bromwich, "Elizabeth Bishop's Dream-Houses," *Raritan*, vol. iv, no. 1 (Summer 1984), 80. The chapter title is taken from the playscript of Robert Wilson's *The Golden Windows* (Munich: Carl Hanser, 1982), 40.

2. Alan M. Kriegsman, "A Robert Wilson Primer," *The Washington Post*, November 16, 1986, Fl. Cf. Elinor Fuchs, in a letter published in the *Village*

Voice: "Robert Wilson is one of the few authentic theatrical geniuses that America has produced. I speak of his entire body of work spanning almost two decades. . . . That he is among these few has long been recognized in Europe" (August 5, 1986, 4).

3. "Into 'The Forest': Surreal Power," *The Washington Post*, December 5, 1988, C9.

4. "Cranking Up a Powerful 'Hamletmachine,' " *New York Times*, May 25, 1986, H3.

5. *Hamletmachine and Other Texts for the Stage*, ed. and trans., Carl Weber (New York: Performing Arts Journal Publications, 1984), 51.

6. A more elaborate version of this story is provided by Robert Coe:

> Once upon a time there was a little boy who worked hard each day in field and barn and shed. But every sunset he went to the top of a hill to see a distant house with windows of clear gold and diamonds. These windows shone and blazed so that the boy blinked to look at them. After a while, when the house was shuttered, he saw that it was actually a farmhouse like any other. Granted a holiday by his father, the boy journeyed to the house on the far hill, where he was greeted by a woman and her pretty daughter, a child his own age. The girl told the boy that he was mistaken about the whereabouts of his vision; she took him to a knoll behind the farmhouse and pointed in the distance to a house with windows of clear gold and diamonds. The boy looked, and realized it was his own house. He gave the girl his most precious possession, a red-striped pebble, but did not tell her what he had learned. Returning home, he saw the lamplight and firelight streaming through his parents' windows. "Have you had a good day?" his mother asked him. "Yes," the boy answered. "I have learned that our house has windows of gold and diamonds."

"The Extravagant Mysteries of Robert Wilson," *American Theatre*, vol. 2, no. 7 (October 1985), 6.

7. For example, "i am just crazy about you do you love me i would do anything to hurt you" (*The Golden Windows*, 16).

8. Coe, "Extravagant Mysteries," 6.

9. *Golden Windows*, 12.

10. The BAM production is the première production of the play in English.

11. The male "characters" seem to be defined by what they do (hang from a rope, sit on a bench); the women, by what they wear (a black or a white dress).

12. Cf. Stefan Brecht's description of Wilson's *Deafman Glance:* "The protagonist does nothing and his outwardness is (like that of all of us, but in this show brashly) a mystery: in which we may attempt to participate. Whereas in conventional drama, words and demeanor tell us the lies one tells oneself, in this show nothing pretends to clear up the mystery." *The Original Theatre of the City of New York: From the Mid-60s to the Mid-70s. Book I. The Theatre of Visions: Robert Wilson* (Frankfurt am Main: Suhrkamp, 1978), 120.

13. *Golden Windows*, 16.

14. *Ibid.*, 36.

15. The assistant to the director tells me during lighting rehearsals, "You'd never think we need a stage crew of forty-five with this [seemingly simple] set."

16. *Robert Wilson: The Theatre of Images*, rev. ed. (New York: Harper & Row, 1984), 105. (Interviewed by Laurence Shyer in December, 1982).

    The treatment of light and actor as equally important members of the company requires the cast to wait on stage or in the auditorium for hours each day during extended lighting rehearsals while many detailed physical adjustments are made. This is a particular hardship for John Bowman ("3") who is attached by invisible wires and a strap surrounding his body to a contraption that raises him high above the stage so that he appears to be hanging by a rope attached to his neck. The actor, who seems to suffer from acrophobia, is compelled to remain in this position while the director adjusts the tilt of his head to conform to the arc of light surrounding it, has the noose knot on the rope tightened, discusses hand make-up and related changes in the lighting of the actor's hand and face, and even has the crease in one leg of his pants straightened out. Rehearsal is temporarily interrupted when the contrivance that raises and lowers the actor jiggles and the lights cannot be properly focused. (It should be noted, however, that while the actor is kept aloft, in visible distress, for long periods of time during lighting rehearsal, the play requires that he remain in this position, sometimes invisibly, high up in the flies, for at least forty minutes during performance.) It is possible that the actor's need to be more securely "grounded," in a theatre piece that itself is not grounded in conventional modes of expression, is betraying him by taking on a physical form.

17. "Lighting that glass" is not so easy as one might think. (A single lit object appears in the same position, downstage left, in each of the three sections of *Golden Windows*: a suitcase in Part A, a glass of milk in Part B, a gun in Part C.) After lighting the glass in different ways, Wilson asks set coordinator Michael Deegan to procure a glass of milk. The next day when the set coordinator asks if the director prefers the real milk, Wilson says that it looks like a lit candle in a glass.

18. In an interview conducted by Margaret Croyden, Wilson says, "Light has its own laws and its own texture. It can actually exist by itself" ("Mystery and Surprise Impel 'Golden Windows,' " *New York Times*, October 20, 1985, H12).

19. Interview conducted by Elinor Fuchs, "The PAJ Casebook: *Alcestis*," PAJ 28, vol. 10, no. 1 (1986), 92–93.

20. Cf. Robert Wilson's silently lying down on the floor next to Charles Whiteside in the playing area.

21. Wilson's tentative attempt to execute his own intricate choreography, previously described, may fall somewhere between experiencing the blocking with the actor and exploring blocking for himself. A clearer example occurs when Wilson simply pauses to experiment in the playing area with various body movements and hand positions before continuing to direct Gaby Rodgers.

22. At one point during rehearsal, the production stage manager whispers to the director that an actress should be moving, not standing still. Wilson whispers to the assistant director who goes into the playing area and whispers to the actress who then begins to move upstage as Warrilow continues to deliver his lines. The scene has not been interrupted; the director continues to watch intently. "Voice-over" blocking directions are also communicated to individual actors by the director.

23. Working with Cynthia Babak, Wilson faces downstage left while the actress faces upstage right. On a diagonal together, standing almost side by side but facing in opposite directions, the director and actress slowly walk in place.

24. Directing Gaby Rodgers, "2," to pretend to let loose a little flying insect, to watch it fly away and return to her finger, Wilson uses his hand to represent the soaring, returning insect, and the actress watches the invisible flight avidly. The director's vision, ideally, lifts up off the ground of the preoccupations and needs of individual actors; soaring, it must always return.

25. "Robert Wilson's Stunning Images: Do they Add Up?" *New York Times*, July 24, 1988, H16. Harlan Foss, playing the role of Abraham Lincoln in the Rome section of Wilson's opera, "the CIVIL warS . . . ," says of the physical demands of the role: "I think performers need a special kind of training to do . . . [Wilson's] work. What is required is the sustaining of a long slow movement through time and space, which is something most of us aren't trained to do and aren't used to seeing. . . . It's a moving painting to music, that's really what it is" (Leslie Bennetts, " 'Civil Wars' Singer Gets Into Harness, Literally," *New York Times*, December 23, 1986, C13).

    Roger Copeland argues that Wilson's "radical conceptions of stage space and of theatrical time are both designed . . . to guarantee the spectator's 'perceptual freedom.' . . . [Images] are presented in a manner that allows us to take them in slowly (*ever* so slowly) rather than to be taken in by them. . . . Wilson's world is fundamentally less manipulative than the environment most of us inhabit in our daily lives" ("Robert Wilson and the Reinvention of Spectacle," *On the Next Wave*, vol. 2, no. 4 [December 1984], 11–12).

26. In addition, there are very few occasions when an actress directly faces the audience as she speaks. The women, even more than the men, enter, exit, and generally perform on the diagonal.

27. *Golden Windows*, 34.

28. Stefan Brecht, *Original Theatre*, 116.

29. Describing Wilson's *Deafman Glance*, performed at the Brooklyn Academy of Music in 1970–71, Stefan Brecht writes, "Formally what is on stage does not present itself as about anything *other* than itself." *Ibid.*, 106.

30. *Golden Windows*, 24. Other self-referential lines in the text are: "i do not get it" (26); "there is nothing coming through do you understand" (27); "exactly what do you mean exactly what happened" (28); "where are we anyway hey where are we anyway hey" (27); "its impossible i need help" (28).

31. Alisa Solomon, "Theater of No Ideas: A Conversation With Robert Wilson and Heiner Müller," *Village Voice*, July 29, 1986, 39.

32. Gaby Rodgers tells me during a break in rehearsal, "When I find something

inside, [Wilson] is very perceptive about seeing it. But I don't talk to him about the private stuff." The director had earlier commented, "Gaby, your interior concentration was great tonight. For the first time I felt there was a reason you were standing up there in the sky." The actress later confirms to me, but not to the director, that she was "gazing at someone" in her mind.

33. Interview with Robert Wilson, conducted by Ronn Smith, "The Night Is For Dreaming," *On the Next Wave*, vol. 3, no. 3 (November 1985), 4, 6.

34. Gaby Rodgers remarks that acting in Wilson's *Golden Windows* is physically confining ("like a strait jacket") but emotionally freeing (Personal communication, October 6, 1985).

35. *Golden Windows*, 28.

36. Wilson's resistance to discussion of intention or motivation appears to stem from his sense of their complexity. During an early October rehearsal, he speaks to the cast of how complicated a split second of human response is, using as an example the time-motion studies of mothers and infants that reveal nuances of expressiveness unseen by the human eye. He says that mothers are horrified to see that the frame of their first split-second response to the baby's crying shows them "lunging with terror."

37. Wilson seems to want to resist his own gifts for creating beguiling beauty in the theatre just as he seems to want to resist the authoritarian tendency in the directorial role he has chosen.

38. Robert Wilson, " . . . I thought I was hallucinating," *The Drama Review*, vol. 21, no. 4 (T76), (December 1977), 78.

39. During a sound runthrough three days before the first preview of *Golden Windows*, the door to the little house upstage opens and David Warrilow fails to appear. Wilson yells from the auditorium, "Fake it, Gaby!" The scene continues. Later the actress says, "*Fake* it?"

40. Costume designer Christophe de Menil is present during technical rehearsals, studying and rearranging the costumes, both stationary and in motion, under different kinds of lighting.

41. Theatre director Tony Giordano describes rehearsal as a "a life-force process" ("The Playwright-Director Relationship," *The Dramatists Guild Quarterly*, vol. 25, no. 3 [Autumn 1988], 15). Playwright-director John Patrick Shanley, making his debut as a movie director, says of his new role: "You're in this situation where if you don't get it, you can go back and get it again. . . . which is probably why they call it a director's medium" (Quoted by Lawrence Van Gelder, "At the Movies," *New York Times*, June 21, 1989, C8).

42. *Hamletmachine*, 57, 58.

43. *Ibid.*, 58.

44. The rehearsal script of the Weber translation contains many small verbal revisions, made by dramaturgs Wolfgang Wiens and Anne Cattaneo, assistant directors Ann-Christin Rommen and Hans-Werner Kroesinger, and the playwright himself who is in attendance during several days of rehearsal.

In his program note for this production of *Hamletmachine*, the playwright says, "The German writer Freilgrath, a close friend to Karl Marx, said: 'Germany is Hamlet, never quite knowing how to decide and because of that always making wrong decisions.' When I wrote *Hamletmachine* after translating Shakespeare's *Hamlet* for a theatre in East Berlin, it turned out to be my most American play, quoting T. S. Eliot, Andy Warhol, Coca Cola, Ezra Pound and Susan Atkins. It may be read as a pamphlet against the illusion that one can stay innocent in this our world. I am glad that Robert Wilson does my play, his theatre being a world of its own" (Heiner Müller, April 30, 1986).

45. Wilson has already introduced minimal lighting effects: dimming and black-outs (the physical structure of the small stage permits no side-lighting); taped music plays in the background.

46. Comments delivered at a public forum at the American Repertory Theatre in Cambridge in March, 1986 (transcript provided by Elinor Fuchs). It is striking that Wilson does not include touching as one of the "primary ways in which we relate to one another." (Robert Coe claims that Wilson is "the son of a . . . housewife who never touched him until the day he left for college" ["Extravagant Mysteries," 6].).

47. "What is disturbing for most of the actors when they work with me is that I usually start with an effect, and I don't know why. I say can you do this, can you move your hand in sixteen seconds, and they say, why? I don't know. I usually start with an effect, and I don't know the cause. But it doesn't matter where you start, because if you start with a cause you'll end up with an effect, and if you start with an effect and you think about it long enough, you'll get causes. . . . But because actors have largely been trained in schools of psychological acting, they want to start with the cause" (Robert Wilson, quoted in "The PAJ Casebook: *Alcestis*," 100).

48. Assistant director Ann-Christin Rommen, with whom Wilson works closely, responds to my question about when Wilson conceives of the perspectival shift: "I never heard of it before we started. . . . He came in with the idea of the table, the chairs, the tree. *As* we began, he began to shift the perspective" (Personal communication, April 26, 1986). During the *Hamletmachine* rehearsals, Wilson says, "I think you waste time by trying to figure it out before you get into it. If you get there and you see the people and you see the room, they tell you what to do" (Interview conducted by Alisa Solomon, "Theater of No Ideas," 39). Of these shifting perspectives, Gordon Rogoff comments, "Once seen, nothing could be simpler than Wilson's ingenious, rational, Cubist solution, but it isn't likely that anyone else could have thought of it" ("Mobilizing the Imagination," *Village Voice*, May 20, 1986, 95).

49. An exception is the actress leaning against the "tree" with both feet flat on the floor.

50. Throughout I am using "visual script" to refer to the director's choreography, and not to the author's literal stage directions.

   Gordon Rogoff notes that "Wilson's images are affinities rather than equivalencies of Müller's politically charged landscape. We are free to make our own associations. Müller wants the public to make up its own mind, Wilson lets the public think" (*ibid.*).

   In Richard Foreman's *Lava*, presented at The Performing Garage in the winter of 1989, the playwright-director's prerecorded voice is accompanied by an oscilloscope picture of sound waves on a screen, an illustration perhaps of equivalence without perceived affinity.

51. Hans-Werner Kroesinger, personal communication, April 26, 1986. Kroesinger, who acted in the earlier production of *Hamletmachine* directed by Müller, showed me the non-consecutive lines he delivered in the monologue of "THE ACTOR PLAYING HAMLET."

52. *Hamletmachine*, 53, 54, 57.

53. Rehearsal version of the script, 4. The Weber translation reads: "After . . . the toppling of the monument," 56.

54. Cf. Jane Hoffman's comment to the director in rehearsals of *The Golden Windows:* "In the middle of something I can't count and get a sense of inner life. That's why I go up [lose her lines]. . . . Maybe I will when I'm more relaxed." Diane D'Aquila recalls her experience in Wilson's *CIVIL warS* as she rehearses the title role in Wilson's production of *Alcestis* at the American Repertory Theatre in 1986: "So many interviewers have said to me, 'Are you still counting?' I haven't counted since the second week of *CIVIL warS*. In fact, there's an element of chance every night. You can't deliver a text the same way twice, it's impossible, not with an emotional content, which you need, even in a Wilson piece" (Quoted in "The PAJ Casebook: *Alcestis*," 100).

55. This kind of request was also made by at least one of the actresses during the *Golden Windows* rehearsals. The distinction made in each case was that between "runthroughs" (which are uninterrupted) and "workthroughs" (which allow for periods of "work" on particular speeches or blocking).

56. The phrase is my own. It is intended to suggest that different kinds of workthroughs occur in rehearsal, especially in Wilson's rehearsals.

57. Smith, "The Night is for Dreaming," 6. I never quite recover the sense of wonder I experience in first viewing the actors rehearse the formalized visual script unaccompanied by the spoken text.

58. *Hamletmachine*, 56.

59. Gussow, "Cranking Up a Powerful 'Hamletmachine,' " H3. James Leverett writes in an essay inserted in the theatre program for Wilson's production of the Rome section of *CIVIL warS* at the Brooklyn Academy of Music in 1986: "This lifting of interpretation—some would call it an irresponsibly arrogant disregard of meaning—is the most controversial aspect of . . . [Wilson's] work. Its radical democracy is simply too much for many who find the world so overwhelmed with matters of life and death that interpretation—active, activist, to-the-rescue interpretation—is everyone's obligation, especially everyone with a public platform" (essay commissioned by the 1986 NEXT WAVE Humanities Program).

60. *Hamletmachine*, 57.

61. Quoted by Carl Weber in his introduction to *Hamletmachine and Other Texts for the Stage*, 16.

Chapter 9

1. Remarks delivered to the New York Shakespeare Society, Columbia University, December 19, 1986.

2. *Ibid.*

3. Interview, during an hour break in rehearsal, February 9, 1986. Remarking that Ciulei describes the rehearsal process as a marriage between an actor and a director, Kline, unmarried at that time, comments, "There were days when I wanted a divorce or at least a good marriage counselor." He adds, "What makes a good marriage work is understanding the needs of the other as well as your own. I think marriage is difficult. It means you have to be attentive to your needs and the other's needs. You have to be clear to yourself and to the other [about] what your needs are. Liviu and I have been that way with each other. . . . It's a dialectic. He says what he thinks it is and as long as I keep saying what I think it is, we'll reach an accord. . . . I won't know until the end whether this is the way I ought to have done it."

   At the time of the writing of this chapter Steven Berkoff was scheduled to direct Kevin Kline in another Public Theater production of *Hamlet*. Enid Nemy reports in *The New York Times:* "Joseph Papp said that Kevin Kline, who is playing the Prince of Denmark, had informed him that he wished to direct his own 'Hamlet' and that Mr. Papp had agreed" ("On Stage," February 9, 1990, C2). His second Hamlet in four years, presented at the Public Theater in the spring of 1990, is directed by Kline himself.

4. Liviu Ciulei, private communication, December 19, 1986. Wilford Leach, who directed Kline in Shakespeare's *Henry V* as well as in the stage and film versions of *Pirates of Penzance*, says of the actor: "I could settle the Middle East crisis in the time it takes to get Kevin to agree to do something." "He changes, he can't decide, he wants to do this, but he wants to do that, and he also wants to do this too. He can think of so many alternatives that he wants to have them all, and he can't make up his mind. He *is* Hamlet" (Quoted by Leslie Bennetts, "In Quest of the Ever Elusive Hamlet," *New York Times*, March 2, 1986, H30).

5. Certain time-consuming bottlenecks in rehearsal—e.g., how to stage the viewing of the portraits of the two brothers, Claudius and Hamlet, in III. iv; the selecting of the "unbated," poisoned foil and the drinking of unpoisoned and poisoned cups in V. ii—are not unique to Ciulei's production of *Hamlet*. Watching these rehearsals at the Public Theater, Joseph Papp speaks of similar practical problems in his own directing of the play. And Peter Hall compares his 1965 and 1975 productions of *Hamlet:* "The same old problems with the gravediggers as I remember in 1965. Where can you keep the spade? Where can you put the coffin? How does Laertes get in and out? How do the gravediggers get in and out? I almost feel like writing a slim paperback entitled *How to Cope With the Grave in Hamlet: To Assist Aspiring Directors and Designers* (*Diaries*, 194).

6. In general, Ciulei does not rehearse scenes in the order in which they occur in the play.

7. For example, in rehearsing IV. ii, Kline unexpectedly introduces a comic way of exiting from the scene that forces Rosencrantz (Randle Mell) and Guildenstern (David Cromwell) to become dupes of his blocking much as Polonius is maneuvered into following Hamlet's verbal gymnastics earlier in the play (II.ii.172–219; III.ii.381–91). Ciulei likes Kline's improvised exit and asks the actor to repeat it. Kline improvises another version of the exit.

The director says, "I like the first one better," and the actor replies, "I can't remember what I did." Ciulei enters the playing area and demonstrates the original version. (The scene is repeated a third time but the actor's inspired zany exit—a zigzagging mockery of all efforts to remove him from the stage in a tidy, efficient, martial manner—never quite recovers its original form and vitality.).

8. An illustration of Smith's focus on intention is her subtextual reading of Gertrude's first speech in the play. After she assures the grieving Hamlet, "all that lives must die,/ Passing through nature to eternity" (1.ii.72–73), the actress immediately speaks aloud her subtext, "I don't care about eternity," and continues the speech as written. Later she begins to rehearse III.iv by uttering only her subtext. At the moment when the actress returns to the scripted lines, Kevin Kline walks over, takes her hand, and together they play the scene as written.

9. In general, Ciulei encourages actors not to introduce "thinking" pauses in lines where there are no caesuras. He speaks of "the fluidity of the Shakespearean verse," continually asks the actors "not to break the [verse] line," finally insists, "There aren't any pauses in the play except where they're supposed to be, . . . which I will say again and again in every rehearsal. . . . The thinking is under the line of the partner [and not during unwanted mid-line or between-the-line pauses]." Cf. Peter Hall, commenting on a readthrough in his *Hamlet* rehearsal: "It had vitality, and it showed conclusively that if you play on the line and keep going, think forward, the full-length play is neither too long nor too complex. I was amazed to find it read at just about three hours. Very encouraging" (*Diaries*, 185).

10. Of his 1968 production of *Macbeth*, Ciulei said, "I replaced truth with reality and destroyed the poetry" (Remarks, December 19, 1986).

11. During the first full runthrough of *Hamlet* on February 8, 1986, I decide to record the work not only of the actors but also of the staff in order to suggest the complexity of fully mounting a play for stage production. This decision is precipitated by Ciulei's asking that all chairs not used in the performance be pulled back as far as possible from the playing area in the rehearsal studio, so that there is a line of seated observers, as if in the front row of the orchestra. The odd sensation this creates, as I am suddenly joined by so many other note-takers, issues in a shift of focus and I find myself taking notes on observers and note-takers as well as on the rehearsal performance. (The following list of working staff is not exhaustive; e.g., neither costume designer William Ivey Long nor his assistant are present.)

   Stage manager Pat Sosnow is acting mainly as prompter and also taking notes on changes in blocking. Production stage manager Alan Traynor is also noting blocking changes and taking down "line notes," as requested by Kline (notes on lines omitted or inadvertently altered). M. L. Geiger, assistant to lighting designer Jennifer Tipton, who cannot be present today, is noting blocking and placement of stage furniture. Vocal and text consultant Elizabeth Smith is checking the reshaped text (cut and otherwise altered by transposed passages and the insertion of an additional scene); her concerns include the pronunciation, pacing, continuity of the verse. Chris Markle, assistant to the director, is taking notes on Ciulei's whispered comments during the runthrough. Prop mistress Frances Smith and assistant Susan

Kappel are taking "prop notes" and "set notes" (notes on new stage properties added during the runthrough and on parts of the set moved into new
positions). B. H. Barry arrives in time to watch the duel he has choreographed in V.ii.

Except for the intensity of his body posture, which few but I can see, and
his intermittent whispers to his assistant, Ciulei is nearly imperceptible,
seated on the edge of his chair, ever-present cigarette in his right hand, the
fingers of his left hand and frequently both arms moving with a silent,
illegible eloquence. During Hamlet's first soliloquy Ciulei is so still that I,
seated next to him, involuntarily hold my breath, move nothing but my
eyes.

12. An exception is Seymour Rudin's review: "One of the few strange cuts in
a more-nearly-complete-than-usual production was of Hamlet's crucially
significant lines in 5.2, 'There's a divinity that shapes our ends, Rough-hew
them how we will . . .' " (*Shakespeare Bulletin*, eds. James P. Lusardi and
June Schlueter, May/June 1986, 10).

13. Examples of cuts made during rehearsal: Laertes's lines on his "terms of
honor" (V.ii.246–52, a cut initiated by David Pierce, the actor playing
Laertes); Hamlet's line in his III.iii monologue, "Up, sword, and know thou
a more horrid hent" (88); Hamlet's and Horatio's lines at the end of I.iv:
"Think of it. . . . roar beneath," "And makes. . . . called!" "He waxes desperate
with imagination," "Have after!" (74–78, 82–84, 87, 89). In V.i, the graveyard
scene, many longer passages are cut: 9–14, 29–37, 98–117, 203–216 (of the
last passage, in which lines 213–16 were sung by Kline, Ciulei says, "With
regret I think we must cut this wonderful scene"). Much-disputed cuts
include the problematic lines in Hamlet's last soliloquy: "Rightly to be
great/ Is not to stir without great argument,/ But greatly to find quarrel in a
straw/ When honor's at the stake" (IV.iv.53–56), and the passage containing
Hamlet's much-quoted phrase, "Hoist with his own petar" (III.iv.203–13;
"There's letters sealed" in line 203 and "Let it work" in line 206 remain). Of
the former cut, Ciulei tells Kline, "Your problem isn't honor. . . . That's
another theme . . . the theme of all the Spanish plays. I think Shakespeare
liked it. . . ." Of the latter, he says, "And we shouldn't speak of Rosencrantz
and Guildenstern because that will be a surprise."

A few further examples of cuts I noted in rehearsal: II.ii.337–75 ("eyrie of
children" section); II.ii.444–52 ("but it was. . . . fine"); III.ii.8–14 ("O, it
offends. . . . avoid it"); III.ii.80–84 ("If his occulted speech . . . Vulcan's
stithy"); III.ii.200–13 ("The violence. . . . his enemy"); V.ii.47–52 ("How was
this sealed? . . . impression," a pointed omission of Hamlet's reference to
"heaven ordinant").

Three other directorial revisions should be mentioned. Despite his desire
to shorten the length of the production, Ciulei introduces two new transitional scenes, one of which is retained in performance. In addition, a lengthy
dialogue between Claudius and Laertes ("Will you be ruled by me? . . . hold
there," IV.vii. 59–162) is removed and placed at the end of V.i. Finally, the
appearance of Fortinbras is held off until V.ii. In IV.iv.1–29, the speeches of
Fortinbras are delivered by a "Norwegian Captain" and the speeches of the
Captain are delivered by Marcellus. In IV.iv.18, "We" is accordingly changed
to "They."

Peter Hall writes of his 1975 *Hamlet* rehearsal: "There is enormous pressure on me from my colleagues not to do . . . [*Hamlet*] as I want to, full-length. . . . Overtime, and the impossibility of matinees, with the consequent loss of revenue. . . . So what am I to do?. . . . I don't want to *interpret* the play by cutting it" (*Diaries*, 176–77).

14. Maynard Mack, "The World of 'Hamlet,' " in the Signet Classic Shakespeare edition of *Hamlet*, ed. Edward Hubler (New York: New American Library, 1963), 237.

15. Later in rehearsal Kline again tears a page from the book he is reading, wets it with his lips, and pastes it on Polonius's bald head in II.ii. In the performance I attended on March 1, 1986, neither this comic staging nor the earlier improvised delivery of his lines while hidden behind a tall chair are retained. Instead, Hamlet mimes sitting on a chair: the chair becomes invisible rather than the actor.

16. Borges, "Pierre Menard," 44.

17. Sometimes these "drafts" are inadvertent. During the first runthrough of the play, the white sheet substituting for the arras which conceals Polonius as he spies on Hamlet's meeting with Gertrude is missing. The murder of Polonius and Hamlet's ignorance of whom he has killed ("O me, what has thou done?" "Nay, I know not. Is it the King?" III.iv.26–27) have an unexpected odd effectiveness when enacted without the concealing curtain. It is as if Polonius is Polonius and Claudius and every treacherous political actor, as if he is so much the actor that even when Hamlet has him visibly in his hands Hamlet doesn't know what it is he's killing. An accident of staging, a missing prop, becomes, for me, an incandescent moment in rehearsal, never to be seen again.

18. David Cole, *Acting as Reading*.

19. The first quote is that of Barnet Kellman ("The Playwright-Director Relationship," *The Dramatists Guild Quarterly*, vol. 25, no. 3 [Autumn 1988], 11). Kellman says, "A writer may not realize that . . . the actors and the director . . . have to recapitulate the writing process for themselves, in terms of their own choices." The latter two quotes are taken from Charles Segal's description of the fundamental principles of baroque composition as enunciated for the plastic arts by Heinrich Wölfflin ("Senecan Baroque: The Death of Hippolytus in Seneca, Ovid and Euripides," *Transactions of the American Philological Association* 114 [1984], 312–13).

What we tend to call "character" in the theatre is often the traces of acting choices and directorial decisions explored, at times laboriously, in rehearsal. Kevin Kline's gifts as an actor are abundantly visible in his improvisatory work, especially in rehearsing Hamlet's instructions to the players at the beginning of III.ii. In this scene in particular Kline is fully at ease as is Hamlet himself with the players. Ciulei responds with delight to one of Kline's inspired improvisations in III.ii: "Keep that," adding, "I'd never have thought of it." Kline's response, "It's frozen," is a chillingly inaccurate metaphor since almost nothing he does is ever set in rehearsal or performance: he is only "frozen" on film. (The desire of the director to preserve the moment is really a cinematic desire and achievement.) What emerges in the midst of rehearsal exploration is as much defined by its context—an ongoing process—as by its intention and can never be repeated in its original form. Although there is always talk of "setting" or "keeping" a successful staging, the creation of "the illusion of the first time" is, of course, itself an illusion. Even the illuminating remark of actor William Roerick that "the surface may change in performance but it's set under the surface: the inner life—the way you see it—is set" (private communication, July 7, 1985) suggests a significant change. Performing in a different way is seeing differently because it is a different way of seeing oneself being seen.

Shakespeare's Hermione uses the word "preserved" to describe her restoration at the end of *The Winter's Tale:* "I . . . have preserved/ Myself to see the issue" (V.iii.125, 127–28). Hermione's "surface" is changed: she is "wrinkled," more "agèd" (28–29), after her sixteen years' absence. The very nature of her being is in question. If she has hidden herself from her husband for all this time, is she still "as tender/As infancy and grace" (26–27)? If she has died and been restored to life, can that uncanny experience have left no trace but wrinkles? (and why wrinkles?) It seems clear, in this famous scene of indeterminacy, that Hermione's use of the word "preserved" is meant to be a theatrical paradox. To "freeze," to "keep," to "set" moments in theatre rehearsal is a theatrical fiction. One can keep organic bodies from decomposing by chemical treatment or freezing (e.g., preserving a corpse); one can prevent fruit or meat from fermentation or decomposition by boiling with sugar, salting, or pickling. In the first case, the life itself is gone; in both cases, that which is preserved is altered in the process of preservation. I am not suggesting that preservation of rehearsal moments in performance is either lifeless or pickled (though these are not entirely ludicrous possibilities) but that the act of preservation of rehearsal moments is always already a reconstruction.

20. III.ii.373–74. This line is plucked out of the play by Ciulei in rehearsal but, fortunately, later restored.

21. See, e.g., Susan L. Cole, *The Absent One*, 41–60.

22. In rehearsal of the Ghost's leave-taking in I.v, Kline grasps the hand of Jeff Weiss (who in a remarkable tour de force performs the roles of the Ghost, the Player King, and Osric). Ciulei rejects this gesture and enters the playing area to discuss, inaudibly, the implications of various forms of physical contact. The final experiment, the Ghost's grasping Hamlet firmly on the shoulders, is retained. In performance, on March 1, 1986, Kline kneels with hand outstretched toward the retreating figure of his deceased father, the only visible remnant of the actor's enactment of his impulse to touch, shake hands with, the Ghost. Kline tells me that he wants a tangible moment between himself and the Ghost (Interview, February 9, 1986).

23. "The prayer scene . . . [was] played casually seated" (Seymour Rudin, *Shakespeare Bulletin*, May/June 1986, 9). More dismissive is Mel Gussow's treatment of the innovative staging of the opening of IV.v: "In his customary fashion, Mr. Ciulei stages the mad scene at a banquet table laden with food and candelabra, adding distraction to an otherwise unconvincing tantrum" ("Theater: Kevin Kline in 'Hamlet' at Public," *New York Times*, March 10, 1986, C13).

24. Ophelia at first appears quite normal as she sits at the banquet table. Suddenly she blurts out, "Where is the beauteous majesty of Denmark?"

(IV.v.21, her first line in the scene). She then begins to sing, as the others continue drinking their soup. Suddenly she rises, looking crazed. The scene as staged is terrifying because it occurs in a conventionally "safe" social context and because Ciulei has intentionally eliminated any transitions between "lucid" and "mad" moments, a characteristic "realistic Ciulei detail."

25. The actress playing Ophelia does not initially feel the necessity of sitting as she delivers her monologue in III.i.

26. Earlier in this rehearsal Ciulei worries that a newly revised blocking "might look stagey." Given the critics' reactions to the production, Ciulei's fear that audiences and reviewers will see either too much (theatricality, *embourgeoisement*, eccentricity, realistic period detailing in costume and properties) or too little (vitality, poetic resonance, mystery, transcendent illumination) is justified. (These examples are culled from reviews of the production.).

27. During rehearsal on February 8, 1986, swords are present for the first time as part of the military costume. When his sword impedes Claudius's rising from his royal seat in I.ii, the actor comments, "Sorry, I'm just not used to it." Often in rehearsal accouterments are added incrementally rather than all at once. Each new piece of clothing, each new prop, requires new moves, new adjustments, on the part of the actor. In performance the audience will see a fully furnished set. But the actor and director create this effect one sword at a time.

28. Leslie Bennetts, "In Quest of the Ever Elusive Hamlet," H30. The following quote occurs during my interview with the actor on February 9, 1986.

29. It seems important to mention the work of choreographer B. H. Barry, who has said: " . . . the heart of what I do is directing" (Interview on the MacNeil, Lehrer Newshour, August 17, 1989). Listed as "Fight Director" in the theatre program, Barry is actually a fight-and-its-context director. During rehearsal Barry either works independently with Kevin Kline and David Pierce in an upstairs studio at the Public Theater or directs the actors on stage, conferring regularly with Ciulei as he refines or suggests blocking. At times Barry himself demonstrates various choreographic options, e.g., the fatal "hit" by Laertes: "I've always thought that hit was the tiniest of movements. . . . There's all sorts of choices, all sorts of things one can color." For 35 minutes Barry rehearses this "nick," so small, so complicated to stage. His only textual aids are Horatio's line, "They bleed on both sides" (V.ii.306) and editorial stage directions, "*In scuffling they change rapiers, [and both are wounded]*" (304). In directing the physical movements of the actors, Barry characteristically voices his sense of psychological motivation and interplay as bases of certain choreographic choices. For example, he suggests to Ciulei that Claudius's interruption of the duel, "Stay, give me drink" (284), is motivated by a sense that Laertes is nervous, possibly out-of-control. Such an interpretation, of course, affects the choreography of Laertes's moves prior to this moment. Ciulei has not offered this view nor do I hear his response to it, but he is concerned earlier with the difficulties in staging the interruption of the match during which the King invites Hamlet to drink with him. Later in rehearsal Barry creates, with Ciulei's approval, a sense

of a "sporting event." Hamlet, scoring a point, deftly taps Laertes on the top of his fencing helmet. The court at first does not know how to respond. Smith asks, "Is that a breach in fencing etiquette?" Reassured that the gesture is not vicious but playful, Smith asks, "Should we react?" Barry responds, "Yes," then secures the assent of Ciulei. The members of the court smile and laugh. Then, in Smith's words, the Queen moves "on the wave" of this moment to toast her son and drinks the poisoned wine. B. H. Barry, officially present to choreograph a duel between Hamlet and Laertes, is drawn into directing the court and Queen as onstage audience, eventually, in collaboration with the actress, motivating Gertrude's fatal exuberant toast to her son, all this conducted, of course, under the eye of Ciulei.

30. Late in rehearsal Ciulei introduces and choreographs two scenes, the first ("I.v.a") to be added as a transitional scene after I.v, and the second ("II.i.b") to be added after II.i. "I.v.a," a silent scene showing the responses of members of the court to Hamlet's "antic disposition" as the Prince enters in their midst and exits, is cut. Ciulei directs this scene in the manner of a silent film director, speaking over the action: "Ladies in, faster, faster. Officers, cross. You stop there. Go very fast. . . . And that's it. Thank you." "II.i.b," retained in performance, shows Hamlet's "antic disposition" at a later stage and contains the dance around the candle. Hamlet enters a crowded set, with officers and court members milling about. He sings lines from III.ii (275–78 and 285–88), followed by a brief dialogue with Horatio:

> *Hamlet.* Would not this, sir, and a forest of feathers . . . get me a
> fellowship in a cry of players?
> *Horatio.* Half a share.
> *Hamlet.* A whole one, I.
> (III.ii.279, 281–84)

No non-Shakespearean lines are added.

Chapter 10

1. David Richards, "Leaving Them Wondering," *The Washington Post*, August 12, 1986, C2. In contrast, Arch Campbell gives the following brief review on the local television news: "It was pretentious, boring, and silly. Two figures in mostly darkness, and that sums up the production" (Channel 4/WRC, 11 p.m. news, August 11, 1986, as reported to me by Alice P. Letzler). Joe Brown, also writing in *The Washington Post*, notes that "Sellars has chosen to stage a brief program of three elegiac prose-poems that taken together sound like a farewell of sorts" (" 'Two Figures': Whispering in the Dark," Weekend section, August 15, 1986, 9a).

2. Wallace Stevens, "Angel Surrounded by Paysans," *Collected Poems*, 497.

3. There is a full house every night, with approximately twenty to twenty-five people turned away from each performance.

4. David Richards writes of *Two Figures:* "It asks spectators to listen first (and above all), and only later allows them to look at what could be a Robert Wilson tableau" (*ibid.*).
   The reliance on natural light in the performance I saw on August 18, 1986

is problematic. My companion cannot see Richard Thomas, attired in a red silk gown, during the Noh play.

5. *Ohio Impromptu*, in *Collected Shorter Plays of Samuel Beckett* (Faber and Faber: London, 1984), 285. All citations to *Ohio Impromptu* are taken from this edition of the play.

6. David Warrilow "has been hailed variously as the 'quintessential,' the 'consummate,' the 'ultimate' Beckett actor" (Jonathan Kalb, "Acting Beckett: Two Versions of *Ohio Impromptu*," *Theater*, vol. 15, no. 3 [Summer/Fall 1984], 48). Kalb notes further: "In fact, I don't know how Warrilow works, what techniques he uses to create his characterizations. As with most great art, analysis breaks down after a point and the honest critic admits to feelings of awe. I must confess that I am amazed at what Warrilow can evoke on the stage, however he comes to it" (53).

7. *Ibid.*

8. The first quotation is from *Ohio Impromptu*, 285; the second is from Wallace Stevens's "Angel Surrounded by Paysans," *Collected Poems*, 496.

9. The director, of course, is not simply audience-surrogate or controlling auditor. In fact, the casting pattern of *Two Figures in Dense Violet Light* offers a series of suggestively linked figures. Richard Thomas, who plays Beckett's Listener, also plays the ghost of Tsunemasa in the Noh play and "the necessary angel of earth" in Stevens's poem. David Warrilow plays the Beckett Reader, the Noh priest, and a countryman in Stevens's poem.

10. *Ohio Impromptu*, 286.

11. *Ibid.*, 287.

12. During the rehearsals of *Ohio Impromptu* attended by Beckett in Paris in the summer of 1986, the playwright corrected the Listener's knock as performed by Jean-Louis Barrault. Beckett used only a fingernail to demonstrate the gentle knock he intended. The effect, as recalled by David Warrilow, was deafening.

13. *Ohio Impromptu*, 285.

14. Jonathan Kalb describes David Warrilow's earlier performance as Reader directed by Alan Schneider at the Harold Clurman Theater in New York: "He reads, eyes ever intent on the book. . . . and the Listener . . . knocks on the table, cutting him off. Warrilow pauses, takes a breath, repeats the preceding phrase, and then pauses again; after a few seconds, the Listener knocks again, and the reading continues. This knock-repeat-knock sequence . . . is the only evidence (before the end) of contact or exchange between the characters, but Warrilow handles the pauses in such a way that he actually develops that slim evidence of contact into intimations of depth and complexity in the characters' relationship" (Kalb, 50). Kalb did not attend rehearsal and seems to ascribe the "handling" of the pauses to the actor alone.

15. Jane Horwitz, reviewing *Two Figures in Dense Violet Light* on WTTG–TV, August 12, 1986, did not realize that both artificially amplified performances of *Ohio Impromptu* are alive: "[The actors] sit virtually motionless at a table, while we listen to a recording of the same Beckett play *again*." In rehearsal Sellars explains his staging of the Beckett play to the actors: "I

need the audience in a tank for awhile, separated from the world. I need to allow their eyes to get accustomed to darkness, I need them to calm down and get centered, and also it's probably the only time in their lives that they'll ever get a chance to comprehend this play [so they will get the play twice]." During the first performance of the Beckett play, the artificially amplified voice of David Warrilow emerges from a speaker placed behind and to the left of the audience. As Sellars says to Richard Thomas, "We [the audience] *hear* the performance from your [the Listener's] point of view . . . right over our left shoulder. So we're in the Listener's position in the first performance of *Ohio*." Placing the audience in the Listener's position during performance is a sign of its appropriation of the director's position in rehearsal.

16. Richard Thomas remarks to me after this rehearsal runthrough: "Rehearsal is solving problems and performance is solving a different set of problems. Performance's problem is maintaining form without losing life."

17. *The Winter's Tale*, IV.iv.90–92.

Chapter 11

1. I regret that I was not able to observe more of the work of this remarkable actress and director, herself a founding member of Mabou Mines. Her rehearsals in New Haven were limited to a few days in the fall of 1988. Unavoidably, her part in the rehearsal process is barely hinted at in this chapter.

2. Wallace Stevens, "Final Soliloquy of the Interior Paramour," *Collected Poems*, 524.

3. Rehearsal script, fall, 1987. The first eight stanzas of this section of *Warrior Ant* were included in the theatre program as hand-outs, along with early versions of several rap verses and a lyric composed for the student chorus by Bob Telson during rehearsal. This line reappears verbatim in the fall, 1988 rehearsal script, 42.

4. At one point in rehearsal work, each of the three American worm puppeteers is successively replaced by the set designer, with the intention of allowing individual handlers to see the puppet's sinuous movements as they might look from the audience's point of view. But the Heisenberg principle works in reverse. The puppeteer, like an actor trying literally to see himself being seen, changes what is seen by absenting himself from the picture in order to see the picture. The puppet rehearsal makes vivid what is true of every theatre rehearsal I observe, with the possible exception of the Wooster Group. The actor knows many things the director can never know but the actor cannot know what is utterly crucial in the theatre: what she or he looks like to the audience.

5. In an interview before the fall, 1988, opening at Yale, Breuer said that "*The Warrior Ant* should be viewed more as performance art than [as] a play" (Quoted by Aninne Schneider, "From Bunraku to Salsa: 'Warrior Ant,' " in "After Hours," the weekend section of the *Yale Daily News*, October 7, 1988, 3).

6. Remarks made during a University of Illinois directing colloquium in the

summer of 1982, transcript by Lorraine Commeret, 14. Speaking of his production of *The Gospel at Colonus*, Breuer says: "What's exciting is how alive it still is. . . . There are many places in the performance where I don't know what's going to happen or who's going to feel like doing what. People change their singing, they change their blocking; they dance one night, they don't dance the next; they go offstage and sometimes they come back, sometimes they don't. The quality of the show is there, but this *looseness* is something I really treasure" (Quoted by Wendy Smith, "Sophocles With a Chorus of Gospel," *New York Times*, March 20, 1988, H17).

7. Characteristic Breuerspeak is this note to the actors: "I think the trip is to hip all these tones, so go more slowly."

8. This is not simply Breuer's technique with a student actor. A year later, in the fall of 1988, Breuer asks veteran Mabou Mines actor and director Frederick Neumann to explore in rapid succession variously accented and unaccented readings of his opening speech (e.g., a slight Indian accent, "a little Russian [accent]," "back to neutral").

9. During rehearsal Bob Telson composes new parts of the score. In the fall of 1987, for example, Telson introduces new music and lyrics. This sung refrain, retained in the 1988 performance at Yale, creates the effect Breuer had been seeking through prolonged experimentation with line delivery. As the director explains to the actor, "The chorus with its refrain is replacing the singing quality we were exploring."

10. This is not at all easy to achieve. Late in rehearsal Tamamatsu attempts to teach a deft rhythmic hand-clapping movement to the chorus of hard-working students who have had to become, in quick succession, dancers, then belly dancers, then puppeteers.

11. The Prologue and Epilogue of the *Warrior Ant* were performed without a full runthrough at Alice Tully Hall. *The Gospel at Colonus* almost opened at the Brooklyn Academy of Music without a full runthrough (Bob Telson, private communication, October 15, 1987). Neither the first work-in-progress performance of *Warrior Ant* at Yale in the fall of 1987 nor the opening performance in the fall of 1988 was preceded by a full runthrough.

12. Eileen Blumenthal remarks, "The inanimate wood-and-cloth beings, somehow, are made to appear more alive than the puppeteers" ("Ants Invade BAM. Puppets in Cahoots," *New York Times*, October 16, 1988, H13). Almost everything that needs saying about life in the theatre is in that "somehow."

13. The shamisen is a small three-stringed musical instrument resembling a mandolin.

14. Barbara C. Adachi, *Backstage at Bunraku: A Behind-the-Scenes Look at Japan's Traditional Puppet Theatre* (New York: Weatherhill, 1985), 11.

15. *Ibid.*, 28–29.

16. *Ibid.*, 149. A narrator with the Osaka troupe remarks: "In Bunraku one is not considered a true performer until one reaches fifty, and not an artist until one reaches sixty. We say it takes three years to learn to laugh, eight years to learn to cry. Well, that's only the beginning" (150).

17. This is my own reconstruction of the hidden operation of the Bunranku doll as she dances, based on the tasks assigned to the three puppeteers. Watching

the dancing female doll in rehearsal, I was certain that it had legs beneath the kimono. I am grateful to Kazuko Hayashi for confirming my later suspicion that the "legs" were an illusion.

18. Carlson, *Goethe and the Weimar Theatre*, 311.

19. Senior puppeteer Bunjaku assigns puppet heads to the chief puppeteers at the National Bunraku Theatre of Japan: "Each puppeteer . . . moves the doll a little differently. Why? . . . The sensitivity of the puppeteers' hands varies remarkably. The tension they maintain . . . and the special fingering they devise to achieve certain effects . . . differ tremendously and affect how the doll comes across on stage" (Adachi, *Backstage at Bunraku*, 90).

20. In the traditional Bunraku theatre of Japan there is no equivalent to Lee Breuer: "No single man is designated the leader of the Bunraku troupe. Responsibility for the affairs of the troupe at present is shared by senior narrators Koshijidayu and Tsudayu and puppeteers Tamao and Kanjuro" (*Ibid.*, 10).

21. Quoted by Eileen Blumenthal, "Ants Invade BAM," H13.

22. I am alluding to Teresa de Lauretis' discussion of "a view from elsewhere," previously quoted in the chapter on Emily Mann. That "elsewhere" de Lauretis refers to as "the space-off," a term borrowed from film theory: "The space not visible in the frame but inferable from what the frame makes visible. . . . Avant-garde cinema has shown the space-off to exist concurrently . . . alongside the represented space, has made it visible by remarking its absence in the frame or succession of frames, and has shown it to include not only the camera (the point of articulation and perspective from which the image is constructed) but also the spectator (the point where the image is received, re-constructed, and reproduced in/as subjectivity)" (*Technologies of Gender*, 25–26). Again, I am adapting her terms for my own purposes in describing the theatre director in rehearsal.

23. The interpreter, Yoko Totani, is also a kind of paradirectorial presence in rehearsal, as indicated by her characteristic position in between Breuer and the performers, and by her voice which follows and sometimes overlaps that of the narrators in rehearsal. Her voice is the mediator of both text and director for the Bunraku puppeteers. Yoko Totani was for six years a professional storyteller in Japan. As she provides a running translation of both the English script and the director's verbal notes during rehearsal, she makes split-second decisions whether to translate the text verbatim, to offer her own condensed or interpretive version, or merely to supply cue words for stage action. Breuer, who does not speak Japanese, cannot know which of the first two functions the interpreter is performing at any given moment.

24. At least six different languages are spoken by the members of the company during the 1988 rehearsals I observe.

25. Cf. Frank Rich's review: "[The Brooklyn Academy of Music's Next Wave Festival's] opening attraction for 1988, 'The Warrior Ant,' is nothing if not a throwback to the smorgasbord esthetics of that totemic artistic happening of the 1950's, the Ed Sullivan show" ("Seeking Truth in an Age of Considerable Boredom," *New York Times*, October 24, 1988, C15). On the other hand, Michael Feingold, reviewing the same production, writes: "In Act One we've experienced the feeling . . . of all cultures, myths and peoples joining into

one happy family, to celebrate one eternally repeating mystery" ("Sailing to Breuersantium," *Village Voice*, November 1, 1988, 103).

26. Rehearsal script, 1988, 62.

27. Cf. Donald Keene: "Unlike the puppets in use in other countries, the Bunraku puppets are often tragic in expression and bearing, and they have a pure intensity no actor could match. They borrow their motivating force from the three men [only men perform in Bunraku theatre] who stand beside and beneath them, but they move of their own, as their tragedies dictate. To say they are incapable of motion themselves is true, but this is not the impression the perfectly coordinated movements of the three operators convey to us; the men seem like witnesses to the actions rather than the cause" (Adachi, *Backstage at Bunraku*, ix).

28. Inserted in the program for the performances of *The Warrior Ant* at the Yale University Theatre, October 10–15, 1988.

29. Rehearsal script, 1988, 22.

30. It is in the 1988 performance of *Warrior Ant*.

31. In the performance at the University Theatre on October 15, 1988, this opening lecture was greatly shortened. The questioning of the lecturer by actors planted in the audience was eliminated altogether.

32. Not unexpectedly, it is as difficult to stage a love scene with puppets as with human actors. While Leslie Mohn narrates the mating of the warrior ant and death moth, six puppeteers, in extremely close proximity to each other, manipulate two puppets. Tamamatsu handles the head and right arm of the moth puppet, Barbara Pollitt manipulates her left arm, and Patrick Kerr operates her legs. Kanju Kiritake handles the head and right arm of the warrior ant (dropping out just before the climactic moment so that Tamamatsu can become the chief handler of both puppets), Eren Ozker manipulates the ant's left arm, and John Ludwig operates his legs. The creation of simultaneous orgasmic shudders, synchronized with the voice of the narrator, is not achieved in the first attempts and, accompanied by some laughter, has to be rehearsed several times. The group-created orgasm might be considered a metaphor for peak rehearsal moments.

   This rehearsal of the primal scene, probably unique in Bunraku, recalls Freud's famous statement that during every act of sexual congress there are at least six persons in the room.

33. In his essay on the marionette theatre, Kleist writes: " . . . so grace returns after knowledge has gone through the world of the infinite, in that it appears to best advantage in that human bodily structure that has no consciousness at all—or has infinite consciousness—that is, in the mechanical puppet, or in the God" ("On the Marionette Theatre," trans. Thomas G. Neumiller, in *The Drama Review*, vol. 16, no. 3 [September, 1973], 26).

Epilogue

1. W. B. Worthen, "Deeper Meanings and Theatrical Technique: The Rhetoric of Performance Criticism," *Shakespeare Quarterly*, vol. 40, no. 4 (Winter 1989), 455.

2. John Donne, "The Ecstasy," *John Donne's Poetry*, ed. A. L. Clements (New York: W. W. Norton & Company, Inc., 1966), 31.

3. The only alteration in the text, suggested by Kathy Schave, is the omission of the following lines, "Take yourself off wherever you wish to go/ free of a heavy charge," spoken by Creon to the guard. Marchitto agrees to omit these lines in order to support his decision to have the guard remain on stage. The translation used in rehearsal is that of Elizabeth Wyckoff, in *The Complete Greek Tragedies*, ed. David Grene and Richmond Lattimore, vol. ii (Chicago: The University of Chicago Press, 1959), 173. All citations are to this edition.

4. In performance on the library steps, each of these movements would place the actor one step higher than his previous position.

5. I am appropriating Donne's phrase in "The Ecstasy," 1. 74.

6. In fact, the library, built in 1904, was originally a family house, a wedding gift to Rebecca Darlington and Louis Stoddard from the bride's parents. It was purchased by Albertus Magnus College in 1924, and designated "an historical building" in 1983. Curiously, one of Louis Stoddard's accomplishments was the building of the Schubert Theater in New Haven (Ann Braun, "The Silver Horn" [Albertus Magnus College publication], October 13, 1954).

7. Marchitto says to the actor playing Haemon, "If you face the audience, we assume that you're talking to Creon. It's a kind of optical illusion on the stage. I don't know why that happens but it's written about in books that that does tend to happen."

8. It seems interesting, in this regard, that there are no speech-tags in the earliest surviving manuscript of *Antigone*, or of any other Greek tragedy.

9. Bernard, in Virginia Woolf's *The Waves*, says: "To be myself (I note) I need the illumination of other people's eyes, and therefore cannot be entirely sure what is my self" (San Diego: Harcourt Brace Jovanovich, n.d. [1931]), 116.

10. The evening rehearsals, arranged out of necessity to accommodate the students' schedules during the day, did not, of course, approximate the natural light that would have illuminated the late afternoon outdoor performance.

11. The director determined before he cast the play to use half-masks, covering only the eyes and nose and worn only by the chorus, a knowing departure from the traditional full-face mask worn in the classical Greek theatre by the principals. In the last days of rehearsal the members of the chorus decide by consensus that these masks seriously obstruct their view of both the scrolls they are reading and the steps they must ascend or descend as they speak. These beautiful rejected half-masks, their tiny variegated earth-colored geometric shapes on a black background reproduced visually on the theatre program, had been designed and created by Marchitto to suggest the permanent ambiguity of the chorus. Partly exposed and partly veiled, the chorus functions as human commentator and interlocutor but also as an element of the set, reshaping the stage space and suggesting perspectives for the viewing audience, thus putting in question certain binary distinctions often applied to theatrical representation, e.g., the foregrounding of

the human actor vs. the foregrounding of the set; being inside the "fourth wall" vs. being outside or even comprising, and thus deconstructing, it.

12. Not here this evening but present at almost every rehearsal is producer Donna Gibson with her nourishing support, tangible and intangible.

13. He explains his inability to lament in rehearsal: "It's hard when you can't speak from experience. I've had a very nice life."

   One of the motivational techniques devised by the director midway through rehearsal is an "exercise" in which Creon is unexpectedly forced to drag across the floor the dead weight of the actor playing Haemon as chorus members are instructed to shout "Murder!" repeatedly. In this rehearsal, but never again, Creon speaks in a voice that is and sounds distressed by, if nothing else, the sheer physical burden of transporting an actor who seems to have lost his stage life.

14. There is a striking similarity in their laments:

    Antigone. I go, without a friend, struck
    down by fate
    live to the hollow chambers of
    the dead. (ll. 919–20)
    Creon. I cannot rest.
    My life is warped past cure. My
    fate has struck me down.
    (ll. 1341–42)

15. That this welling up was, in fact, involuntary was later confirmed by the actress in conversation.

16. Sher, *Year of the King*, 237.

17. José Quintero, *If You Don't Dance They Beat You* (Boston: Little, Brown, 1974), 114.

Selected Bibliography

Articles and reviews cited in the notes are not generally repeated in the bibliography. Bibliographical information about plays appears in the notes.

Aaron, Stephen. *Stage Fright: Its Role in Acting*. Chicago: University of Chicago Press, 1986.

Adachi, Barbara C. *Backstage at Bunraku: A Behind-the-Scenes Look at Japan's Traditional Puppet Theatre*. New York: John Weatherhill, 1985.

Bartow, Arthur. *The Director's Voice: Twenty-One Interviews*. New York: Theatre Communications Group, 1988.

Benedetti, Robert L. *The Director At Work*. Englewood Cliffs: Prentice-Hall, 1985.

Bergman, Ingmar. *Four Screenplays of Ingmar Bergman*, trans. Lars Malmstrom and David Kushner. New York: Simon and Schuster, 1969.

Berry, Ralph. *On Directing Shakespeare*. London: Hamish Hamilton Ltd., 1989.

Blumenthal, Eileen. *Joseph Chaikin*. New York: Cambridge University Press, 1984.

Borges, Jorge Luis, "Pierre Menard, Author of the *Quixote*," in *Labyrinths: Selected Stories and Other Writings*, eds. Donald A. Yates and James E. Irby. New York: New Directions, 1964.

Brecht, Stefan. *The Original Theatre of the City of New York: From the Mid–60s to the Mid–70s. Book I. The Theatre of Visions: Robert Wilson*. Frankfurt am Main: Suhrkamp, 1978.

Brockbank, Philip, ed. *Players of Shakespeare: Essays in Shakespearean Performance by Twelve Players with the Royal Shakespeare Company*. Cambridge: Cambridge University Press, 1985.

Brustein, Robert. *The Theatre of Revolt*. Boston: Little, Brown, 1962.

Callow, Simon. *Being An Actor*. New York: St. Martin's Press, 1984.

Carlson, Marvin. *Goethe and the Weimar Theatre*. Ithaca: Cornell University Press, 1978.

Cixous, Hélène and Catherine Clément. *The Newly Born Woman*, trans. Betsy Wing. Minneapolis: University of Minnesota Press, 1987.

Clurman, Harold. *The Fervent Years: The Story of the Group Theatre and the Thirties*. New York: Hill and Wang, 1945.

Clurman, Harold. *On Directing*. New York: Macmillan, 1972.

Cole, David. *Acting as Reading*. Ann Arbor: University of Michigan Press, 1992.

Cole, Susan Letzler. *The Absent One: Mourning Ritual, Tragedy, and the Performance of Ambivalence*. University Park: The Pennsylvania State University Press, 1985.

Cole, Toby and Helen Krich Chinoy, eds. *Actors on Acting*. New York: Crown, 1962.

Cole, Toby and Helen Krich Chinoy, eds. *Directors on Directing: A Source Book of the Modern Theatre*. Rev. ed. New York: Bobbs-Merrill, 1963.

Corrigan, Robert W., ed. *Theatre in the Twentieth Century*. New York: Grove Press, 1963.

Craig, Edward Gordon. *On the Art of the Theatre*. New York: Theatre Arts Books, 1956.

Darwin, Charles. *The Voyage of the Beagle*, ed. Millicent E. Selsam. New York: Harper & Brothers, 1959.

Davy, Kate, "Foreman's *PAIN(T)* and *Vertical Mobility*." *The Drama Review, Rehearsal Procedures Issue*, vol. 18, no. 2 (T62), June, 1974, pp. 26–47.

Davy, Kate. *Richard Foreman and the Ontological-Hysteric Theatre*. Ann Arbor: UMI Research Press, 1981.

Davy, Kate, ed. *Richard Foreman: Plays and Manifestos*. New York: New York Unversity Press, 1976.

Deák, František, "The Byrd Hoffman School of Byrds: Robert Wilson." *The Drama Review, Rehearsal Procedures Issue*, vol. 18, no. 2 (T62), June, 1974, pp. 67–73.

de Lauretis, Teresa. *Technologies of Gender: Essays on Theory, Film, and Fiction*. Bloomington: Indiana University Press, 1987.

Drakakis, John, ed. *Alternative Shakespeares*.New York: Routledge, 1990.

Edwards, Christine. *The Stanislavski Heritage: Its Contribution to the Russian and American Theatre*. New York: New York University Press, 1965.

Fenichel, Otto. *The Psychoanalytic Theory of Neurosis*. New York: Norton, 1945.

Flaubert, Gustave. *The Temptation of Saint Antony*, trans. Kitty Mrosovsky. New York: Viking Penguin, 1987.

Foreman, Richard. *Reverberation Machines: The Later Plays and Essays*. Barrytown: Station Hill Press, 1985.

Freud, Anna. *The Ego and the Mechanisms of Defense: The Writings of Anna Freud*. Rev. ed. 2 vols. New York: International University Press, 1966.

Fuchs, Elinor, "The Death of Character," *Theatre Communications*, vol. 5, no. 3 (March 1983), pp. 1–6.

Goldman, Michael. *The Actor's Freedom: Toward a Theory of Drama*. New York: Viking Press, 1975.

Gorchakov, Nikolai M. *Stanislavski Directs*, trans. Miriam Goldina. New York: Grosset and Dunlop, 1962.

Gould, Eric, ed. *The Sin of the Book: Edmond Jabès*. Lincoln: University of Nebraska Press, 1985.

Hall, Peter. *Peter Hall's Diaries: The Story of a Dramatic Battle*, ed. John Goodwin. London: Hamish Hamilton, 1983.

Houghton, Norris. *Moscow Rehearsals: An Account of Methods of Production in the Soviet Theatre*. New York: Harcourt, Brace, 1936.

Johnson, Mark. *The Body in the Mind: The Bodily Basis of Meaning, Imagination, and Reason*. Chicago: University of Chicago Press, 1987.

Jones, David Richard. *Great Directors at Work: Stanislavsky, Brecht, Kazan, Brook*. Berkeley: University of California Press, 1986.

Kaplan, E. Ann, "Is the Gaze Male?" in *Powers of Desire: The Politics of Sexuality*, eds. Ann Snitow, Christine Stansell, and Sharon Thompson. New York: Monthly Review Press, 1983.

Kaye, Kenneth. *The Mental and Social Life of Babies*. Chicago: University of Chicago Press, 1982.

Kott, Jan, "Theater—The Eternal Art of the Particular Moment," *New York Times*, September 2, 1984, H5.

Lacan, Jacques. *The Four Fundamental Concepts of Psycho-analysis*, ed. Jacques-Alain Miller. Trans. Alan Sheridan. New York: Norton, 1978.

Laplanche, J. and J.-B. Pontalis. *The Language of Psycho-Analysis*, trans. Donald Nicholson-Smith. New York: Norton, 1973.

Loney, Glenn, ed. *Peter Brook's Production of William Shakespeare's* A Midsummer Night's Dream *for the Royal Shakespeare Company*. Chicago: The Dramatic Publishing Company, 1974.

Magarshack, David. *Chekhov The Dramatist*. New York: Hill and Wang, 1960.

Malpede, Karen, ed. *Women in Theatre: Compassion and Hope*. New York: Drama Book Publishers, 1983.

Mann, Emily. *Execution of Justice*, in *New Plays 3*, eds. James Leverett and M. Elizabeth Osborn. New York: Theatre Communications Group, 1986, pp. 40–112.

Marowitz, Charles. *Prospero's Staff*. Bloomington: Indiana University Press, 1986.

Marranca, Bonnie. *Theatrewritings*. New York: Performing Arts Journal Publications, 1984.

Molière. *L'Impromptu de Versailles*, in *One-Act Comedies*, trans. Albert Bermel. Cleveland: World, 1964, pp. 95–118.

Mulvey, Laura, "Changes: Thoughts on Myth, Narrative and Historical Experience," *History Workshop*, Issue 23 (Spring 1987), pp. 3–19.

Mulvey, Laura, "Visual Pleasure and Narrative Cinema," *Screen* 16, no. 3 (Autumn 1975), pp. 6–18.

Nemirovitch-Dantchenko, Vladimir. *My Life in the Russian Theatre*, trans. John Cournos. New York: Theatre Arts Books, 1968.

Olivier, Laurence. *Confessions of An Actor: An Autobiography*. New York: Simon and Schuster, 1982.

Olivier, Laurence. *On Acting*. New York: Simon and Schuster, 1986.

Quintero, José. *If You Don't Dance They Beat You*. Boston: Little, Brown, 1974.

Ragland-Sullivan, Ellie. *Jacques Lacan and the Philosophy of Psychoanalysis*. Chicago: University of Illinois Press, 1986.

Savran, David, "Adaptation as Clairvoyance: The Wooster Group's *Saint Anthony* [sic]," *Theater*, vol. 18, no. 1 (Winter 1986–87), pp. 36–41.

Savran, David. *In Their Own Words: Contemporary American Playwrights*. New York: Theatre Communications Group, 1988.

Savran, David. *The Wooster Group, 1975–1985: Breaking the Rules*. Ann Arbor: UMI Research Press, 1986.

Selbourne, David. *The Making of* A Midsummer Night's Dream, *An Eye-Witness Account of Peter Brook's Production from First Rehearsal to First Night*. London: Methuen, 1984.

Sher, Antony. *Year of the King: An Actor's Diary and Sketchbook*. London: Chatto & Windus, 1985.

Snow, Edward. *A Study of Vermeer*. Berkeley: University of California Press, 1979.

Snow, Edward, "Theorizing the Male Gaze: Some Problems," *Representations*, no. 25 (Winter 1989), pp. 30–41.

Spolin, Viola. *Theater Games for Rehearsal: A Director's Handbook*. Evanston: Northwestern University Press, 1985.

Stanislavski, Constantin. *An Actor Prepares*, trans. Elizabeth Reynolds Hapgood. New York: Routledge/Theatre Arts Books, 1989.

Stanislavski, Constantin. *Building a Character*, trans. Elizabeth Reynolds Hapgood. New York: Routledge/Theatre Arts Books, 1989.

Stern, Richard L. *John Gielgud Directs Richard Burton in* Hamlet: *A Journal of Rehearsals*. New York: Random House, 1967.

The Theater of Images, rev. ed. The Contemporary Arts Center, Cincinnati, and The Byrd Hoffman Foundation, New York. New York: Harper & Row, 1984.

Toporkov, Vasily Osipovich. *Stanislavski in Rehearsal: The Final Years*, trans. Christine Edwards. New York: Theatre Arts Books, 1979.

Turner, Victor. *The Anthropology of Performance*. New York: Performing Arts Journal Publications, 1986.

Worthen, W.B., "Deeper Meanings and Theatrical Technique: The Rhetoric of Performance Criticism," *Shakespeare Quarterly*, vol. 40, no. 4 (Winter 1989), pp. 441–55.

Index

Author's Note: I only list actors or other company members whose work in rehearsal has been important to the points I make.